THE DOMINICAN MISSION FRONTIER
OF LOWER CALIFORNIA

The Dominican Mission Frontier of Lower California

✠

By Peveril Meigs, 3d

University of California Press

Berkeley, California

1935

University of California Publications in Geography

Volume 7. Pp. vi + 1–232, plates 1–19, 24 figures in text, 1 map

Issued November 30, 1935

Price: Cloth, $2.50; paper, $1.75.

University of California Press

Berkeley, California

————

Cambridge University Press

London, England

CONTENTS

LIST OF FIGURES

Contents

LIST OF PLATES

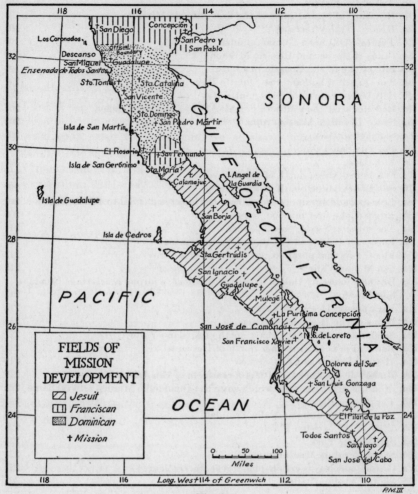

Fig. 1

PART ONE

THE CONQUEST OF A FRONTIER

INTRODUCTION

THE NETWORK OF MISSIONS founded under the Dominicans in the latter part of the eighteenth century in northern Baja California established there a new and distinct culture landscape. Although at the very doorway of Alta California, these missions have remained almost unknown. A geographic analysis of them has not heretofore been attempted, and history has so greatly neglected them that the very existence of the last two missions has been overlooked or questioned.* The present study, based upon field work from 1925 to 1929 and upon such written knowledge as is available, delineates this almost forgotten scene of activity.†

I. AN INHERITED FRONTIER

A BREAK IN THE MISSION CHAIN

THE MISSION SYSTEM of the Californias, starting from the original foundation at Loreto in 1697, grew link by link under the labors of Jesuits until it included the entire Peninsula as far north as Santa María (just south of 30° N; see fig. 1). In 1768 Franciscans replaced Jesuits as the directors of the Californian establishments. The first mission founded by the newcomers, San Fernando de Velicatá, merely extended by a few leagues the area conquered by their predecessors and served as a base for further conquests to the north (Sauer and Meigs, 1927). Instead of continuing north slowly and steadily, however, the Franciscans built their second mission, San Diego, one hundred twenty leagues beyond Velicatá, leaving open the intervening gap.

In the exploratory trips north from Velicatá and San Diego in 1769, numerous attractive sites for missions were noted by the several Franciscan diarists, who also observed that gentiles existed in numbers along the entire route. The Franciscans favored continuing the chain unbroken, but the new civil policy of Gálvez, requiring immediate occupation of the two great ports, prevailed, and Serra, president of the California missions, soon became a most ardent advocate of the prior settlement of *Nueva California*.

The strategic northern bases once occupied, both civil and religious authorities were anxious for the speedy occupation of the intervening

---

* The statement by Engelhardt (1908, 1:513), quoting Bancroft in part, that "the Dominicans have left no account of their labors," fails to consider the interesting letters by the Dominican, Luis Sales, published in 1794.

† The Board of Research of the University of California contributed support to the later field expeditions.

areas. Viceroy Armona lamented the long, unprotected gap,[1] and on November 12, 1770, ordered that new missions be founded with all possible haste, five between Velicatá and San Diego and five between San Diego and Monterey.[2] By the end of 1772 three new missions had filled in the northern gap, between San Diego and Monterey, but the southern gap remained open, and bad weather for nearly a year prevented the friars destined to found the latter missions from reaching California (Palóu, 1874: 126). In November, 1772, they finally arrived at Loreto, the political and religious headquarters of the Peninsula, but no soldiers were available there for the proposed foundations, so the new arrivals were distributed among the missions already existing in Baja California, and expansion was perforce temporarily suspended (*ibid.:* 163–164). The Franciscan authorities demanded more soldiers (*ibid.:* 153), but before the necessary steps were taken the mission field of the whole Peninsula, in April, 1772,[3] was assigned to the Dominicans.

THE ADMISSION OF THE DOMINICANS TO CALIFORNIA

The Dominican order of Preaching Friars, though never so powerful in New Spain as the Franciscans, had nevertheless a venerable background of missionary experience. The very invention of the mission system had been made by a Dominican, the Vicar Pedro de Córdova, about 1512, as a substitute for the *encomienda* system. Under the direction of the Dominican, Bartolomé de las Casas, the mission idea was tested between 1537 and 1539, with complete success, in Guatemala (Richman: 36–41).

The principal Dominican field of activity in New Spain was Oaxaca. In the north the Dominicans were the first to make successful headway in the Sierra Gorda region (now Querétaro), where by the end of the seventeenth century they were operating at least six successful missions, and later they worked here in coöperation with Franciscans of the College of San Fernando. The Sierra Gorda experience may have served at least in part as preparation for the later harmony between the two orders in California, and for the great similarity in the mission foundations of Alta and Baja California.

The extension of the Dominican field to California seems to have been brought about by the activity of the Dominican Procurator of Mexico, Fray Juan Pedro de Iriarte y Laurnaga. Upon the expulsion of the Jesuits, he petitioned for a share in the conversion of the west coast of California. He requested in particular the possession of the missions in the vicinity of San Ignacio and, with these as a foundation, the privilege of extending the spiritual conquests to the north, explaining that the many good ports of that part of California would thereby be more secure against foreign encroachment (Sales, part 3: 10–16).

[1] Letter to Croix, June 30, 1770:7.

[2] Palóu, 1874, 1:126–129; the standard authority on the Franciscan period.

[3] Palóu (chaps. 29–30) gives the history of the transfer from the Franciscan, and Sales (1794, part 3:8–49) from the Dominican point of view.

His Majesty immediately wrote to the Viceroy of Mexico demanding advice on the matter. The Viceroy consulted Gálvez, who, in a letter of June 10, 1769, replied that it would be inadvisable to grant the Dominican petition, as the Franciscans were making as rapid progress as could be desired in the Peninsula, and had every prospect of continuing to do so (Palóu, 1874: 229–233). To this reason the Viceroy, in his report to the King, added that mixing the two orders would give opportunity for inquietude on the Peninsula (Sales, part 3: 9). Nothing daunted by the adverse reports from the royal representatives in America, Iriarte renewed his plea, emphasizing the argument that "it was not right that one order alone, and much less a single monastery or college, should occupy a peninsula as large as that of California" (*ibid.:* 234). Gálvez and the Viceroy then decided that there was plenty of work for both Franciscans and Dominicans in California, and the King, in a decree dated April 8, 1771, commanded the Viceroy to assign to the Dominicans, in the person of Iriarte, "the districts and places that are suitable of those that they request, with total separation and independence from those which the Franciscan Religious occupy" (Sales, part 3: 10–17).

Iriarte immediately circulated among the Dominicans in Spain an appeal for volunteers to serve in California. The response was ardent. Two hundred men answered the call, though only twenty-six, the number granted by the King, could be accepted. Of those who came to America (one became sick and was left behind in Cádiz), thirteen were from Castille, eight from Aragón, and four from Andalucía.[4] They reached Vera Cruz on August 19, 1771, and from there went to Mexico City to await the division of California between the two orders (Sales, part 3: 45–47).

THE DIVISION OF CALIFORNIA

The Viceroy permitted the Dominican and Franciscan leaders to discuss the division among themselves. The result was a "Concordat," signed on April 7, 1772, by Verger, Guardian of the Franciscan College of San Fernando, and Iriarte, Dominican Procurator (Palóu, 1874: 236–240). By its terms, the Dominicans were to take charge of the old Jesuit missions of Peninsular California and the frontier of Velicatá, extending their new conversions north nearly to San Diego. Their last mission was to be placed on the arroyo of San Juan Bautista (later San Miguel), selected, no doubt, because it had been the last good mission site found south of San Diego on the exploring expeditions of 1769.[5]

This agreement gave the Dominicans more than they had asked for. The Franciscans, too, were satisfied, for they had noted on the expeditions of 1769 that much of the Peninsula was of scant utility,[6] not only

---

[4] The practice of employing only native Spaniards in the Dominican missions of California was continued later. At no time were *criollos* (Mexican-born) used.

[5] For a full discussion of this boundary, see below, pp. 111–113.

[6] An anonymous paper, dated August, 1773, quotes Portolá, a member of the expeditions of 1769, as saying that he had never seen a country more frightful than the Peninsula. The same paper emphasizes that Gálvez had tried every means

as a mission field, but also as a route for sending supplies to the more valuable country beyond. Trouble with the civil authorities further detracted from its desirability. The first difficulty arose from a system of regulations imposed by Gálvez which made the support of the missions almost impossible. This led all the missionaries toward the end of 1769 to beg Palóu to resign the temporal care of the missions, so that, should the new regulations result in their ruin, the Franciscans would not be blamed (*ibid.*: 90–93). He agreed, but his messenger failed to reach Gálvez. By the end of 1771, interference of Governor Barri with the management of the Indians at the Mission of Todos Santos had resulted in such insubordination on their part that Palóu felt compelled to resign control of that mission and to ask that measures be taken to remedy conditions. As a result, the Guardian requested of the Viceroy (December 23, 1771) that seven of the southern, former Jesuit missions (which he enumerated) be taken over by the Dominican Fathers, or others, the Franciscans to retain Loreto, San José Cumundú, San Ignacio, Santa Gertrudis, and San Borja (*ibid.*: 151–154). An examination of the condition of the missions, as set forth by Palóu himself in a report of February 12, 1772, shows that the missions which the Franciscans wished to hand over to the Dominicans were the ones of least value, because of poor site, unruliness of Indians, or scanty population, and that those which they wished to retain were the strongest in number of inhabitants or desirability of site. Had the Franciscan request been granted, a distinct mixing of the two orders would have resulted, contrary to the express orders of the King.

After writing to his College, Palóu sent Fray Ramos de Lora, former missionary of Todos Santos, to communicate directly with the Viceroy, to see if some other religious group might take charge of the southern missions. Leaving Loreto in January, Fray Ramos reached Mexico in March, and his influence undoubtedly hastened the decision of Fray Verger to renounce the whole of the Peninsula, for the Concordat was signed early that month (*ibid.*: 168, 212).

Perhaps the best statement of the Franciscan attitude at the time of the division is that of Palóu himself, in a private report which he made to Verger, dated February 12, 1772 (too late to affect the decision, though completely in accord with it). He states that in the three years and four months that his order had been in charge, the number of Indians in the old missions decreased by 2055 (29 per cent) owing to epidemics, and "if it goes on at this rate in a short time Old California will come to an end." Furthermore, a total of fifty-four missionaries

---

possible to get an income from Lower California, but had failed utterly. Armona, in a letter of January 2, 1771, states that "the Peninsula of California which was in my charge [as governor] appears to me a *Bank of Sand*, from its narrowness, bareness and aridity." Bishop Diego writes on May 14, 1769, "De la California y sus riquezas, ya nada, nada se espera, mas que la total ruina de las Misiones, y misioneros." The Dominicans seemed unfamiliar with such pessimistic reports (Gálvez Transcripts).

would be needed, twenty-six north and twenty-six south of Velicatá, besides supernumeraries: a heavy charge for one College alone. Also should be considered

the great harvest which the College has awaiting it in the heathendom of Monterey: while from San Borja to Cape San Lucas [i.e., the Southern District of Lower California] there is not a town in which the Faith can be newly propagated [and] ... these towns are not and never will be fit to be delivered to the bishop, for the land is so poor that it does not yield enough for the natives to support a curate. Consequently, I believe it is best to make every effort to give up these missions, and if the resignation is not accepted, at least to make it evident for the future that we are stating beforehand that they will never be fit to pass over to the bishop, so that it may not be said that the missions have been ruined by the missionaries of this apostolic College.—*Ibid.*: 211–213.

Apparently Palóu wanted Velicatá to be the point of division between the two orders, but Verger, in order to get rid of the decadent missions of the south, had to acquiesce to the reasonable Dominican demand for at least some new territory and the result was the boundary described above.

THE ARRIVAL OF THE DOMINICANS

The difficulties connected with California, so fully appreciated by the Franciscans,[7] soon began to be experienced by the Dominicans. Even before they had reached Loreto one of their vessels was shipwrecked, and three of the friars died, including their leader, Iriarte, who thus never set foot on the shores of the land for whose control he had so persistently labored.[8] On May 12, 1773, however, the last of the Dominicans reached Loreto and the missions were turned over to Fray Vicente Mora, who had replaced Iriarte as president (Palóu, 1874: 278–279).

The new Dominican field, as already noted, included the decadent area south of Velicatá and the virgin territory north. We are concerned with the cultural landscape developed by the Dominicans on this northern frontier, or, as the early records call it, *La Frontera.*

---

[7] The announcement that they were to leave the Peninsula was received by the Franciscans in California with ringing of bells and a Mass giving thanks to God (Palóu, 1874:255).

[8] Sales (part 3:49–54) describes the terrible journey across the Gulf, and Palóu (1874, chap. 32) the delays occasioned by it.

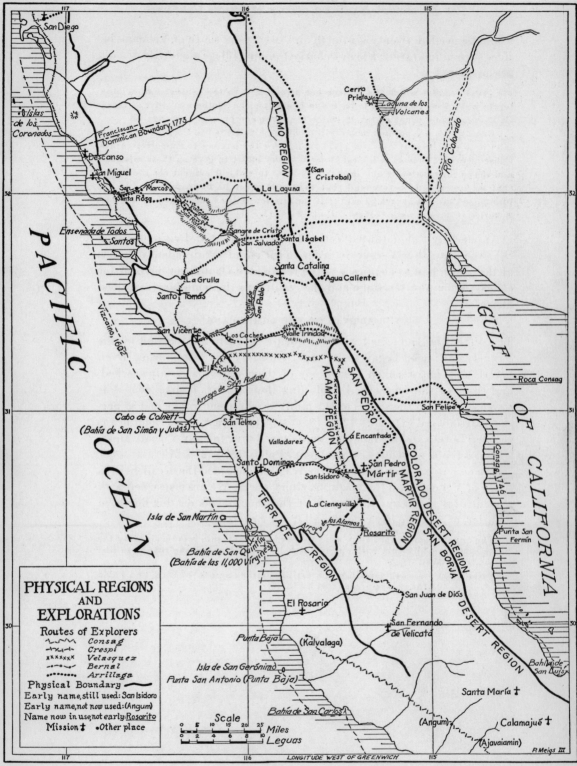

PHYSICAL REGIONS
AND
EXPLORATIONS
Routes of Explorers
〜〜〜 Consag
✕ Crespi
✕✕✕✕✕✕ Velasquez
— Bernal
••••••• Arrillaga
— Physical Boundary
Early name, still used: San Isidoro
Early name, not now used: (Angum)
Name now in use, not early: Rosarito
Mission ✝ •Other place

Scale
0 5 10 15 20 25
Miles
0 2 4 6 8 10
Leguas

LONGITUDE WEST OF GREENWICH

P. Meigs III

Fig. 2

II. PRE-DOMINICAN KNOWLEDGE OF THE FIELD

WHEN THE DOMINICANS, in 1773, were ready to occupy their new frontier, there was available to them a considerable body of knowledge concerning it. At least the western part had been explored to the degree that its desirable mission sites were known. The Franciscans had contributed most to the exploration of the Frontera, but its margins had been touched more than two hundred years before their time.

EXPLORATIONS BY SEA

The first explorers to approach the area were navigators, who, sailing along the coasts with occasional stops, got some idea of the country close along the shores. The observations on the west coast known to the missionaries were in particular those of Sebastián Viscaino and Cabrera Bueno (Richman: 81). The work of Cabrillo does not appear to have been known to the land explorers, but Crespi and Serra refer frequently to Viscaino and Cabrera Bueno,[9] and several of the place-names given by Viscaino are still in use. San Gerónimo, San Martín, and Todos Santos Islands appear first under those names in Viscaino's charts of 1603. The Punta Baja and Cape San Quintín of the modern maps appear also on these charts, but the first referred to the present San Antonio Point and the last to Cape Colnett. Torquemada's account of the expedition adds another lasting place-name, the Coronados Islands (Torquemada: 710). Cabrera Bueno, following another account of the Viscaino expedition (Carrasco y Guisasola: 89), adds Ensenada de Todos Santos as the name of the bay which is still so known. He also used the term "San Quintín Bay," though this bay has become since the time of Vancouver "Colnett Bay" (Vancouver, Atlas, chart no. 8) and "San Quintín" is used to denote the bay known by all the Viscainic accounts as Ensenada de las Vírgines, or Bahía de las 11,000 Vírgines. Islands were named more permanently than shore points, though even in the names of the islands there was some confusion in the early accounts, a result, probably, of the fact that dense fogs overtook Viscaino's ships near San Gerónimo and lasted beyond Las Vírgines.

The Gulf coast of the Dominican area had also been explored early by water. Though Ulloa, in 1539, and Ugarte, in 1721, had examined it in some detail, it was the expedition of the Jesuit, Consag, in 1746 which gave to the Franciscans and Dominicans, through Venegas, a description of that coast. Venegas (vol. 2, app. 3) gives the complete diary of Consag's voyage, as well as a map whose gulf portion is taken, in large measure, from Consag. Along his route, shown in figure 2, Consag affixed many place-names that still persist—for example, the bays of San Luis Gonzaga, San Fermín, and San Phelipe. Consag's description of the country indicated the futility of founding missions in the Colo-

---

[9] For example, Bolton, 1927:101, 246; Serra: 517.

rado Desert region. He reported a great scarcity even of drinking water, no anchorages except very rocky or sandy ones, and untractable, even hostile, Indians.

JESUIT LAND EXPLORATIONS

Consag was also the first explorer to approach the interior of the future Dominican Frontier. With San Ignacio as a base, he set out May 22, 1751, to seek a site for a new mission to the north near the Pacific.[10] The farthest point that he reached in traveling three and a half weeks, mostly to the northwest, was *Kalvalaga.* The location of this place may be ascertained with some exactness. He says it is nearly in 30° latitude, two *leguas* from the shore. "Toward the southwest is seen a high island not very large, and it appears to be that which the navigators call Guadalupe." On his return, however, he noticed it to the northwest, and therefore concluded that "if it is Guadalupe, it is not so far out as the map shows." Since his map showed no other island between Cerros (Cedros) and Cenizas (San Martín), he concluded that the island had simply been mapped too far from shore. In the light of our knowledge of the coast, Consag's difficulty is explained: Guadalupe Island is 135 miles from the nearest land, but in latitude 29° 47′, six miles from shore, is a small island (San Gerónimo) not given on Consag's map, and this island is undoubtedly the one he saw. A line drawn northeast from San Gerónimo Island, in accordance with the direction given by Consag, reaches a point two leagues inland at the Penga Quemada Cañon, in latitude 29° 58′ N, ten miles southeast of the site of the future mission of El Rosario. This cañon is probably his Kalvalaga. With its dry arroyo and barren surrounding country, it gave no indication of the running water of the Arroyo Rosario just a few miles to the north, and Consag returned to San Ignacio with the belief that the west coast region offered little in the way of mission sites. The only possibility he saw was to use the two arroyos *Ajavaiamin* and *Angum* (apparently the present arroyos Amargoso and San Julio) for the support of a single mission.

Having found no good place for a mission either along the Gulf shore or near the west coast, Consag, in 1753, undertook to explore the land toward the east side of the Peninsula. The details of this expedition are not known, except that it reached, according to Consag's measurements, the latitude of 31° "without finding more than great *pedregales*" (Clavigero: 98). It must have passed to the east of the Velicatá site and come to an end in the dry Llanos de Buenos Aires, toward the northern end of the San Borja Desert, without reaching the well-watered valleys that lead down from the San Pedro Mártir region.

The explorations of Consag were continued in 1766 by another Jesuit, Father Link, the minister of the San Borja Mission. He had already undertaken, in 1765, an expedition to the Island of Angel de la Guardia,

---

[10] The detailed account of this expedition given by Ortega (pp. 487–533) is here followed.

and, in the following year, had led an expedition north by land with the purpose of seeking a new mission site and exploring the country as far as the Colorado River (*ibid.*: 102, 106). Unfortunately, Link's diary, if still in existence, has not been discovered in modern times,[11] though his immediate successors have left accounts of his journey which let us know that he found a desirable mission site (Velicatá), though he failed to reach the Colorado. The chroniclers of the Franciscan expedition of 1769 followed his route for a considerable distance and used the place-names he had given, thereby perpetuating some of these names to the present day, and making possible the reconstruction of his route (see fig. 2) as far as La Cieneguilla, the point where they left his trail.[12] The present arroyos of San Juan de Dios, Los Mártires, Las Palmas, and Los Álamos, north of San Fernando, were named by Link (Bolton, 1927: 63–70). La Cieneguilla, according to Crespi, is about seven leagues southeast of San Isidoro, twenty-five leagues beyond San Fernando. Beyond that place, Link's route is uncertain. Palóu (1787: 74) quotes one of Link's soldiers as saying that from La Cieneguilla Link went north several days until forced to turn back by a high sierra where the animals could not go. Crespi (Bolton, 1927: 63) says that Link, from La Cieneguilla, climbed the Sierra and came out on the coast of the Gulf of California. Clavigero, who gives the fullest account available of Link's work, says that he went to 33° or a little more, and then turned east to cross the mountains and go down to the Colorado River. The mountains were so rough and steep that he had to turn aside to look for a better pass, and came to such a large sandy stretch that, lacking water and fearful of incapacitating the horses, he decided to abandon the enterprise. As Link gave the latitude of San Fernando two degrees too high, it is probable that he attempted to pass the Sierra about ten leagues north of La Cieneguilla. He cannot have done much exploring after reaching La Cieneguilla, for time did not permit. He reached San Juan de Dios on March 8 (Clavigero: 105–106), having averaged four leagues a day from San Borja. Assuming that he covered the twenty leagues to La Cieneguilla at the same rate, he reached there about March 13, which left him only fourteen days to get back to San Borja, eighty-five leagues away, by March 27 (when his journey is known to have ended), or six leagues a day, a reasonable rate for the return. Whatever his exact route, his expedition was the first to penetrate to the San Pedro Mártir region and the mountainous country west of it, and to make known the existence of a well-watered country to the north of the inhospitable Desert of San Borja.

[11] In Arch. Cal., P. S. P., Benicia, Miscellaneous, 1:21, the diary of Link's voyage, February 20–March 27, 1766, ten pages long, is mentioned. As the original Archives of California were destroyed in 1906 in the San Francisco fire, this copy, at least, is no longer in existence. North says he found "old chronicles" concerning Link at San Borja (North, 1907b: 545). Clavigero (p. 107) says that a copy of the diary was sent to the Viceroy.

[12] Palóu, 1787:74; Bolton, 1927:72; Serra: 516.

THE FRANCISCAN EXPEDITION OF 1769

Link's explorations led to the founding of the San Fernando Mission at Velicatá by the Franciscans, and chiefly determined the route followed by their famous expedition of 1769 to San Diego. Because of the direct relation of this expedition to Alta California history, several good diaries of it have been collected by Californian historians.[13] The diary of Father Crespi will be cited here as a rule, as it is the most complete, containing not only Crespi's observations, but also a summary of Serra's. The route taken can be traced quite accurately from his excellent descriptions by using the directions and distances that he gives and with the aid of the place-names given by him that are still in use (see fig. 2).

The permanent names which Crespi gave are: San Isidoro[14] (Serra: San Fernando), an arroyo of good water in a grassy plain; Valladares (Serra: Arroyo de San Andrés Hispelo), another arroyo with good water;[15] San Telmo (Serra: Los Santos Mártires Gorgoniensis), a deep pond still known near the present town of San Telmo; and San Rafael (Serra: Santa Margarita), an arroyo north of San Telmo (Bolton, 1927: 84, 87). Beyond San Rafael, all the names given by Crespi have been replaced by others. Identification of the sites of these names is possible by means of surveys in the field. Names thus identified by the writer are the following:

Present name	Crespi's name	Serra's name
El Salado	San Bernabé	San Bernabé
San Vicente	Marsh of Santa Isabel	San Guido de Cortona
Santo Tomás	San Francisco Solano	San Antonio
La Grulla	Valley and Marsh of San Jorge	San Antonogenes
Arroyo de San Carlos, mouth	Hollow of the Holy Apostles	
Ensenada de Todos Santos	Holy Cross of the Pools of the Bay of Todos Santos	Visitación de Nuestra Señora María Santísima
El Sausal de Camacho	Pools of Santa Monica	Ranchería de San Juan
San Miguel	Valley of San Juan Bautista	San Juan Capistrano
Descanso	Wells of the Valley of San Antonio	San Francisco Solano
Rosarito Creek	El Vallecito de San Pío	San Benvenuto
Vicinity of Tahiti Beach	Pool of the Holy Martyrs	Carcel de San Pedro
Tijuana River	Sancti Spiritus	

[13] Of the advance party of the expedition, which left San Fernando on March 24, we have the account by Father Crespi, available both in Palóu's *Noticias* and Bolton's *Crespi;* also the valuable unpublished account by José de Cañizares, the geographer of the expedition. Of the second party of the expedition, which left San Fernando on May 15 and followed the trail of the first party to within six leagues of San Diego, we have the accounts of Father Serra and of Portolá.

[14] Bolton (1927:76) calls it San Isidro, but as Crespi arrived there on April 4, the day of San Isidoro, Archbishop and Doctor, the latter is correct. May 15 is the saint's day of San Isidro. The present occupants of the ranch call it San Isidoro.

[15] Crespi named it San León, but its permanent name was received accidentally because an Indian on the expedition, Manuel Valladares, died and was buried there by Crespi. The second party, which saw the name over his grave, was probably the first to refer to the locality as Valladares (Bolton, 1927:82; Serra: 636).

The locating of Crespi's Holy Cross of the Pools of the Bay of Todos Santos at the site of the present town of Ensenada is based on Cañizares' statement that it was east-northeast of the Todos Santos Islands. The Pools of Santa Monica, which Cañizares locates northeast of the islands, are the lagoons at the mouth of the present Arroyo del Sausal de Camacho.

Briefly, Crespi and his party followed the trail of Link across the plains and arroyos of the San Borja Desert as far as Cieneguilla, where they turned to the northwest. From Cieneguilla to the San Telmo Plain they went through rough country; from there to San Vicente, mostly over fairly smooth terraces; from there to Todos Santos Bay, through very rough country; and the rest of the way to San Diego mostly over the level coastal terraces (see fig. 2).

In summarizing the expedition in a letter to Palóu, Crespi writes:

Almost all of the road was through the mountains, some of them very rough, but we found water and good pasturage in them on every day's march. We always travelled in the mountains because the captain had a complete aversion to going down to the seashore, until finally the mountain forced us to descend because of its height, steepness and roughness, and he was obliged, in spite of himself, to allow us to come down to the beach. In my opinion all our good fortune in not perishing was due to this, because the beach gave us a good and very easy passage by land, was well supplied with pasturage, and had sufficient fresh water for all.—Bolton, 1927:6.

The insistence of Captain Rivera y Moncada on keeping to the mountains rather than the coast is probably explained by his knowledge of them gained in the explorations of Consag and Link. As captain in the Consag expedition of 1751 (Clavigero: 96) he had seen the dryness and roughness of the coastal mesas south of El Rosario, and he had no reason to suspect the existence along the coast to the north of smooth plains and favored valleys like that of El Rosario. The soldiers from Link's party, on the contrary, had found the mountainous region to be full of well-watered valleys and abundant pastures. It is not to be wondered at that the notes of the navigators were ignored.

The Franciscan expedition discovered for the first time the merits of the coastal lands. It broke a trail that has been used, substantially unchanged, until the development of motor transportation. Along that trail, Crespi and Serra definitely noted and recommended the four sites that were used later for the Dominican missions of San Vicente, Santo Tomás, San Miguel, and Descanso. Crespi's strong suspicion, on the basis of information from the Indians, of the existence of another desirable site near the sea on the San Dionisio River (now San Antonio River, Bolton, 1927: 8, 79) was proved well founded by the establishment there, later, of the Santo Domingo Mission.

LATER FRANCISCAN EXPLORATION

The Santo Domingo site was probably discovered by the Franciscans shortly after the expedition of 1769. Certainly Viñaraco, the site of El

Rosario Mission, had been found before the entry of the Dominicans into Baja California, for in July, 1773, Palóu speaks as a matter of course of traveling north by way of Viñaraco. This coastal road was the outcome of explorations of the coastal region made under the Franciscans toward the end of 1771 or beginning of 1772. Of these explorations no record has been discovered. We know only, from the fragmentary account left by Palóu, that the present names, Santa Úrsula, La Grulla, and Médanos, were in use at the time of his departure from Baja California in 1773 (Bolton, 1926, 1:216, 299–301).

Even without the details of these particular explorations, it is clear that by the time the Dominicans were ready to begin establishing new missions, the rough exploratory work for the five missions that were to unite San Diego and Velicatá had already been done.

III. THE FRONTIER AS A FIELD FOR MISSIONS

SELECTION OF SITE

THE GENERAL LOCATION of mission establishments north of Velicatá was determined as a matter of policy by the civil authorities. The Dominican Fathers, however, were responsible for the selection of the exact sites to be used, their selection being subject to subsequent approval by the Viceroy (Sales, part 3 : 60, 61).

The ostensible and primary reason for the mission system was the desire to convert Indians. The first requirement, then, was a supply of gentiles. From the secular point of view, the saving of the souls of the Indians was only incidental; the chief value of the missions to the King was in the protection of Alta California against foreign encroachment by facilitating communication from the north. By pacifying the Indians, the missions made travel safe, and as convenient stopping-places for travelers, they made it easier.

In addition to the Peninsular route to California, along which were situated most of the missions, another was contemplated, to go to the Colorado River and thus provide an all-land communication between California and Mexico. As part of this second plan, which was never completed, two Dominican missions were established.

For success both in converting heathen and in maintaining a line of communication it was necessary that each mission be at a place capable of supporting at least a part of its people. This involved, in the first place, a constant supply of water close to a mission—something not to be found in every league, nor even in every dozen leagues. There must be land suitable for raising crops of wheat and maize, either by means of rainfall or irrigation. In the surrounding country there must be fire-wood for the mission and pasture for the livestock. The character of the surrounding country as a contributing source of human sustenance through its wild fruits and shellfish was important, too, though apparently this factor did not enter into the selection of the various sites.[16]

QUALIFICATIONS OF THE AREA

Indians.—According to all early accounts, the entire area north of Velicatá was well populated with Indians. Even on a rapid journey to carry south the news of the occupation of Monterey in 1770 (Richman : 88), one soldier counted along his route between San Diego and Velicatá nineteen Indian *rancherías,* with an estimated population of 2000 (Velazquez, MS). Indians were to be found in almost all parts of the area, and were particularly numerous along the coast.

Physical landscapes.—The physical characteristics of the area were widely different in different parts, a fact of great importance in deter-

---

[16] A specific statement of the requisites for a mission site is contained in the instructions for reconnoitering the site of the Santa Catalina Mission, outlined on p. 32 below.

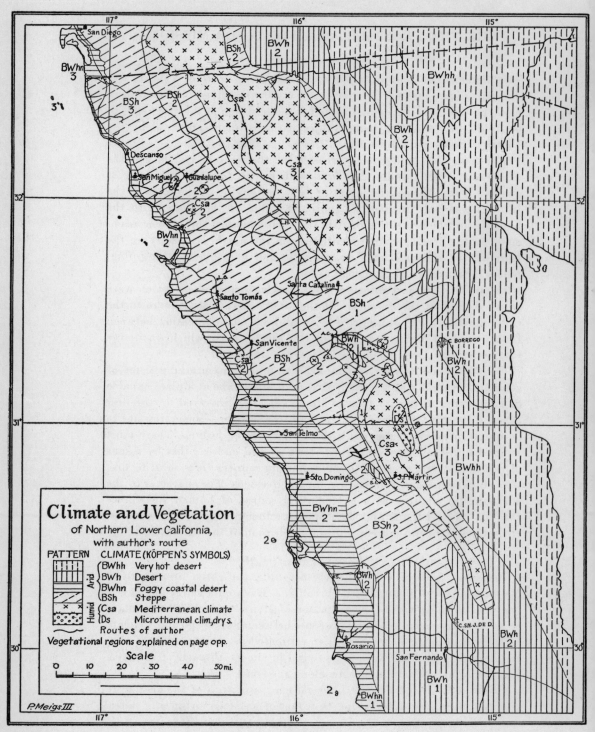

Fig. 3

EXPLANATION OF FIGURE 3

Life-Zone (Nelson)	Climate	Distinctive vegetation (names of plant associations in capitals) of average exposure.
Lower Sonoran	BWhh	DESERT SHRUB. Creosote bush, ocotillo, cactus, mesquite.
	BWh-1	DESERT "FOREST." Cirio, elephant wood, tree yucca, cardón, other cactus, mesquite.
	BWh-2	DESERT SHRUB. Creosote bush, desert agave, yucca, ocotillo, biznaga, mesquite.
	BWhn-1	DESERT SHRUB. Guayule, yucca, vidrío, siempre vive.
Upper Sonoran	BWhn-2	MESCAL CHAMISO (mescal, guayule, Indian burr, *Eriogonum fasciculatum*, cactus). Siempre vive, vidrío.
	BWhn-3	COASTAL SAGEBRUSH (California sage, *Ramona nivea*, etc.). Vidrío.
	BSh-1	STEPPE-DESERT TRANSITION. Yucca, biznaga, mesquite, and, locally, juniper. No live oaks.
	BSh-2	MONTE (manzanita, palo colorado, *Adenostoma*). Occasional yucca and mesquite. Live oaks in cañons.
	BSh-3	CHAPARRAL (*Adenostoma*). Grass, live-oak groves common.
	Csa-1	PARK LANDSCAPE (live oak). MONTE.
Transition	Csa-2	CONIFEROUS GROVE (Prickle-cone pine, cypress, with monte underbrush).
	Csa-3	CONIFEROUS FOREST (yellow pine predominant, with piñon lower and mixed cedar-pine-fir higher).
Canadian	Ds	CONIFEROUS FOREST (lodgepole pine predominant; scattered sugar pines).

mining the location of the *camino* and consequently of the missions, between San Diego and Velicatá. A brief characterization of the physical subdivisions, together with the accompanying map (fig. 2), will be helpful in explanation of the locations selected.

Colorado Desert region.—The part of the Dominican Frontier least suited for missions was the Colorado Desert region, a series of basins and plains near sea level, with occasional isolated mountain ranges.[17] This entire region has so arid a climate (largely *Bwhh:* see fig. 3) and so deficient a supply of surface water that large permanent settlements, to say nothing of the raising of crops, would have been impossible, unless in the vicinity of the Colorado River itself. Even had water been abundant, the region was distinctly peripheral to any direct line between San Diego and Velicatá, and the way between the Colorado Desert and Velicatá would have been difficult. The San Pedro Mártir mountain mass was a formidable obstacle to eastward travel, as the first explorer north of Velicatá discovered,[18] and westward travel from the desert would have encountered the high, steep escarpment which extends from north of the present international boundary to south of Velicatá.

San Pedro Mártir region.—The San Pedro Mártir Sierra, lying to the west of the southern half of the Colorado Desert (see fig. 2) at an elevation of from 5000 to 9000 feet above sea level, is in some respects suitable for settlements. It consists, for the greater part, of a series of broad, moist, grassy flats, surrounded by granite knobs covered with coniferous forests, mostly of yellow pine. In respect to water supply, level land, and abundant timber, this region is unexcelled in the entire Peninsula. The severe winters, however, were an obstacle against which the Spanish Fathers, with their Mediterranean agricultural background and limited resources, were little willing to struggle. The highest part of the region has microthermal climate; the lowest, a cold-margin mesothermal (see fig. 3). Finally, as part of a through route this region is worthless, being surrounded on all sides, with the possible exception of a part of the south, by extremely difficult escarpments. The one mission established in this region[19] was placed on its southwest margin, near the inland north-south route, at about the lowest, warmest part of the region.

Álamo region.—To the west and north of San Pedro Mártir lies a region better suited than either of those already mentioned for a chain of missions. It is a country of rough hills and mountains of granitic, volcanic, and metamorphic rocks, interspersed with broad valleys, basins, and smooth plains. The name "Álamo" is here applied to this region (see fig. 2) from one of its most centrally located places (at present a dormant mining camp). It contains excellent sites for settlement, with abundant water in arroyos arising mostly in the San Pedro Mártir or Juarez sierra; sufficient irrigable land; wood in abundance, in gallery forests

[17] Kniffen (1932) analyzes the natural landscape of much of this region.

[18] See a discussion of Link's exploration in Sec. II, above.

[19] The mission San Pedro Mártir, from which the Sierra received its name.

of cottonwood, willow, sycamore, and live oak, and local growths of pine, juniper, and mesquite; and sufficient pasture during most of the year. The climate (see fig. 3) is semi-arid, with more humid high spots, and desertic depressions. Most of the rain comes in winter, but occasional summer thunderstorms are usual.

A road through this area could be used only with difficulty because of the roughly dissected land masses intervening between the easily traversable plains. As a matter of fact, the road used by the first parties going to San Diego by land (1769) kept within this region most of the way as far as the Ensenada de Todos Santos (see Crespi's route, in fig. 2). That this route was difficult and not satisfactory as a permanent one is shown by the diaries and letters concerning the journey (Bolton, 1927: 6–7).

Terrace region.—A much better route was soon[20] discovered, lying for the most part west of the Álamo region. Whereas the second party of the expedition of 1769 had taken forty-seven days to reach San Diego from Velicatá,[21] a similar party, using the new route in 1773 and traveling slowly, required only twenty-eight days. To this saving of time, ease of traveling as well as a shortened distance contributed. Palóu states that the distance from Velicatá to San Diego by the old road was 119 leagues, and by the new one, 100 (Bolton, 1926: 206, 299–302).[22]

The distinctive feature of this region is a series of plains (mesas) which rise in broad steps from the sea level to an altitude, inland, of more than 2000 feet. These marine terraces fringe the Álamo region in almost continuous, roughly parallel strips. In most places the terraces are uninterrupted by mountains, but from San Vicente to Socorro a broken mountain chain, parallel with the coast, breaks the terraces into a seaward strip and a series of connected landward reëntrants behind the mountain barriers. A group of flat, shallow, elevated plains in the vicinity of San Miguel is mapped within the Terrace region in figure 2, here of fault rather than marine origin (see Sec. X, below).

On the whole, the terraces afford a good location for a road. The chief obstacles, aside from one interruption by the approach of mountains to coast near Santo Tomás, are the steep-sided cañons, arroyos, and gullies. In the lowest terraces, which are the ones most recently exposed to subaërial erosion, the walls of ravines are generally steeper than in the older, higher terraces, but also more of the original surface remains. The Terrace region is distinctly superior to the other parts of the Frontera for north-south communication, and has determined the course of the main road at least from the beginning of 1772.

[20] At least before February 12, 1772, according to Palóu's report of that date (Bolton, 1926, 1:216).

[21] Serra. According to Crespi's diary, the first party, exploring the route, took fifty-two days. An unencumbered rider could of course go much more rapidly: Velazquez (MS) in 1770, took only seven and one-half days.

[22] The present automobile road covers 306 miles.

The Terrace region was also well adapted to the existence of missions along the route. Gentiles were more numerous here than in any other part of the Frontier. In 1769, Crespi noted thirteen villages, most of them large, in the last quarter of his journey (thirty-one leagues), all situated on the terraces between Ensenada, where he first reached the coast, and San Diego; whereas in the first eighty-eight leagues of his journey, in the interior from Velicatá to Ensenada, he saw only five small villages (Bolton, 1927 : 62–116). The southern part of the Terrace region appears also to have been well populated. Accounts of Viscaino's expedition of 1602 mention Indian villages at frequent intervals along the coast. At San Quintín Bay (Ensenada de las Vírgines) three villages were seen (Carrasco y Guisasola: 84). The attraction of this region for the Indians is easily explained by the abundance of fish and shellfish. Early accounts[23] mention the fishing, and numerous shell heaps along the coast show the importance of gathering shellfish. On the mesas the abundance of mescal (*agave*) (pl. 1a), the roasted hearts of which were another principal Indian food, made the region still more desirable.

Water, a critical factor in a region such as this with an annual rainfall of from five to ten inches, is found at the surface in many of the arroyo beds, or in springs near the arroyo level. As these sources of water are all considerably below the level of the main terrace plains, the plains could not be irrigated without storage facilities far beyond the resources of the missionaries. Yet, with so arid a climate, it is impossible to raise most crops without irrigation; therefore the padres could use the terraces only as grazing land. In many places, however, the arroyos run through broad valleys, with flat bottoms of good soil, and usually one or more additional valley terraces lie above the valley floor. The valley floor or first terrace can often be easily irrigated by arroyo or spring water, and the second terrace provided, for the mission buildings, a location safe from attacks by the shifting arroyo. Consequently, the missions were built in valleys, never on the main coastal terraces.

Wood for building and burning was supplied by the sycamores, cottonwoods, and willows growing along and in the arroyos. North of San Vicente, live oaks on floors and sides of valleys and a few small groves of cypress on mountains provided an additional supply. Other, smaller forms of woody growth, particularly *Rhus laurina* near arroyos and some members of the tall chaparral on the hillsides, were good for firewood. The hillsides, where not too steep, and the main terraces, supplied grass for grazing during the winter rainy season and for a while after, and some species of the low chaparral provided forage at all seasons. The quality of grazing lands grows better in general from south to north, as the climate becomes less arid. As in all arid regions, the variability of rainfall is great, and in some years there is a painful scarcity of feed.

[23] *Ibid.*: 85, for San Quintín, and Serra (p. 71) for the vicinity of Ensenada.

The greater part of the region is a true desert, but lacking excessive temperatures and evaporation rates such as characterize the deserts of the Gulf. This Pacific-margin desert is tempered by the westerly winds and their accompanying fogs. Its advantages were deemed sufficient, and seven of the nine missions of the Dominican Frontera were founded either in or on the margin of this small region.

IV. THE FOUNDING OF THE MISSIONS

GENERAL PROCEDURE—GATHERING INDIANS

AT LEAST FIVE of the nine mission sites used by the Dominicans agreed approximately with sites that the Franciscans had noted, although it does not appear that this existing knowledge was used by the last comers. Before each foundation, the Dominicans made a careful, independent exploration, but they naturally followed the road that had been laid out by the Franciscans, and the choice of the suitable sites along this road would probably have been the same by any persons of good judgment.

The procedure followed by the Dominicans in the actual founding of a mission has been described by Sales, who speaks from personal experience:

The missionary, observant of some place with water, firewood, stone and other supplies for founding, informs the Señor Viceroy. Having the consent of His Excellency, he notifies all the missionaries to give alms and help the founding of the settlement. Some send beef cattle, others cows, mules, horses and converted families to begin the work. Then he takes an escort of soldiers, for without them (though harmful) it would be an imprudence for the missionary to expose himself . . . with this train he goes out to the place selected, begins to sow, to make corrals and a stockade of sticks to defend himself; and this concluded he goes out around barrancas, caves and mountains to seek Heathen. And this is the transaction of the most difficult sort, for the Indians are wont to lie in ambush to attack the soldiers and missionary, and wound them, as happened to me. Having the fortune to meet some Indians, he talks to them of their unhappiness, with some little gifts. If the missionary does not understand the language, he talks to them through an interpreter, and assures them that he has arrived at that place to make them happy in soul and body. Some receive the proposal with pleasure; others, although they are aware of the advantages that can be gained for body and soul, after the missionary is tired of talking to them answer: "Who knows, father?"; others, urged by their neighboring Christians for instruction, flee; others (and they are the most) show themselves taciturn; and some at the first insinuation join the missionary and go to the place where he is established. It is noteworthy that the heathen Indians, although they may be forty [*sic*] leagues distant, once they are instructed and baptized, remain members (*vezinos*) of that recently-founded pueblo. These sallies the missionary repeats when he finds it convenient, and in this manner the number of Christians goes on increasing.—Sales, part 3:60–63.

Tradition among the present Indians says that where the Indians were wild and inapproachable, food was left along trails known to be frequented by them, in the hope of gathering them in. At first the Indians would not eat the unfamiliar forms of food, saying of the corn, "It is human teeth," and of the beef (quite different from the accustomed venison), "It is human flesh," but eventually some favorable response might be received.

Such gentle methods of persuasion, together with gifts, may have been all that were necessary in the days when the Indians were numerous, and it was not felt to be necessary, even if possible, to convert every individual. Later, when the Indian population grew meager, and the missions were short-handed, converts were brought in by force, just as under the Franciscans in Alta California (Blackmar: 120). Thus, one Indian gives a graphic account of being lassoed and carried prisoner to San Miguel Mission (Rojo: 9), and an important revolution among the northern Indians of the Dominican area was started by one of their leaders, ostensibly because he was enraged by the enforced baptism of his people (*ibid.:* 37–49). Such tactics are not to be regarded as characteristic of the principal period of missionary activity, especially in the southern part of the Dominican area, where the Indians had the reputation of being "humble, peaceful, and docile" (Sales, part 1 : 37).

ROSARIO

The nearest suitable location for a mission on the main highway beyond Velicatá was at the point where this trail first approached the coast of the Pacific. This place, known to the Indians as *Viñadaco*,[24] was carefully inspected by President Mora toward the end of 1773, a few months after the Dominicans had taken over the Peninsula. On his way to Viñadaco he stopped overnight five leagues from Velicatá at a place which he called *Aguas Amargas* (the Santa Úrsula of Palóu; Browne, 1896*b*: 109) and on the following day he crossed an arroyo which he named *San Vicente* (Mora: 67), a name which it still bears.

Apparently he made no new explorations, except of the immediate vicinity of Viñadaco. There, in the bottom of a broad valley, he found a dense willow thicket, running west-southwest toward the ocean across a plain which he called *Nuestra Señora del Rosario*, as it was here that the mission of that name was later to be established. In the plain was a large pool with much water and *tule, carriso*, and *junco*. The next day he followed down the arroyo and came to another beautiful plain, which he called *Santo Tomás* (the inspection being made on the saint's day, December 21), where the willows were so thick that the flow of the water was impeded. Below this was the plain of *San José*, with another pool of water and another willow thicket. Beyond this he found and named still another beautiful plain, *Santa Rosa*. On rounding the last point of land, which he named *Santa Catarina*, he saw an extensive lagoon, sweet in its upper part, though somewhat salty toward the ocean beach (*ibid.:* 68–69).

After reaching the mouth of the valley, Father Mora's party returned to the first plain to examine more carefully the water resources of the future mission. He was of the opinion that the water in the pool did not come directly from the arroyo, but from the outer borders of the plain. Acting upon this theory, he set his Indians to digging several wells in the arroyo, and from one of them water flowed with great force. He then went some two hundred *varas* away from the arroyo, opposite this well,

---

[24] This spelling is used by Mora, who gave the first complete description of the place. *Viñaraco*, Palóu's spelling, would be pronounced nearly the same by a Spaniard. Sales calls it *Viñatacot*.

and again encountered abundant water. From here he climbed a hill (probably a lateral terrace) about on a level with the tree tops and had the Indians dig a trench one and one-half varas wide and three varas long. (A vara is thirty-three inches.) At a depth of two and one-half varas they struck about a *brazo* of water, which flowed from a sierra toward the northwest. The water came out with such force that two Indians could not stop it up, and Mora concluded that with a little effort much water could be obtained, even should the water in the willow thicket dry up when the brush should be removed. It is probable that the spring which he tapped determined the exact location of the mission.

So pleased was the Father President with the results of his reconnaissance that he wrote, ". . . it seems to me that in all California, at least in that which I have seen, there is not a place more suitable for a mission, nor is it possible that farther on a better one may be found" (*ibid.:* 70). The authorities apparently approved his selection of a site, for his diary was sent to the Viceroy June 26, 1774, and later in the same year[25] the Dominicans founded at Viñadaco their first mission, that of Nuestra Señora del Rosario.

The site occupied by the mission was used for about thirty years, when it was abandoned in favor of another, on the opposite side of the valley, two miles nearer the ocean. The reason for the change, as stated to the writer in 1926 by Señor Santiago Espinosa,[26] was the drying up in 1802 of a spring near which the mission had been originally founded. An independent statement by Señorita Dorotea Ortíz[27] agreed that it was the failing of the spring which caused the change of location, but that the spring was buried as a result of a flood.

SANTO DOMINGO

Rosario had been in existence a little over a year when the second of the "Five Missions" was founded. Of the exploration for the site for this new mission almost nothing is known. In a letter of August 10, 1775, Governor Neve reported that a site had been reconnoitered a day and a half by road from Viñadaco, and had been given the name of Santo Domingo; and that its waters, lands, heathen, and so forth made it very acceptable for the establishment of a mission (Arch. Cal., P. R., 1:359). This place, identifiable only through present local traditions, is situated at the mouth of the Santo Domingo Cañon, at the foot of the well-known Red Rock. On August 30, Fathers Manuel Garcia and Miguel Hidalgo arrived on the spot to found the mission of Santo Domingo, and it was established on or about that date (*ibid.:* 377).

---

[25] Probably in July, for the first entry in the Mission *Libros* was dated July 31. Arch. Cal., S. P., M. & C., 1:281–323, gives January 7 as the date, but as all the other dates of foundations given by this report are wrong, that for El Rosario is doubtless wrong, too.

[26] Grandson of the original purchaser of the Rancho Ex-Misión Rosario.

[27] Granddaughter of one of the Mission Indians of Rosario. Age in 1928, 62 years.

This mission, like the preceding one, did not remain in its original location. It was moved two and a half miles up the Santo Domingo Cañon to a place where two confluent cañons had made a fairly wide flat. The date of its removal is not known. Engelhardt gives one clue when he states that in 1798 the Fathers put up a large building which contained a chapel, private rooms, a kitchen, all the workshops needed at a mission, and a granary, at the Rancho de San Anselmo, a league from the old mission site, apparently with intent to remove the mission to the new site. Water being abundant, sufficient land was also plowed to plant eight *fanegas* of maize (Engelhardt, 1908, 1:557). If, as the distance given might suggest, San Anselmo is to be identified with the final location of the mission, the removal would appear to have taken place in the same year (1798) or soon thereafter. The writer is of the opinion, however, that "San Anselmo" is a corruption of "San Telmo" (sixteen miles northwest of Santo Domingo), a place where, as Engelhardt goes on to state, *additional* building was carried on in 1799, in which year all the buildings erected previously were whitewashed. San Telmo was a subsidiary of the main mission. The removal of the mission itself probably took place very shortly after its original foundation, a theory borne out by the lack of remains at the original site. Furthermore, Engelhardt gives the clinching proof that the mission was moved before 1798 when he says that in 1793 the church was 8 by 18 varas, which agrees with the measurements of the ruins at the second site today. The reason for the change, as stated by Negrete (p. 350), was lack of water. In summer the water of the Santo Domingo River sinks into its sandy bed before reaching the first mission site at the mouth of the cañon.

There was a delay of five years before the next Dominican foundation, a result, probably, of bad conditions in the new establishments. These conditions arose, according to Father Hidalgo, of the new Mission of Santo Domingo, because of an insufficient garrison for the three frontier missions. The Indians were disorderly and many of them deserted. In fact, he believed that the best step would be to retire the Padres of Santo Domingo, though he admitted that this would make impossible the continuance of the conquest of the frontier (Arch. Cal., P. S. P., 1:265–266). Apparently, conditions soon improved, the seventeen officers and men in the three frontier missions at the time of Hidalgo's complaint (May, 1777; *ibid.*: 277) having been increased to twenty-seven within four months (Arch. Cal., P. R., 1:33–34). Nevertheless, Santo Domingo grew very slowly (fig. 24; see page 136), and this fact must have further discouraged continued expansion.

SAN VICENTE

At last, says Sales, ". . . vanquished many difficulties which were offered in the Province, the year 1780 arrived, in which the missionaries, desirous of advancing their conquests, examined another place some twenty leagues distant from the last for establishing the Mission of San Vicente

Ferrer, which was accomplished with all success, although with many assaults on the part of the heathen, for they are arrogant, and always inclined to do evil" (Sales, part 3 : 65). The governor reported that the mission was started on August 27, 1780, at the place of Santa Rosalia, which "has much and good land of irrigation and 'humedad,' plentiful water, and much and near-by pasture" (Arch. Cal., P. R., 2:77–81). Crespi had described this same place (which he called Santa Isabel) as a large plain, with green grass, a marsh, plenty of water in the arroyo, and arable land: a good site for a mission (Bolton, 1927 : 89). Results confirmed his judgment, for this mission proved to be one of the few which the Dominicans did not move to a new site.

SAN MIGUEL

Hostile Indians, an annoyance to the founders of San Vicente, were also a chief cause of a delay of seven years in founding the next mission, for in 1781 the Yumas destroyed two "pueblo missions" which the Franciscans had founded on the Colorado River, massacring priests, colonists, and soldiers, including Rivera y Moncada. To quote Sales, "This sad occurrence attracted the attention of the Commander General, and no longer did he think of extending the conquest, but of restoring and fortifying that already conquered" (Sales, part 3 : 67). As San Vicente was believed to be only a day and a half distant from those bloodthirsty Indians, the concern of the authorities is not surprising. To make matters worse, the Frontera was retarded by a severe epidemic of smallpox which reached its maximum in 1780 at San Fernando, in 1781 at Santo Domingo, and in 1782 at El Rosario and San Vicente (fig. 24). Regardless of the condition of the Peninsula, however, the camino had to be protected. The King, on October 24, 1781, had commanded that some new missions be at once established to connect the settlements of Old and New California (Bancroft, 1884b, 1 : 722). The Viceroy reported that the establishment of the fourth and fifth missions had been proceeding "since 1784" (Revillagigedo, 1789).

The explorations were apparently undertaken by Fray Luis Sales, the missionary at San Vicente. According to his account, which is sadly deficient in dates and place-names, a first reconnaissance was hampered by storms. A second resulted in the discovery of a satisfactory site some thirty leagues from San Vicente. After the Viceroy had been informed of the site and had approved the building of a mission there, Sales and the Governor set out to found the new establishment. "But look you," says Sales, "how great an affliction did I not have when, entering the places already reconnoitered, in which there had been so many possibilities, nothing was to be seen but banks of sand and beds of rock, the result of a furious flood which stopped up all the springs of water." Then they moved to another site, which they found "at an arroyo called 'encina,' which place, though of small size, would be able to serve provisionally." A search of the neighborhood failing to reveal a better site, the foundation was begun there.[28]

Fages gives a somewhat different version of the selection of this site. A letter of his dated May 4, 1785, two years before the mission was founded, indicated that "el Encino" was already his choice as a site. He wrote:

In the reconnaissance that has just been made[29] to found the fourth mission which should cover the road between the frontier and San Diego, no better place has been discovered than the "Encino," which is halfway between San Diego and San Vicente. This place is very advantageous because of its plentiful and rich lands, much and very accessible water, pastures and woodland, a clear building site, and beautiful climate, and the *camino real* passes through it.—Arch. Cal., P. R., 1:517–520.

Here, on March 28, 1787, the Mission of San Miguel Arcangel was founded[30] and became generally known as San Miguel Encino, or San Miguel de la Frontera. The instructions for founding the mission were directed chiefly toward preventing any antagonism of the surrounding Indians, who, according to Fages, had until then shown themselves the most "bronco" of any (Arch. Cal., P. R., 3:642–646).

The precise location of El Encino, the site of the original San Miguel Mission, is not known. From Fages we know that it lay on the main road. In another letter, dated two days earlier than the one quoted, Fages states that the new road to El Encino goes by way of the high plain (Arch. Cal., P. R., 2:417–419). Still another manuscript states that El Encino is three leagues from the later site of the San Miguel Mission (below, pp. 26 ff.). In the same general vicinity, the writer, in the summer of 1928, passed a Russian ranch house whose occupants declared that their place was known as "La Misión." There is a possibility that this name was handed down from the original foundation at El Encino, and that this was its approximate location. The distance of the ranch from Misión Vieja, the later San Miguel Mission (about seven miles by an old road), and its situation on the eastern edge of one of the high plains peculiar to this area, just above an *encina*–(live-oak) filled cañon, tend to support this notion.

---

[28] Sales, part 3:77–79. *El Viagero Universal* (26:184) states that the search for a better site than the Encina ended because the Governor grew tired and went away.

[29] Engelhardt (1908, 1:527) states that Fages selected the Encino early in 1783.

[30] Arch. Cal., P. S. P., 7:103. Bancroft (1884b, 1:725 ff.) says that San Miguel is mentioned in a letter dated 1777 (Arch. Cal., S. P. Sac., 8:260–296; p. 45 of the Bancroft Library copy) and that it must therefore have been founded by that date. Bancroft's confusion arose from the fact that the document is signed "Fr. Anto. Cruzado, Predicador del Colegio de Propaganda y ministro de San Miguel Arcangel. June 19, 1777." Fray Cruzado was a Franciscan, but the Franciscan Mission of San Miguel was not founded until July 25, 1797. The mission at which he was actually stationed, however, and which is repeatedly mentioned elsewhere in the same document, was San Gabriel Arcangel (see Bancroft, 1884a, 1:181). Evidently, Fray Cruzado or the copyist confused the two Archangels and originated the discrepancy noted by Bancroft.

On the same page, Bancroft makes the contradictory statements that the explorations for El Encino were made in 1785, and that the mission was founded there in March, 1784. Sales gives 1787 as the date of founding.

The original dissatisfaction of Sales with El Encino proved to have been well grounded, for while the buildings were being constructed and the first crops sown, the supply of water dried up. While they were in this predicament, says Sales, a heathen appeared, bitten by a rattlesnake. Sales cured him "with common oil," and the Indian, who was captain of a place called San Juan Bautista, showed his gratitude by inviting the party to his own land, where, he said, all the conditions were suitable for founding a *pueblo*. The entire pack train immediately moved to the new place, where work was begun to great advantage.[31] According to the statement of Arrillaga, in a letter of 1793, the removal to the new site was not made until 1788 (Arch. Cal., P. R., 1: 632–633), a statement which is borne out by the fact that approval for the change was not given by Comandante General Loyola at Arizpe until September, 1787. Loyola concluded his letter of consent with the admonition that, in future, care should be taken to make "prolix reconnaissances, so that changes will not have to be made" (Arch. Cal., P. S. P., 7: 68–69), a warning that seems to have had little effect in stabilizing subsequent foundations.

The change of site of San Miguel again vindicated the good judgment of Crespi, who had said that the Valley of San Juan Bautista was suitable for a good mission; indeed, that with its verdure and houses it looked like a mission already established. He had noticed in it plenty of water, land, and pasture, and many little Indian houses, which appeared like a town, all very near the shore. This ideal valley, surprisingly enough, does not seem to have been known at first to the founders of San Miguel, which indicates that the Dominicans were almost wholly ignorant of the early Franciscan explorations. In the present matter Sales seems not to have known even of the division agreement of 1772 between his order and that of the Franciscans, in which it was expressly stated that the last Dominican mission should be in the Arroyo de San Juan Bautista (Bolton, 1927, 7: 105).

SANTO TOMÁS

The distance of San Miguel from San Vicente, the previous Dominican outpost, was two long days of riding. It had been intended at first to build a mission at La Grulla, between Todos Santos and San Vicente. Had it not been that "very serious difficulties were noted" at La Grulla, the fourth mission might have been founded there instead of at El Encino, and a temporary gap in the Dominican line would have been prevented (Revillagigedo, MS). The elimination of the La Grulla site was a result of an exploration made in April, 1785, by Fray Luis Sales

---

[31] Sales, part 3:79–81. An account of the change, by Arrillaga, February 14, 1789 (Arch. Cal., P. S. P., 10:205–209), simply states that a more suitable place having been found in the arroyo of San Juan Bautista, some three leagues from El Encino, the old works were abandoned and the mission was founded at this new place. Bancroft (1884b, 1:725 ff.) misquotes Negrete as saying the mission was later restored to the original site; and misquotes Sales as saying that San Juan was the original site.

accompanied by Ortega. The place, they decided, was utterly unsuited for a mission. A hot spring was the only source of water, cultivable lands were limited and alkaline, and wood was scarce.

Although La Grulla was unsuitable, a site considered ideal for a mission was discovered along the near-by arroyo of San Francisco Solano, about two and one-half leagues from the *aguage* of that name. Ortega reported that it contained more than a *buey* of water, flowing from a marsh, enough good land for the planting of more than ten fanegas of maize, a good place for building houses, and an abundance of willows, sycamores, and live oaks—"enough for three missions." Pasture abounded in the main valley of San Francisco Solano and at La Grulla.[32] Two and one-half leagues below the aguage is a widening in the cañon with a smooth floor of eight or nine fanegas (at present chiefly made up of sandy arroyo bottom, which has probably increased with heavy loss of the original silty floor, remnants of which are still to be seen along the sides). At the time of the writer's visit (July, 1926), the arroyo at this point was dry, though a small spring, of much less than a buey, just above the valley floor at one side, maintained a marshy pool of water. According to the present inhabitants of Santo Tomás, the arroyo generally has running water throughout its length. Certainly in April, the time of Sales' reconnaissance, there must have been a fair amount of water. That the site described by Ortega was peripheral to the existing road is indicated by his statement that it would be necessary to reconnoiter a new road from it to Todos Santos. As the location is exactly that given by Ortega, and its appearance agrees well enough with his description, we may safely assume that it is the one that he and Sales selected.

In spite of their favorable report, Governor Fages considered the site unsuitable for a mission. His objections were that the site was a narrow cañon, with few lands and those exposed to floods, and that it would lack the sun a third of the day because of the height of the hills (Arch. Cal., P. R., 2: 468–469). He was in favor of locating the mission in the open valley, near the San Solano aguage, though the Dominican President favored a site at the lower end of the San Solano Valley, between the cañon site and the aguage site (Arch. Cal., P. S. P., 21: 193).

The upshot of the disagreement was that the fourth mission was not built at any of the San Solano sites, but instead, as we have seen, at El Encino, fifty miles nearer to San Diego. Finally, however, the President's choice of location was adopted for the fifth mission, which was thus founded at the lower end of San Solano Valley, on April 24, 1791, with the name of Santo Tomás de Aquino (Arch. Cal., S. P. Sac., 5: 846–847). With this mission, the protected line of communication between Old and New California, which had been contemplated for more than twenty years, became at last an accomplished fact.

[32] Arch. Cal., P. S. P., 5:446–448. Sales (part 3:84) mentions this exploration briefly, and speaks highly of the site.

Negrete, writing in 1853, says that it was founded at a place called *Copaitl coajocuc* (crooked sycamore), "on the skirt of the hills on the north of the arroyo, about a league to the west of where it is today" (Negrete: 352). This, beyond all possibility of doubt, identifies the site with ruins still observable. Arrillaga describes the site as being a league from San Solano, toward the coast of the Mar del Sur, "in the greatest abundance of water, provided by a marsh or lagoon which is near by. It ·is suitable for sowing maize, as it is more toward the lower end of the plain" (Arch. Cal., P. S. P., 21:193–195). This new mission would facilitate communication between the two Californias, and for this reason the Viceroy, although aware of Fages' adverse opinion, resolved to approve the foundation (Arch. Cal., S. P. Sac., 1:103–104).

The mission site soon proved to be unsatisfactory, not from a dearth, but rather from a superabundance of water. According to a letter of the Padre's, all went well the first year. In 1792, sickness began to develop, and by August only three men and two women remained well. This the Padre attributed to the proximity of the tule marsh, the air of which he believed to be noxious. He noticed that

the heathen did not live where the mission is, but farther up the plain, where the air is pure and there are no mosquitoes or gnats because the land is clearer. That furthermore it has lands more sufficient, and good, permanent water that has not decreased in twenty years. That its products will be able to support the neighboring heathendom, which is great.

Consequently, he wished to have the mission moved to this better site, which would result in enough improvement to justify the abandonment of the work already accomplished.[33]

This report led the Viceroy in 1795 to decree the change of the mission to the upper plain, in order "to avoid the complaints of the natives against the mosquitoes and bad climate" (Arch. Cal., P. S. P., Benicia, Military, 20:303). Upon receipt of the Viceroy's order (Arch. Cal., P. S. P., 21:283), Arrillaga passed it on to Ortega, emphasizing as reasons for the change the unhealthfulness of the old site, which was "so infested with mosquitoes that the heathen Indians would never live there," and the fact that the new site had purer air and clearer soil which was not less suitable for the sowing of wheat (Arch. Cal., P. R., 1:632–633). Ortega received the order in November (Arch. Cal., P. S. P., 11:338), and in June, 1794, the Santo Tomás Mission was reëstablished (Engelhardt, 1908, 1:559) at the site which it has occupied ever since.[34]

The place where the mission finally came to a rest after years of exploration, argument, and trial was the very one which Crespi, twenty-five years before, had discovered and characterized as an excellent place for a mission. His description of this original San Francisco Solano site

---

[33] Arch. Cal., P. S. P., 21:193–195. Bancroft (1884b:728 ff.), as usual, misquotes Negrete, locating the new site a league west instead of east of the old.

[34] Engelhardt (1929, 1:625) states that the mission was moved again, in 1799. In the absence of evidence of a new site, the present writer assumes that the mission was rebuilt near the same site.

might be used today : two springs suitable for irrigation a stone's throw apart in the middle of a large valley two leagues long and one-half league wide (Bolton, 1927 : 92). Fages had from the first favored the building of the mission at these springs. The opposition of the President, occasioned perhaps by the unimpressive volume of water at the springs as compared with the marsh below, had yielded only after an expensive trial elsewhere.

SAN PEDRO MÁRTIR

The Fathers being "well assured with them [the "five missions"], the transit from one to the other California, the founding of that of San Pedro Mártir was proceeded with for the purpose of reducing the heathen who remained wild in the Sierra and on the shores of the Gulf" (Gentil, MS). This seems indeed to have been the only reason for the foundation of San Pedro Mártir. If so, it is the only Dominican mission that was established purely to Christianize heathen. Its situation at a pass in the Sierra (see below, p. 31) could be accounted for by the easy access to the Gulf Indians, though the protection of a route to the projected Colorado settlement may also have been considered.

It was one of three missions which the Father President Gomez had proposed to found in the plains among the mountains to the east. The sites are listed by the Viceroy as : between Rosario and Santo Domingo; in one of the nearest valleys to the north of Santo Domingo and San Vicente; and in another valley east-northeast of San Miguel and Santo Tomás (Arch. Cal., S. P. Sac., 1 : 103–104). Arrillaga advised, on November 7, 1792, that permission should be given to occupy the first of these sites (the future San Pedro Mártir), the other two to be reconnoitered more carefully (Arch. Cal., P. S. P., 21 : 202–210).

In November, 1775, the pine-covered Sierra was explored by José Velazquez, whose route must have passed near the mission site, though his four-page diary, related from memory at the conclusion of the trip, is not sufficiently detailed to permit identification of individual places. Ordered by Neve to explore the northern coast of the Gulf in search of a port more accessible to the northern missions than that of San Luis Gonzaga, Velazquez set out with a party from San Fernando, passed through Cieneguilla, and continued north and northeast, for two days. Then, passing through many pines, and taking note of numerous Indians along the way, he climbed a mountain and saw the Colorado River, the plains about its mouth, the plains of Sonora, and the mountains beyond. Though the river appeared to be only ten or eleven leagues away, the party was deterred from descending to it by the thought that salt water might extend up its mouth for some distance, and consequently no drinking water be available. From the mountain they traveled west for three days, and struck the *Camino Real* of the new missions between Santa Ysabel (San Vicente) and San Rafael Arriba, probably at El Salado, for that evening they made camp at San Telmo (Velazquez, MS).

Velazquez' route (fig. 2) was north from Cieneguilla along the west foot of the Sierra San Pedro Mártir. He probably did not pass through the site of the San Pedro Mártir Mission, for he mentions pines only at the northernmost point of his trip. This point, in the latitude of El Salado, must have been one of the massive peaks between San Pedro Mártir "Mountain" and Valle Trinidad. Although this expedition failed in its purpose and for a while put an end to attempts to find a new port, it nevertheless contributed to geographical knowledge of the Sierra and, above all, brought back news of a rich harvest of heathen waiting to be gathered in.

There is evidence that soon after the expedition of Velazquez, and probably influenced by it, choice was made of a site for a mission near the Sierra. The evidence is the title of a document in Mexican archives, given by Bolton as follows: "Complaint of the Dominicans that they have not sufficient help to found a border mission at Cieneguilla. 1779."[35] As there are no other references to founding a mission at Cieneguilla, the matter must have dropped here, and serious consideration of sierra missions was postponed until the "five missions" were in operation. After that, Cieneguilla was no longer considered as a mission site, or was eliminated in the course of explorations.

Of the three places mentioned by President Gomez as suitable for sierra missions, a further reconnaissance sent out by Arrillaga from May to October (the dry season and quite timely for forming a judgment of aguages), 1793, reduced the number, in the Governor's opinion, to two: the site east of Santo Domingo, and a place known as *El Portezuelo*, at a pass near the eastern edge of the mountains, north of Valle Trinidad. As the latter site could be made usable only "by means of art," Arrillaga held to his first impression (see p. 29, above), and reported, in a letter of January 15, 1794, that the Mission of San Pedro Mártir would be founded east of Santo Domingo in the following April (Arch. Cal., P. S. P., 21:321). As the Viceroy had already resolved, on the basis of Arrillaga's report of 1792, that the next mission should be founded "between El Rosario and Santo Domingo" (Arch. Cal., P. R., 1:633), no further obstacle remained, and on April 27, 1794, the Mission of San Pedro Mártir de Verona was begun, at the place selected.[36]

On July 18, 1794, the very day after acknowledging congratulations on having founded the mission, Pallas wrote to Governor Borica:

The new foundation has not continued with the happiness with which it began. The crops have frozen and I have determined to move it to work at another place, situated on the western slope of the Sierra about three leagues distant from the other.

The next day he wrote that

the missionary at San Pedro Mártir says that he will move the week that now ends, because of frosts and annoyances.

---

[35] Bolton, 1913:71. Unfortunately, this and other documents have not been procurable.

[36] Arch. Arzob., 1:82; Arch. Cal., P.S.P., 21:434. *Ibid.*, 13:236 gives the date erroneously as April 29, 1795.

Ten days later, he requested permission to execute the transfer from the place called "Casilepe" to the second, called "Ajantequedo" (Arch. Cal., S. P. Sac., 9:306–308, 312–317, 322–325). Borica promptly responded, August 10, permitting the transfer of the mission to another site more fertile and sheltered (Arch. Cal., P. R., 6:583).

Concerning the location of Ajantequedo, the final site of the mission, there is no doubt. It is marked by extensive adobe ruins which are known as those of San Pedro Mártir by the present inhabitants of the Sierra. It is at an elevation of about 5500 feet, seven miles to the east of San Isidoro. The exact location of Casilepe is rather uncertain. The name is not now known to the Indians. The notes in the preceding paragraph indicate that Casilepe was at a much greater elevation than Ajantequedo and that they were three leagues apart; Casilepe therefore occupied one or the other of the two grassy parks known at present as La Grulla and Santa Rosa. Both are about eight miles from Ajantequedo, and at an elevation of nearly 2000 feet above it. The writer strongly favors Santa Rosa as the probable original place of foundation, for it lies on an old missionary trail leading through a pass across the Sierra and is, besides, much more easily accessible from Ajantequedo than is La Grulla. A pass so situated would explain the statement (see p. 29, above) that one of the objects in founding the mission was the reduction of the heathen inhabitants of the lowlands bordering the Gulf of California.

SANTA CATALINA AND NORTHERN EXPLORATIONS

As soon as San Pedro Mártir was founded, explorations were undertaken to select sites for the second and third of the missions desired by President Gomez and approved by the Viceroy. That very year (1794) Sergeant Ruiz, with Fray Tomás Valdellon, examined the aguage of Santa Catalina[37] (which had apparently been known some time before),[38] near El Portezuelo, and reported plentiful water there in October (Arch. Cal., P. S. P., 12:316). Although the Indians told them that the water was permanent (Arch. Cal., P. R., 5:569–571), Ruiz saw reason to doubt it, for the summer rains had been copious that year, and another aguage that had not received rain was nearly dried up (Arch. Cal., P. S. P., 12:316). As a result of this expedition, President Pallas immediately (January 22, 1795) recommended that a mission be established at El Portezuelo (frequently, as here, confused with Santa Catalina). A year should be allowed, he thought, for a padre and guards to go among the Indians and pacify and prepare them for religion before the actual foundation of the mission (Arch. Arzob., 1:112).

Governor Borica, however, was not willing to approve the foundation of a mission at Santa Catalina until the question raised by Ruiz con-

---

[37] Known to the Indians as *Jaca-tobojol* (Arch. Cal., S. P. Miss., 2:115). Santa Catalina is still called by the Indians "Jactobjol."

[38] Possibly Fages was its discoverer, for in a letter of May 2, 1785 (Arch. Cal., P. R., 2:417–419) he says that from San Vicente he crossed the sierra and came out near the outlet of the Colorado where the Cucupas and other Indians live.

cerning the permanence of the water should be satisfactorily answered. In a letter to Arrillaga (March 10, 1795) he ordered that additional explorations be made, before the season of rains, and in another letter (March 11) gave minute instructions for the exploration not only of Santa Catalina but also of other possible sites (Arch. Cal., P. R., 5 : 569–573). Arrillaga detailed Ensign Bernal to lead the expedition. Borica wrote Bernal a list of the prime essentials which a site must possess in order to be suitable for a mission, upon which he was to report fully. Suitable places were defined as those with a constant supply of water, land fit for raising wheat and maize, whether by rainfall or irrigation, near-by firewood and pasture, and numerous available heathen. Much latitude was allowed in the general location of the two prospective missions : one should be from fifteen to twenty-five leagues from Santo Tomás or San Vicente, to the east; the other, a similar distance from Santo Tomás and San Miguel. Nearness to the Colorado was stressed as of great importance (Arch. Cal., P. S. P., 13 : 556–571), though it is doubtful if this consideration entered very much into the selection of the site.

Bernal and his party, which included Ruiz, left San Vicente on October 18, 1795, before the winter rains had begun, and headed directly for Santa Catalina by way of the San Vicente Arroyo. From Santa Catalina, he examined the country west to the Pacific near Mission San Miguel as carefully as was possible in the nine days of the journey. As his diary gives the first known description of a large area, and as most of the places first mentioned (though probably not named) by him are still known by the names he used, the following list of the places on his route mentioned by him, in the order visited, is here inserted, supplementing the representation of his route in figure 2.

Name of place	Distance from the preceding in leagues	Name of place	Distance from the preceding in leagues
San Vicente (misión)	....	*La Alameda	....
*San Pablo (cañada)	8	*San Francisco (arroyo)	5
Santa Catalina (aguage)	7	*San Marcos (valle)	4
*San Joaquín (aguage)	4½	*Santa Rosa	5
*San Salvador (cañada)	5	San Miguel (misión)	....
*Sangre de Cristo (cañada)	5	*El Tigre	....
*San Rafael (valle)	6	Santo Tomás (misión)	....

* Names in italics are still in use. Asterisk indicates that the name first appears in this diary.

Among all the places examined, Sangre de Cristo and San Rafael were the only two, besides Santa Catalina itself, that had enough water for a mission. The water at Sangre de Cristo, gathered from several marshes, flowed in a stream 3 *cuartas* (a cuarta is one-fourth of a vara) and 4 *pulgadas* wide, and 5 pulgadas deep (72 × 12 cm.), but unfortunately most of the good lands were not irrigable, unless some of the higher marshes could be made to yield enough water. Level land, firewood, and pasture abounded. The *alameda* (cottonwood grove) in the Valle de

San Rafael, six leagues distant over a level road, was considered near enough to supply building wood. San Rafael was better equipped than Sangre de Cristo as a mission site, having many marshes and water holes, broad grassy plains, and the above-mentioned alameda. Both of these places, however, shared the irremediable defect of being entirely without Indians. At Sangre de Cristo the nearest sign of Indians was clouds of smoke in the sierra three leagues to the north, while at San Rafael not even a trace of Indians was seen (Arch. Cal., P. S. P., 13: 305–307).

Ruiz confirmed the belief that "the best site for a new mission, as far as the Río Colorado, is Santa Catalina." He described the water supply as a spring, originating in a little marsh. The irrigable land adjacent to the spring amounted to only ten *almudes de maiz de sembradura* (six and one-fourth acres), but one-fourth league down the arroyo, beyond a narrow cañon, was a flat of some ten *fanegas de sembradura* (seventy-five acres) of good land, which could be irrigated only if the supply of water from the spring were impounded by the construction of a dam at a suitable place in the cañon (*ibid.*, 13 : 553–555). That the water was permanent was indicated, in Arrillaga's judgment, by the fact that heavy rains on September 22, 23, 24 did not augment the volume of flow, which in that month was only two *naranjas* (a little less than the amount observed by the writer on July 18, 1926). Bernal further described the Santa Catalina site as having open land, surrounded by low hills with white boulders, pastures, and firewood in abundance, pine wood in the sierra one league to the north, and a "large heathendom," living on the seeds of *tunas* and *dátiles* and many other plants. He characterized the climate as cold, with north winds. According to Ruiz, Santa Catalina was one and one-half days by good road from Santo Tomás, an equal time by worse road from San Vicente, and three days from San Pedro Mártir, though he hoped that a road might be found by way of the sierra that would shorten the latter time to two days. Additional information concerning the merits of the site can be obtained from Arrillaga's summary of the results of the Bernal reconnaissance. El Portezuelo, he said, was not suitable for a mission, though Santa Catalina, three leagues away, was. The latter place was situated in a plain three or four leagues wide and eight or ten leagues long, level in some places and with low hills elsewhere, bordered to the north and east by sierras. Although land for dry farming was abundant, it was doubtful if rainfall was adequate, for it was reported that the only months of rain were May, June, September, and part of October. Snow fell from November to April. There was plenty of pasture for livestock, but places with water to drink were rare. Of Indians, there were five rancherías around the plain, with a total of from five hundred to six hundred souls, and not far to the north another ranchería which might be within reach of the new foundation. In addition, four rancherías in "el parage de la Trinidad" (first mentioned here), some six or eight leagues to the south, with at least five hundred souls, would be available for this mission (*ibid.*, 13 : 305–307, 547–555, 576–577).

Arrillaga, however, wished to see the place for himself, and make sure that no better was to be found in hitherto unexplored territory. In 1796 he personally conducted a series of expeditions that for area covered and detail of observation are without parallel in the early history of the northern part of the Peninsula. In three months in the late summer and autumn he covered on horseback a distance that he estimated as five hundred leagues, much of it in unknown territory. He made four journeys, with San Vicente as the main base. In the first, he visited Santa Catalina and explored the country south of it, particularly Valle Trinidad. In the second, he surmounted the Sierra San Pedro Mártir, descended its east slope, and crossed the formidable desert to the port of San Felipe on the Gulf of California, examining on his return the arroyos at the base of the Sierra as far as Valle Trinidad. On the third, he surveyed the pine country to the north of Santa Catalina, a part of the east base of the sierras in that latitude, and the Valley of San Rafael. In the fourth and last journey of the series, the longest of all, he went by way of Santa Catalina to the Río Colorado, and returned by way of San Diego. The diary of his "reconnaissances," an important document in respect not only of missionary expansion but also of development of geographical knowledge, has not been published. The following condensed itineraries outline his explorations (Arrillaga, 1796) ; the symbols used are the same as those for the Bernal expedition (p. 32, above).

Journey 1. July 21–July 27
 Misión de *San Vicente* (salida) ; thence up the San Vicente Arroyo to
 San Pablo
 Santa Catalina
 El Portezuelo
 Llano de *la Trinidad*
 *Agua Caliente (in Llano de la Trinidad)
 *Los Encinos, or Nuestra Señora del Pilar
 *San Luis, or de *los Coches*
 *San José
 Misión de *San Vicente*

Journey 2. August 22–August 30
 Misión de *San Vicente*
 Misión de *Santo Domingo*
 Misión de *San Pedro Mártir* (salida)
 *La Encantada; thence north for five hours, down a steep arroyo on the eastern
  face of the sierra, and across the desert to
 San Phelipe de Jesús; thence back to the foot of the sierra (at modern Cañon
  Diablo) and north to
 *San Elias (modern Esperanza Cañon)
 *Arroyo de la Vieja (arroyo heading in San Matías Pass)
 *San Matías
 Llano de *la Trinidad*
 Agua Caliente

Encinas
San Luis
San José
Misión de *San Vicente*

Journey 3. September 11–October 3
Misión de *San Vicente*
Misión de *Santo Tomás* (salida)
La Grulla; up the La Grulla Arroyo for a short distance and across to
San Salvador
*Jesús María (now Sangre de Cristo, as Bernal had called it)
**Santa Ysabel;* thence east to the foot of the sierra, then north for a while, then
south to
*Arroyo Caliente (now Agua Caliente)
El Portezuelo
Santa Catalina
Santa Ysabel
**La Laguna*
*San Mauricio (named by Arillaga)
San Rafael
La Alameda
**Arroyo del Maneadero*
San Marcos
El Tigre
**El Carmen*
Ensenada de Todos Santos
*Las Ánimas
La Grulla
Misión de *Santo Tomás*
Misión de *San Vicente*

Journey 4. October 15–November 21
Misión de *San Vicente* (salida)
San Pablo
Santa Catalina
El Portezuelo
Agua Caliente
*El Galletal, or Zacate Toboso; thence east to
Río Colorado; thence south toward the outlet, then north to
Una laguna (now Laguna de los Volcanos) ; thence north a short distance, then
retracing steps to the foot of the sierra, then north to
*San Cristóbal (named by Arillaga; now Las Palmas)
San Sebastián (now Fish Creek Mountain) ; thence west up the now-called Car-
risso Creek to
San Phelipe (just east of the headwaters of the San Diego River)
Arroyo San Luis
Misión de *San Diego* (arrived Oct. 27) ; thence along the coastal route to
Misión de *San Vicente*

The details of Arrillaga's expeditions were apparently little known
among the Lower Californians, for none of the few place-names of
which he was the maker have been retained. His explorations were important in other ways. His diary shows clearly that in the selection of
the Santa Catalina site more importance was attached to the ability of
the locality to support a mission than to its desirability as a connecting

link with the Colorado River, as has commonly been supposed. Though Fages, after personal explorations in 1785, reported the existence of good land near the Colorado River (Arch. Cal., P. R., 2: 417–419; above, p. 31), Arrillaga, on visiting the same area ten years later, was more impressed (Arrillaga, 1796, October 21) with the number and hostility of the Indians who occupied these good lands. The idea was much discussed of erecting a presidio at Laguna de Santa Olalla, probably part of the channel of the old Abejas River (Bolton, 1930: 269). Arrillaga's report could only have confirmed the Viceroy's opinion, expressed in a letter of 1789 to the Council of the Indies, that the founding of a presidio near the Colorado to facilitate an all-land route from Mexico was not advisable, because the expense would be greater than the advantages, and the risk from Indians, whose character had been shown in 1781, would be very great (Revillagigedo, MS).

The permanence of the spring at Santa Catalina was amply corroborated by Arrillaga's observations. He visited it three times, in July, September, and October, and always found a small but steady flow of water (Arrillaga, 1796, October 16). Furthermore, in his four extensive expeditions, no other place impressed him as suitable for a mission. The founding of the mission was therefore undertaken as soon as all the conditions were ripe. This was not until near the end of 1797, for in the early part of that year, according to Padre Loriente, there were "invincible difficulties in the way of proceeding to the new foundation, through lack of various indispensable utensils, and through the inability to supply it, even with the seeds which el Rosario is contributing, and through the lack of pasture which there is in the country." He thought, however, that the troops and Indians supplied by the other missions should begin at once the work of constructing the guardhouse, church, and priest's house (Arch. Cal., P. R., 5: 704). Accordingly, on August 6 the building began (*ibid.:* 716). Three months later, on November 12, with great precautions against attack by the Indians (*ibid.*, 6: 223), the mission was officially founded with the name of Santa Catalina Virgen y Mártir (Arch. Cal., S. P. Miss., 2: 115).

As might well be expected after such a thorough series of explorations, Santa Catalina Mission was never moved to a new site.

After Santa Catalina, no more of the missions then contemplated for Lower California were founded. Plans for the third sierra mission which the Viceroy had ordered appear to have been abandoned, perhaps simply because the numerous explorations had disclosed no suitable site.[39] The idea of a Colorado-Gulf settlement did not die so easily. Suggested as long before as the time of Kino (1701), and strongly advocated by others from that time on (for example, by Venegas, 2: 193–194), it resulted in

[39] Another, though less probable reason, is suggested by a letter of Borica, March 10, 1795 (Arch. Cal., P. R., 5:569), in which he tells Arrillaga not to explore for the third mission ordered by the Viceroy, but only for the second, because of the number and hostility of the Indians.

the ill-fated Franciscan establishments at the Gila-Colorado. Renewed plans, including a strong presidio, continued to be discussed. Even in 1797, Borica was urging the minister at Santa Catalina to do everything possible to increase the amount of food supplies so that aid might be given to "the intended establishment on the Colorado River" (Arch. Cal., P. R., 6: 689–690). In 1800, the Dominican Provincial made an ardent plea for such an establishment (Gentil, MS), but the King steadfastly refused to approve another Colorado attempt.

DESCANSO

It is not true, however, as is commonly stated, that Santa Catalina was the last mission founded by the Dominicans in Lower California. Two others were founded between 1812 and 1834 near the Mission of San Miguel: Descanso, and Nuestra Señora de Guadalupe. Most of the published statements concerning these missions contain serious errors. Thus, Lassepas (pp. 91–105), whose valuable book must be used with caution, includes them in a list of missions founded between 1770 and 1796, and even gives a 1778 population figure for Descanso! Alric (p. 28), uniformly unreliable, lists Descanso and Guadalupe as having been founded in 1779 and 1790 respectively, and adds to the absurdity by giving each a population of 1500 in the year 1800. Guadalupe was doubtless confused with the Guadalupe Mission of the southern part of the Peninsula, which was discontinued in 1795 (Lassepas: 76).

Fortunately, we have the statement (undated) of the missionary who founded Descanso, Fray Tomás de Ahumada, that the San Miguel Mission lost its irrigable lands by floods, and he moved it to El Descanso, eight (*sic*) leagues to the north, where there was also some "tierra de humedad" (Troncoso: 21 ff.). As Ahumada was stationed at San Miguel from 1812 to 1814 and probably later, but had left the Frontera at least by 1822 (Engelhardt, 1929: 624–629), we may date the move at approximately 1817, with the knowledge that it was certainly within five years of that time. Negrete (p. 354) says that the San Miguel Mission was moved to Descanso and then changed back to its first location, and that afterward Fray Felix Caballero moved it back again to Descanso, where he made a new church. This fits the detailed first-hand account of the Descanso and Guadalupe missions in a manuscript collection of "relaciones" of old Baja Californians who had lived in the time of Caballero, collected in 1879 by Manuel C. Rojo. According to these "relaciones," "la Misión del Descanso" was founded by Caballero in 1830, four leagues to the north of San Miguel Mission. The latter "began from that time to be called Misión Vieja, which name has remained, leaving almost forgotten that of San Miguel, which was applied at the time of foundation" (Rojo: 78–79). Clearly, the Descanso mission was built twice.

While it appears from the foregoing that Descanso was simply the San Miguel Mission at a new site, there is sufficient evidence to show that the two existed concurrently and were considered as separate establishments, though they were always under the command of the same priest. Thus, the livestock of the Missions Guadalupe, El Descanso, and San Miguel is mentioned (*ibid.*: 23, 25), and two Indians escaped from Misión Vieja in 1837. In addition, the 1919 Goldbaum blueprint, upon which the principal landholdings are shown, labels two adjacent properties as "Misión del Descanso" and "Misión San Miguel ó Misión Vieja." Emphasis did shift to Descanso, for in 1837 it had an *escolta* (garrison), while Misión Vieja apparently had a more limited guard (*ibid.*: 25).

Descanso Valley had not escaped the observant eye of Crespi. He had described it under the name of "San Antonio" as a valley as green and pleasant as San Juan, with a thick wood of tall saplings, good for a town if the woods were cleared away (Bolton, 1927: 108). Descanso was the fourth mission to be established at a site which he had recommended. Junípero Serra's independently formed opinions as a member of the second party of the expedition of 1769 agreed with Crespi's. Such excellent judgment on the part of the members of the Franciscan expedition can be at least partly explained on the basis of their considerable frontier experience, an experience which the Dominicans, fresh from Spanish convents, lacked.

GUADALUPE

Guadalupe was unquestionably a mission. It is constantly referred to as such in Rojo's documents; its church was large enough to have a choir loft (Rojo: 37); it is called a mission as a matter of course by Señora Barré,[40] who lived in the building after it had passed from the hands of the church; and finally there is in the Bancroft Library a letter in President Caballero's own hand inscribed: "Mn. de Ntra. Sa. de Guadalupe, June 25, 1839" (Archivo de las Misiones, Papeles Originales, 2:903).

Rojo also says (p. 79):

in the month of June, 1834,[41] he [Caballero] began to found the mission of Nuestra Señora de Guadalupe, nearly in the center of a beautiful valley which is found four leagues to the east of the northern part of the Ensenada de Todos Santos, with many lands "de humedad" in the upper part of the said valley, and with running water for the planting of an orchard of fruit trees. Furthermore, the said valley has waters and pastures sufficient for the raising of livestock.

The valley was the one that had been known at least since the time of Bernal as Valle de San Marcos (above, p. 32), a name which, since the founding of the Guadalupe Mission, has been restricted in its use to the lower end of the valley. Bernal, in 1795, had dismissed it with the brief notice that it was a valley of about four leagues with some swamps of very little water, with good enough pastures, cottonwoods, and willows,

---

[40] For the fifty-two years previous to her death in 1928 a resident of Guadalupe Valley.

[41] According to Negrete, 1819–1820, but that may be disregarded, since Caballero was not yet stationed in the Frontera, and Guadalupe is not mentioned in the reports of these decades.

and some heathen (Arch. Cal., P. S. P., 13 : 305–307). Apparently, the mission was built to serve as a cattle ranch and for the raising of grain on the level lands round about, at the same time making possible the conquest of the numerous heathen who lived in and near the valley.

If the last act of the "vast colonization plan of the Spanish people was in the occupation and settlement of California" (Blackmar : 9), the last scene of the act was the founding of Guadalupe Mission.[42] The conquest of new territory by means of the mission system ended in 1834.

SUMMARY

	Founded	Site changed	Reasons for change of site
Main route missions:			
1. Nuestra Señora del Rosario......	1774	1802 (*circa*)	Water deficiency
2. Santo Domingo..............................	1775	1798 (?)	Water deficiency
3. San Vicente Ferrer.........................	1780	unchanged	
4. San Miguel Arcángel....................	1787	1788	Water deficiency
5. Santo Tomás de Aquino..............	1791	1794	Unhealthful lagoon: mosquitoes
Sierra missions:			
6. San Pedro Mártir de Verona......	1794	1794	Coldness of climate
7. Santa Catalina Virgen y Mártir	1797	unchanged	
Late missions:			
8. Descanso...	1817 (*circa*); reëstablished, 1830		
9. Nuestra Señora de Guadalupe....	1834	unchanged	

Seven of these nine Dominican missions were within a short distance of the Pacific Coast, and only two were far in the interior. This unsymmetrical distribution came about in the first place because the coastal terraces provided the most easily serviceable route from Velicatá to San Diego. Secondly, the plentiful sea food resulted in a marked concentration of Indians near the coast. Thirdly, sites with favorable water and land were most numerous in this part of the area. That access to the sea was not in itself an important factor is shown by the fact that missions were not founded near either of the two principal harbors, Todos Santos and San Quintín. The reason for the Dominican avoidance of the ports was simply lack of fresh water.

The two interior missions were built to gather in the otherwise inaccessible harvest of heathen of the sierras, and, especially Santa Catalina, to protect a line of communication to a contemplated Colorado River settlement.

The changes of site (always within a radius of three leagues or less) were made three times because of a decrease in the expected water supply, once because of the unhealthfulness of an adjacent marsh, and once owing to the severity of the climate.

----

[42] San Francisco Solano, the last mission founded in Alta California, was begun in 1823, eleven years earlier than Guadalupe.

PART TWO

THE DEVELOPED LANDSCAPES

V. ROSARIO—THE TYPICAL MISSION CULTURE

PRE-MISSION CULTURE

SO FAR AS IS KNOWN, cultivation of the soil was not practiced by Indians anywhere west of the Colorado River lowlands, prior to the European invasion. The Indian economy was entirely of the "gathering" type. The principal plant used as food was the mescal (*agave*) (above, p. 18), of several varieties, which was pretty well distributed throughout the area except in the western half of the Álamo region. The core or "head" of the mescal roasted in a pit is delicious and nourishing. The tall mast, or stalk, when young and juicy, was sometimes chewed for moisture as a substitute for water. The stem of the little coastal *siempre vive* (*Dudleya*) served the same purpose. Deer, got with bows and arrows or pitfalls, and rabbits, killed with arrows or thrown sticks, were generally available sources of meat. Wild honey formed a regular part of the diet. Other important sources of sustenance were distinctly localized. Chief among these were the mountain sheep or *borregos* of the Great Escarpment, the pine nuts of the piñon fringes of the forested sierras, the fruit of the spiny *pitahayas* (*Lemaireocereus gummosus*) of the coastal terrace-land, and the acorns (ground, leached, and eaten as mush) of the north. Most localized and probably most important of all was the sea food. Clams or mussels, obtainable along the greater part of the coast, were gathered in quantities, and often carried inland many miles, in large carrying-nets made of the twisted, treated fiber of the mescal *penca*. Fishing with hook and line and the occasional catching of sea otters was carried on with the aid of navigation on crude tule *balsas*, at least on the Pacific Coast. Even dead whales, which now and then were washed up on the beach, were not scorned. One "Forty-niner" saw one hundred or more Indians eating the putrid, stinking flesh of a dead whale on the coast north of Rosario (Cleland: 495).

Though the gathering of food must have necessitated a fair amount of daily traveling, the Indians appear to have lived in at least semi-permanent small settlements or rancherías consisting of crude huts made by inserting long willow or other branches into the ground in two roughly parallel rows, bending and fastening the tops of the rows together, and piling other branches and brush upon and at one end of the framework so formed. These easily built huts were no great incentive to permanency of settlement, especially since the movable possessions of the Indians were few and light. Away from the coast with its stable food supply, abandoned rancherías were frequently seen by the early explorers. Seasonal movements of the Indians brought about some of the changes in settlements. At the time of the piñon harvest in the fall, whole rancherías sometimes moved to the piñon woods of the sierras for a period of a month or more. In the winter, some of the inhabitants of the sierras moved down to the Colorado Desert region, or, possibly, toward the Pacific.

Freedom of travel was hampered by hostility between tribes of adjacent areas, but travel for limited distances appears to have been very common. This travel often followed definite lines, from a ranchería to the coast, to a water hole, to a friendly neighboring ranchería, or to the San Quintín or other *salina,* in quest of salt. There resulted a network of well-beaten trails in most parts of the area, particularly through passes across the Great Escarpment. The Indian trails were of great help to the Spanish exploring expeditions, as well as to travelers in the mission period following.

Establishment of the mission culture was further favored by the weak political and military organization of the natives. Although the Indians of the entire Peninsula except the Cape region belonged to the same linguistic stock, namely, the Yuman, differentiation had proceeded so far that languages of adjacent small groups of people were often mutually unintelligible. Even within a language group a spirit of unity or coöperation was strikingly lacking, as was true in general in Alta California also. Each ranchería had a "captain," but his position was little more than honorary, for the people obeyed him or not as they saw fit. It is not surprising that the Spaniards met with little concerted opposition to their early activities. It was only after the mission system had become widely spread that sentiment for general uprisings gained ground, and by that time the system was so firmly established that it could not be uprooted by the hordes of primitive warriors.[1]

OUTLINE OF MISSION CULTURE

Under the mission régime, as before it, Indians still constituted the major part of the population; and all within reasonable distance of a mission were considered as members of the community of that mission and subject to the orders of its padre or padres. The primary duty of these religious leaders was the conversion and improvement of the Indians. Toward the permanent fulfillment of this charge the padres were made absolute dictators over their subjects, in material as well as spirit-

---

[1] Concerning the Indians in the area covered by this paper, very little has been written. The accounts of Baegert, Venegas, and Clavigero apply only to the area farther south. Sales gives the most numerous data of any one author, but the value is lessened by the lack of definite localization of the greater number of the culture traits described. In the preparation of the present brief summary of the outstanding facts of native geography, the writer has relied chiefly upon notes of early travelers—Viscaino, Consag, Crespi, and Serra—and upon his own researches in the field, both along the Pacific Coast and, more especially, among the remaining Keliwas of the Sierra region, under the guidance of the Department of Anthropology of the University of California. The anthropological results of this research are to be published later.

ual matters, with a small but effective body of troops to see that their will was obeyed. Within the sphere of influence of each mission, the primitive, unsystematic, individualistic utilization of the land, which had been characteristic of aboriginal days, was replaced by a conscious, systematic, directed development of resources, with Indians as laborers and padres as leaders. The padres were the original regional planners of the West, and with a great advantage over modern regional planners, namely, that the natural area and its inhabitants were theirs to manipulate to the extent of their ability, irrespective of established institutions.

The regional pattern developed by the Spaniards was based upon two great economic systems which until then had been foreign to the area: agriculture, and stock raising. The former involved as its corollary the innovation of permanent localization of centers of population and buildings. The construction of massive buildings of sun-dried adobe bricks near the land to be cultivated was the first step in the transformation of the culture landscape. Since the arid climate precluded the possibility of successful cultivation of the soil without irrigation, except in the north, and since the combination of level soil and sufficient water for irrigation occurred only in the valleys, the principal buildings were always put up in the valleys. The general pattern of development was similar in the missions, being modified in each just enough to suit local conditions. A description of Rosario, the first mission founded by the Dominicans, and its valley, will therefore bring out the characteristic elements of the typical landscape pattern.

ROSARIO VALLEY AND ITS TERRACES

The original mission, the ruins of which are still recognizable (pl. 1*b*), is situated three and one-half miles from the ocean up the broad Rosario Valley (see fig. 7). The floor of the valley (including in the term "floor" the low, level, relatively undissected area of arroyo bottom and the minor valley-terraces between the high, steep sides) averages half a mile in width (pl. 1*b*) and is bordered on both sides at a distance of from one-half to one mile by impressive mesas, some of them eight hundred feet high (fig. 4). For the greater part of their height these mesas are composed of tilted strata of conglomerate and very soft Tertiary sandstone and shale, so soft, indeed, that they can almost be spoken of as unconsolidated. A nearly horizontal unconformable cap of slightly cemented conglomerate surmounted by *caliche* protects the mesa summits from erosion, and explains the retention of their strikingly smooth, level tops. At the edges, however, where the protective layer has been removed, the soft, exposed older material has been etched by storm water into steep ridges, cañons, and gullies, making access to the mesa tops well-nigh impossible at most points. Belts of these sharply dissected sediments, amounting sometimes to actual badlands, border Rosario Valley on both sides.

The mesas and their broken-down margins were of scant utility to the mission. The scattered desert vegetation furnished but meager forage for livestock, while some plants provided supplementary food for the Indian population. The area of real importance to the mission was the valley floor.

In producing the present features of the valley floor three sets of factors appear to have operated:

(1) From every lateral cañon and gully, in time of rain, sediments have been washed out into the valley and deposited in fans and aprons

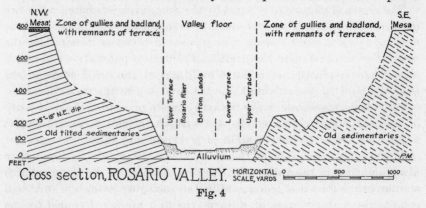

Cross section, ROSARIO VALLEY.

Fig. 4

of fine sandy silt (coarsest at the upper edge) gently sloping toward the valley center.

(2) Transverse to this action is that of the river. This is dry throughout most of its length except at the time of storms in the winter rainy season, or of occasional summer thunderstorms. At such times the swollen stream may erode the land at its margins, truncating the alluvial deposits on both sides so as to leave them in the form of lateral terraces. Today it carries from its headwaters an abundance of granitic sand, which is deposited as the water subsides, forming the sandy arroyo bottom in the central part of the valley. In its lateral swinging during many years, the stream has covered with sand a rather large area, which may be called the "bottom lands."

(3) The third factor is fluctuation in land elevation. After the deposition of the material composing the earliest lateral terraces, a general rising of the land occurred, permitting downward erosion by the stream, followed by another period of rest, during which new silty plains were deposited at lower elevations between the fronts of the early terraces. The most clearly recognizable of these early floor levels—no longer a part of the valley floor—lie at elevations of some three hundred feet and one hundred feet above the present valley bottom, the former apparently in large part a cut terrace, and the latter a fill, deposited as fans or as deltas at times of former submergence (fig. 4). During the successive uplifts of the land, these two terraces have been dissected by erosion until little of the original surfaces remain (fig. 7).

The highest valley terrace (Upper Terrace) that retains considerable stretches of smooth, undissected surface was the site of the two Rosario missions. It forms the margins of the valley floor in almost continuous strips, sloping valleyward at an angle of from one to two degrees. Its rear elevation averages fifty feet above the bottom lands. That the Upper Terrace was deposited as an estuarine fill rather than as alluvial fans is indicated by the uniformly fine silt loam that composes it. The terrace is no longer growing, and drainage from side cañons cuts through it in deep gullies.

At several places, notably for a distance of a mile and a half near the second mission and for a mile near the first mission, the Upper Terrace is skirted by a still lower terrace, only a few feet higher than the bottom lands. This terrace, the most important cultivated part of the valley floor, we may call the "Lower Terrace." In many places, as, for example, the large side-cañon at Santo Tomás, where the Upper Terrace has been cut through by gullies or small cañons, the Lower Terrace extends without any break up these channels, forming thus the floor of the side cañon as well as a terrace of the main Rosario Valley (pl. 2a).

That the Lower Terrace of today is a remnant of an unbroken valley floor that existed within historic times is indicated by old and by modern statements. Mora, in his original explorations of Rosario Valley, described its beautiful plains, with pools and reed thickets (lacking today), but mentioned no terraces or sandy wash (see above, p. 21). The present inhabitants of Rosario say that many years ago there was no sandy arroyo in the valley; the floor extended unbroken from side to side of the valley. "Then," they continue, "there came a great flood from the Sierra [date given varies between 1840 and 1875], and the river washed away large areas of good land," leaving remnants of it in the present Lower Terrace. Castro, who visited the valley in 1849, said that two years earlier a great flood of the arroyo had carried away half the land and many people (Castro: 367). There can be little doubt that at least one such flood occurred, nor that even at present, to judge from the recency of scars in the terrace fronts, the stream, during and following heavy rains, is still further cutting into the valley floor. Very likely the clearing and disturbing of the valley floor by man made possible the erosion that created the Lower Terrace, which would then be a cultural development.

Because of flooding, the bottom lands are not suitable for costly permanent developments, and even the Lower Terrace, as has been explained, is exposed to losses of territory by stream cutting. The Upper Terrace, however, is rarely subject to attacks by the stream, and consequently has been the site of most of the human habitations in the valley from pre-mission days down to the present time. Heaps of shell fragments mingled with chips of rocks and charcoal (pl. 2b), found at frequent intervals at the edge of the Upper Terrace, mark the sites of

Indian encampments. That these deposits are lacking on the bluffs of the Lower Terrace is another indication of the recency of the Lower Terrace.

The location of the middens at the tops of cliffs overlooking the lower levels of the valley (see fig. 7) suggests that the shells may have been obtained from an arm of the sea formed when the valley was at a lower level than at present, and that the present Upper Terrace cliffs were sea cliffs. There is, however, no convincing physiographic evidence that the valley has been invaded by the sea since the formation of the Upper Terrace. The Lower Terrace is rather an alluvial apron than an old estuary floor. The clams and mussels composing the middens are of types which live only by the open sea, not in estuaries,[2] and they must have been carried inland to their present locations from the shore, in accordance with the general practice all along the coast. Furthermore, there are no rocks in the valley below the Upper Terrace to which mussels could have clung; and the Lower Terrace, which would have been the floor of the supposed estuary, shows no clam deposits in its cuts.

THE FIRST MISSION

The mission buildings, like the Indian shell heaps, were built on the protected Upper Terrace. So safe from floods is this terrace that in all the one hundred fifty-nine years since the founding of the mission, none of the buildings has been undermined, though built very close to the terrace bluff. The original mission was built on a narrow remnant of the terrace, on the north side of the valley opposite the mouth of the Cañada de San Fernando (pl. 1b). The terrace is here traversed by two gullies, a little more than a hundred yards apart, which leave between them an unbroken platform with a surface that was almost entirely included within the walls of the mission structures (fig. 5). The outlines of the buildings can be traced only rather roughly now, for though the walls are two and one-half feet thick, the air-dried earth of which they were made washes away rapidly when unprotected against rain; treasure hunters have destroyed some sections of the walls; and all that now remain are small fragments, and low ridges of earth where other walls once stood.

The plan reconstructed on this evidence by Professor Hendry (fig. 5) shows that the main feature of the arrangement was a large enclosure or patio, around which the buildings were grouped on three sides, while all openings not closed by buildings were filled in by sections of wall. Such a court, characteristic of all the Dominican missions (as well as the Franciscan missions of California), was not at all original with the missions. It was an old Spanish style of Moorish-Roman origin (Blackmar: 129), in fact, a common feature of old European monasteries (Newcomb: 93), and it was admirably adapted to the frontier conditions

---

[2] Statement of Professor Bruce L. Clark, Department of Paleontology, University of California, who examined sample shells from the Rosario middens.

in Lower California. Within the court, activities could be carried on free from thieving or other interference by untamed Indians and at the same time be concentrated in a place where one of the padres could

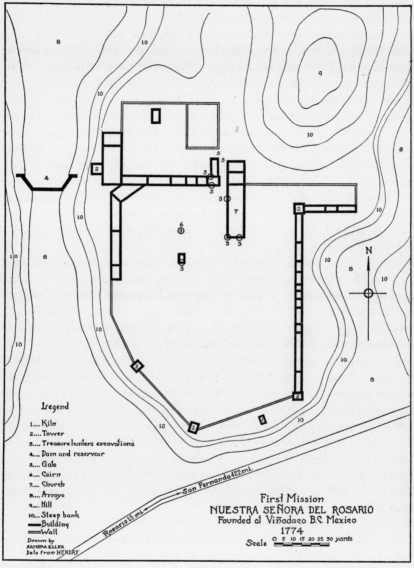

Fig. 5

readily keep an eye on them. Perhaps the enclosed court helped to keep down the number of runaway Indians. It served, too, as a walled castle in times of actual or threatened attacks by the savages, though we have no record that Rosario was ever troubled in this way.

On the north side of the court and projecting into it was the largest building, the church, alongside the main entrance. This edifice is identifiable, by its measurements as given in an annual inventory, as the one built in 1793.[3]

The use to which each of the other twenty-eight rooms shown in the plan was put, is hard to determine from the meager accounts that have been handed down. Other, later buildings mentioned by Engelhardt were an oratory, storeroom, kitchen, forge, and weaving room, which were 16, 12, 10, 10, and 10 yards long respectively, and all of them were 6 yards wide. They are thus identified as part of the group in the northwest part of the quadrangle, and may be spoken of as the industrial part of the establishment.

The long line of rooms four yards wide on the east side of the court very likely held sleeping quarters for those of the Indians who lived at the mission, for the plan suggests the "galleries" mentioned by Rojo in his manuscript collection of statements of "ancianos" of Lower California (p. 8). In describing the mission system in general he says that the Indians were shut up in galleries at night, the married people in one gallery, the bachelors in another, and the unmarried women in the "Mongerio" (convent?). At Rosario, apparently, the people were divided into smaller groups.

In the rear of the main court the plan shows another, smaller, attached quadrangle, which was probably the military headquarters, for it seems to have been customary to keep the soldiers somewhat removed from the rest of the establishment. Defense of the mission was further strengthened by small structures, described by Hendry on the plan as towers, at several strategic points along the walls of the courts.

Although the traces of walls make possible partial reconstruction in the field of the plan of the mission, there is no corresponding evidence to give an idea of its vertical profile. Furthermore, so far as the writer is aware, there has not been preserved (if ever made) a single sketch or other picture of this or any other of the Dominican-built missions of Baja California before they were destroyed. We know that the Rosario buildings had roofs of poles covered with earth. This might have been suspected, since no fragments of roof tiles are found near the buildings. The walls were probably plastered like those of other missions, since near the outer embankment are found remains of a kiln, probably for burning lime. The lime may have been derived from the plentiful shell accumulations near at hand, or, of poorer quality, from caliche. Both are occasionally used at present.

One other element of the plan of the Rosario Mission remains to be noted: the dam across the gully just west of the military court. The gully is now dry. Possibly the dam was simply intended to store water for use of the livestock in winter. It seems likely, however, that it was kept filled with water from the original spring tapped by Mora at the

---

[3] These measurements are 44 by 9 yards including the sacristy in the rear. Engelhardt (1908:556) gives its dimensions as 46 by 9 varas. (A vara is 33 inches. See App.) The main room, where services were held, was 29 by 8½ yards.

time of his explorations for a mission site. It is about on a level with the tree tops in the arroyo, as stated by Mora, and there is at present no trace of any other spring in the vicinity. That such a spring existed, and that it dried up, has already been shown (see above, p. 22). The water stored here could not have been very large in amount, to judge from the smallness of the gully dammed (see fig. 5). Its chief importance, probably, was as a domestic supply for the mission, though it may also have been used for occasional irrigation of some small patch of land.

The Indian population probably lived in other parts of the valley as well as at the mission. The names given by Mora to four plains of the valley from the mission to the sea—El Rosario, Santo Tomás, San José, and Santa Rosa, respectively—are no longer known as he gave them, and in fact seem to have been somewhat confused from the very first by the occupants of the mission. This is not surprising since there are no strong natural transverse demarcations between the different parts of the valley. At present, "Santo Tomás" is the name applied to the land a thousand yards west of the second mission, where a large cañon enters the valley on the south side; and "Santa Rosa" designates the first mission. The other names are not now in use. According to the original book of burials of the Rosario Mission, there were three rancherías: Santa Rosa, Santo Tomás, and El Rosario (*Libro de Entierros*, Rosario, 1776–1777, MS). El Rosario must have been at the mission site, Santo Tomás at the place still known by that name, and Santa Rosa on the most seaward plain in the valley, for such a location could hardly have been confused with others. The supposition that these three localities contained the principal rancherías of this part of the valley is supported by the fact that they include the principal shell middens observable (see fig. 7). The other plain named by Mora, namely, San José, does not appear in the records as a ranchería. Engelhardt (1908: 556) states, however, that "in 1799 a building containing several rooms was constructed at San José, a ranch in the district where the grain was raised." As the principal cultivated lands today are in the vicinity of the second mission, between the first mission and Santo Tomás (see fig. 7), it is likely that San José was in this neighborhood. Thus Mora's names were used, though the middle two were transposed in order, and they have been inserted in the map according to usage rather than original application.

THE SECOND MISSION

From the dates given for the construction of the building at San José (1799) and the removal to a new mission (1802; above, p. 22), it is certain that the two are identical. The second site had important advantages over the first, especially after the first dried up. It was nearer the coast and the supplementary supply of sea food, it had much more cultivable land near at hand, and it was less crowded for space, for it crowned the bluff of the Upper Terrace at a place where that terrace, smooth and unbroken by gullies, is nearly two hundred yards wide.

The plan of this mission (fig. 6), as recognizable from the extant ruins, is less unified and pretentious than that of its predecessor. At the very edge of the terrace bank and part way down stood a somewhat detached building, measuring 5 by 19 yards (probably cut up into rooms), which may have been the storehouse. Higher up, completely on the terrace, was

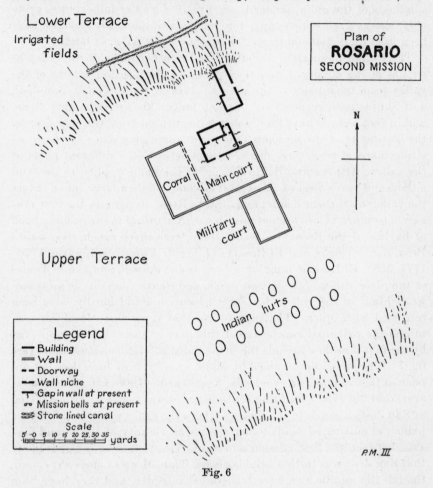

Fig. 6

the main walled court, with one end shut off as a corral,[4] and with a three-room building at the opposite end. The largest room in this build-ing is believed to have been the church, for not only does it surmount the first-mentioned building in elevation and open upon the main court, but also it seems to have been constructed with more care. The room adjoining, measuring 7 by 11 yards, was probably the sacristy, and the little chamber measuring 2 by 3 yards a cell or (and?) confessional. Behind the main court, as usual, was the military court, in one corner of which, as tradition has it, the soldiers' house was placed.

[4] According to Señorita Ortíz, already quoted (above, p. 22), who is now living in a house near the mission ruins.

Between the military court and the inner edge of the Upper Terrace the ground is dotted with barely distinguishable, shallow, roughly oval excavations, about 5 by 4 yards in major and minor axes respectively, arranged in regular rows. These, according to Señorita Ortíz, who pointed out among them the very "pozo" occupied by her grandfather, are the remains of the huts in which the Indians of the mission lived. The huts, she said, were partly dug out, and the upper part was made of willow branches bent over and tied—the same technique as was used in pre-mission days. As there is no trace of a wall surrounding these living quarters, we may conclude that the Rosario Indians had become so docile in the course of thirty years that any danger of their attempting to escape was not feared. Close under the hill behind the village is the cemetery. There was no cemetery near the first mission, probably because the dead were buried in the mission floor, whence many human bones have been removed; but in 1789 the King commanded that all establishments build cemeteries outside of the settlement, since the practice of burying the dead in churches was believed to cause epidemics (Arch. Cal., P. S. P., 10 : 411–413).

On the whole, the remains of the second mission have deteriorated less than those of the first, as we might expect, and it is possible to gain a better idea of details of construction. The foundations of the massive earthen walls are of water-rounded stones, loosely bound together by a mortar of adobe. The superstructure is of adobe bricks (composed of a mixture of mud and chopped organic refuse), mostly 12 by 12 by 3 inches, laid in rows and held together by one and one-half inches of mortar of the same material. Such wood as was used in the mission for rafters, door frames, and the like, has entirely disappeared either through decay or through use as fuel. Wood cannot have been an important element in the structure, for the supply available here was small, weak, willow trunks. For one, at least, of the doorways, no wood was necessary—a graceful, pointed arch, 9 feet high and 3 feet wide, opening into the main nave from the sacristy, perfectly preserved even now (pl. 3*a*). This detail is of special interest because the Roman-Moorish architecture of the Alta California missions did not include the pointed Gothic arch (Blackmar : 127) represented here. Small pointed niches also remain in the sacristy and cell. As there is no trace of a tower foundation, the mission bells probably hung in a terraced pediment ("Texas fashion") rather than in a pierced campanile. At present the bells (the only ones that have not yet been stolen from the Dominican missions) hang on a T-post on the old walls. The floor of the mission was formerly tiled, with well-made unglazed red tiles, 10½ inches square and 2 inches thick. The walls, both inside and out, were protected with a thick layer of white plaster, fragments of which still adhere. The dazzling white mission, in its position overlooking the broad expanse of the valley, must indeed have been a beautiful and venerated sight, visible for miles around.

FIELDS AND CROPS

The land that has certainly been cultivated in Rosario Valley within recent years—327 acres in all—is shown in figure 7. Much of it is under cultivation at present, and the rest is recognizable as having been cultivated because it is covered with a thick growth of *vidrío* (*Mesembryanthemum crystallinum*), an ice plant common along the Pacific Coast for at least three hundred miles south of San Diego. It thrives on rather hard silt or sand loams wherever the surface has been disturbed, and it is rarely found mingled with other vegetation. Thus, the mission courtyards and the surrounding trampled areas are covered with a dense mat of vidrío (pl. 1*b*), and it flourishes vigorously even on the tops of the ruined walls (see pl. 3*a*). Often it takes complete possession of fields that are left uncultivated for a year or two. To the investigator of past conditions this trait is a help, for the blood-red fields of vidrío mark, strikingly, areas of former cultivation. It seems to be almost independent of rainfall, and to thrive upon the heavy fogs characteristic of the coastal belt.

These same fogs make possible even dry farming, at least in some years, and at Rosario (where the average annual rainfall is certainly not more than five inches) it is said that when post-war prices were at their highest around 1919, the large fields of vidrío a mile east of the first mission were cultivated to wheat and beans, without irrigation. Castro, in 1849 (p. 367), remarked that above the arroyo were lands that could be cultivated without irrigation. The indications are, however, that all the valley crops of mission days were raised by means of irrigation, since there was plenty of water and plenty of land at the right elevation, and the principal crop was maize. Furthermore, though the winter rain was reported as very plentiful in the 1785–1786 season (Arch. Cal., S. P., Miss. and Col., 1 : 92), the wheat crop was unusually poor in 1786, which it would hardly have been had the wheat been dependent upon direct rainfall. Granting that no dry farming was carried on, we may at once eliminate from possible mission fields all land east of the first mission. Below, water flows continuously to the ocean, whereas above there is running water only at the time of winter storms. It also eliminates the broad Upper Terrace at the mouth of the Cañada, which is too high above the bottoms to have been irrigated.

The only direct evidence discovered concerning the lands irrigated is a short stretch of stone-lined irrigation canal, now overgrown with brush, at the foot of the bank overlooked by the second mission, and thus at the rear of the Lower Terrace. This means that the 118-acre field of the Lower Terrace ("g," fig. 7) was cultivated. To divert the arroyo water to this canal there was formerly, according to the present inhabitants, a dam across the valley at the narrows about six hundred yards below the first mission. A low dam here could easily have raised the water to the level of field ("g"), and even that of the 30-acre field ("e") of the Upper Terrace on the north side of the valley, and the 27-acre piece ("j") of the Upper Terrace west of the second mission. In addition, the pieces of bottom land now in use below the dam (9 and 28 acres, "d" and "f" respectively) were probably cultivated earlier. The more distant lands toward the west were probably not used. This gives, then, as probable mission fields, a total of 212 acres, or considerably less than one acre per capita in the prosperous years of the mission.

This acreage would be insufficient to supply the maximum crops reported for Rosario. In the best year of which we have any report, 1786, the crops were: corn, 5590 bushels; wheat, 62 bushels; barley, 576 bushels; beans, 312 bushels (see table 1). The probable yields upon soil of average fertility under mission conditions have been estimated at about 24, 18, 25, and 15 bushels, respectively, for these crops,[5] which means that the total land required for the big year would have been 284 acres. This indicates that the area under cultivation was greater than the fields now discoverable. But in 1780 a report states that there were 60 fanegas de sembradura (445 acres) in tilled fields at Rosario—more than at any other mission of Lower California (Croix, *Estado*, May, 1780, MS). This former large area is accounted for through lateral erosion by the central stream of the valley. The amount of such land destroyed between San Fernando Cañon and Santo Tomás, as indicated by the present extent of the sandy or marshy bottom lands, is about 250 acres. Allowing twenty acres for originally sandy and swampy unusable arroyo land, we get a total figure of cultivable land closely approximating the 445 acres of 1780. Unfortunately, we have no crop report for that year. If that amount of land was cultivated every year, the yields given above would have to be revised downward considerably. Very likely, however, in most years some fields were left fallow.

The largest crop of wheat or barley recorded for any year was 676 bushels; the maize crop often amounted to more than 3000 bushels. The average harvest in the prosperous period was about 2875 bushels of corn, 360 bushels of barley, 190 of wheat, and 180 of beans. Corn crops were larger at Rosario than at any other mission—at first glance a rather strange anomaly in view of the fact that Rosario is the farthest south and consequently the driest of all the Dominican foundations. The abundance of water for irrigation and the higher temperatures here afford a partial explanation.

In addition to the foregoing staple crops, fruits and vegetables were raised in a *huerta* in the field below the second mission. Fig trees and large grapevines, said to have been planted by the *frailes*, are still pro-

---

[5] Estimates of Professor G. W. Hendry, agronomist, College of Agriculture, University of California. The accuracy of these estimates is interestingly borne out independently by the crops at Rosario in 1776, probably the first year of approximately normal conditions there. The area under cultivation that year (data not generally included in the *estados*) was 14 fanegas or 104 acres (*Estado*, May 27, 1777, Calif. Transcripts, MS); the crops raised that year, with the corresponding acreages based upon the yields given, were: corn, 1820 bushels, 76 acres; wheat, 546 bushels, 30 acres; barley, 26 bushels, 1 acre; total, 107 acres.

ducing fruit there. Small tomatoes being raised near by are also said to be descendants of ones originally cultivated here by the frailes, an assertion which seems likely, since similar tomatoes were seen by the writer growing wild in several former mission fields, but nowhere else, in the Dominican area.

GRAZING LANDS AND HERDS

Rosario was not simply an agricultural center; it also maintained herds of livestock. In the period of prosperity from 1784 to 1800, these herds averaged about 75 horses, mules, and burros, 200 cattle, 800 sheep, 135 goats, and 60 hogs (see table 1). The preponderance of sheep over cattle is in harmony with the desert character of the surrounding vegetation. Only near the surface water-table of the arroyo is there a nonxerophytic growth of vegetation dependent upon ground water, ranging from the 12-foot tules (*Scirpus*) growing in the standing water of the lagoon and marshy places, to the delicate-leaved *romerillo* (*Hymenoclea monogyra*) thriving in the sandiest parts of the arroyo bed. Where the soil is somewhat finer and firmer and the water table still close to the surface, especially near the lower end of the valley, salt grass (*Distichlis spicata*) and perhaps other grasses cover the ground with green. Most important of all the elements of the bottom-lands vegetation are the willows, which occur in all gradations from shrubs less than a yard high to 25-foot trees, forming dense thickets along much of the arroyo. Probably the "gando mayor" ("larger cattle") spent most of their time in the bottom lands, living on herbaceous plants and partly on willow leaves, which when dry are relished by livestock when other food is scarce.

The plants native to the valley terraces (Upper and Lower) had little value as stock food. The prevailing plant association of these silt-loam terraces consists especially of shrubs of stiff, thorny *frutilla* (*Lycium*), bitter-leaved Indian burr (*Franseria chenopodiifolia*), and a small *Atriplex* (one of the plants known as *chamiso* to the Mexicans), probably eaten somewhat by sheep.

This "valley chamiso" association merges at the valley sides into "mescal chamiso" (as we may call this, the southern representative of Cooper's "coastal sagebrush" of California; Cooper, 1922), in which mescal (*agave*) is the dominant individual. On the high mesas and fairly level stretches of lower mesas, the mescal chamiso association also includes a *guayule* (*Euphorbia misera*), a small plant with almost leafless, bent, swollen-jointed stem, the juicy interior protected by smooth, shiny bark; *siempre vive* (*Dudleya*); *Eriogonum fasciculatum; Franseria chenopodiifolia;* and occasional plants of several types of cactus. These plants, all except the mescal apparently small from dryness (meteorologic, from deficient rainfall, and physiologic, from the cold and wind of the sea), form a fairly open formation. On the less arid, northward-facing slopes, however, the formation sometimes becomes extremely dense and changes its character by substituting for the mescal the dwarfish Parry buckeye (*Aesculus parryi*), a sprawling deciduous shrub five or six feet high, and the leathery-leaved *jojoba* (*Simmondsia*). Here and there north slopes are covered with an almost pure formation of *Adenostoma fasciculatum*, the plant which, farther north, is the principal element of the California chaparral. As the *Adenostoma* of southern California tends to give way to coastal sagebrush through the action of fire (Cooper: 82), so it must tend to give way even more easily near its arid southern limit to the mescal chamiso, remaining now only in scattered, isolated patches. South slopes in the mescal chamiso area, such as those behind the first Rosario mission (pl. 2*a*), have large spaces of bare ground between plants, and the most xerophytic members of the association dominate: mescal, *pitahaya* (*Lemaireocereus gummosus*), *cholla* (*Opuntia*), and other cacti. Another element of the vegetation on all exposures, but especially those near the ocean, is the gray lichen, *orchilla* (*Rocella*), which, apparently related to the drenching fogs along the coast, forms masses of drapery on living plants. Frutilla and guayule are the plants generally singled out as the hosts of orchilla; they may be densely covered while adjacent plants of different species are entirely free. It will be seen that, on the whole, Rosario is barely within the Upper Sonoran lifezone, though the Lower Sonoran, characteristic of San Fernando de Velicatá, begins but a short distance to the south and east (fig. 3; Nelson: 121–130). Modified by proximity to the sea and its fogs, the plant life in the Rosario area may be spoken of as belonging to the coastal district of the Upper Sonoran zone, within the *BWhn* climate that terminates near San Diego in the north (Russell, 1926: 79).

The mescal chamiso provides a considerable amount of forage for livestock. Cattle and mules are said to eat the dry *pencas* of the mescal, and to like the leaves and rich "beans" of the jojoba, of which the same or a similar species is reported to be an important source of food for goats and deer on Cedros Island (Goldman: 344). Even the thorny cholla may have been used, as it is important cattle forage in Sonora. Sheep could graze on the chamiso lands north and south of Rosario Valley.

Assuming a 40 per cent annual increase in cattle,[6] 75 per cent in sheep[7] and goats, and 200 per cent in hogs (rather conservative figures), the mission would have averaged in its period of prosperity an annual meat supply of about 80 cattle, 700 sheep and goats, and 120 hogs, in addition to the seed harvest of 3600 bushels. Some of this surplus, both of livestock and of grain, was sent to other missions as they were established, for it was the custom for existing missions to contribute to the stocking and early support of new foundations, but the greater part was doubtless used locally.

[6] A survey in California in 1924 revealed among range cattle an average "calf crop" (proportion of calves to breeding cows) of 67.3 per cent, which would mean an increase of about 40 per cent in an entire herd.—Hart and Guilbert: 3, 8.

[7] Estimate for range conditions, by Professor Voorhies, College of Agriculture, University of California.

POPULATION

The consumers of Rosario included the small governing group of *gente de razón* and the much larger one of Indians. According to Sales (statistical table), the former consisted in 1787 (an ordinary year) of two missionaries (later, in 1797, there was only one—Arch. Cal., P. R., 8:665) and an escolta (guard) of five soldiers. The Mission Indians, according to scattered estados which have been preserved, ranged in number between three hundred and four hundred during the last fifteen years of the eighteenth century. Fluctuation in numbers, from year to year, graphically represented in figure 24, was occasioned by the irregular alternation of periods of great success in baptizing wild Indians with other years of severe mortality, the result of epidemics of contagious diseases. Figure 24, based upon the original Mission *libros* of baptisms and burials, shows that the conversion of Indians was highly successful from the very beginning, with 419 baptisms in the first full year of the mission's life. At the end of the third year the population numbered 557, the highest in its entire history. In the following year, 1777, however, more burials were recorded than for any other year, and they were two and one-half times as numerous as the baptisms, though the 84 burials of this peak were much fewer than the 365 of the worst year (1780) in the neighboring mission of San Fernando (Sauer-Meigs: 288). For six years (1777–1782) the population declined, numbering at the end of that time, in the year of a great smallpox epidemic, only 251. Then followed twelve years of steadily mounting numbers, slightly interrupted in only two years. At the end of the twelve years a second maximum was reached, just how high we do not know, for although the accumulated differences between baptisms and burials up to a given year might be expected to give the population for that year, a comparison with the actual populations as recorded in the estados shows that after 1776 the actual population figure was considerably less than that to be obtained from the accumulated differences (fig. 24). The reason for this is simply that many of the Indians died far from the mission (Sales, part 3: 68) and lay unburied, or were cremated according to the Indian custom,[8] so that their deaths remained unrecorded, and others, after the first great epidemic of 1777, fled to the *monte* (Arch. Cal., P. S. P., 1:267, 276), apparently attributing the disease to the Spaniards (Sales, part 2: 96). By interpolation of the accumulated difference with the last previous census, we know that the secondary maximum of population in 1794 must have been close to 412.

Entries in the baptism book of the age of newly baptized Indians show that the year 1794 also marked the close of the active period of conversion, for after that year the baptisms were nearly all of *párvulos* (in-

---

[8] In the *Libro de Entierros* of San Vicente, Sales records such burnings on January 28 and March 4, 1785. In that of Rosario, a burning is recorded after burial number 72, in 1776.

fants), which would indicate that they were born of converted Indians, whereas in the earliest years baptisms had been in larger measure of adults and children. The following figures, selected at random and roughly calculated, of the proportion of párvulos to the total number of new baptisms, illustrate this tendency:

	Approximate percentage		Approximate percentage
First year	10	1794	50
1776	24	1796	100
1777	65	1797	60
1780	54	1807	100
1790	65		

The years at and immediately after the turn of the century were especially black at Rosario. Failure of water and change of site together with the severe epidemics of 1800 and 1805 had led to pitifully small crops: 312 bushels of wheat and corn in 1800, and 187 bushels in 1801. In 1805 Shaler found Rosario producing nothing, and dependent on its neighbors for support (Cleland: 477).

It is interesting to observe that in by far the greater number, probably in all the years, the death rate exceeded the birth rate (the latter calculated on the number of párvulos baptized). After 1794, the population, augmented by little more than the offspring of the Christian Indians, declined steadily, with burials averaging at least twice and, in the epidemic years of 1796, 1800, 1805, and 1808, from five to ten times the number of baptisms. Births were very few in proportion to the population. In 1800, for example, among a total population of 257, only five baptisms were recorded—a rate as low as in our most modern civilizations. Syphilis (*mal gálico*), for the spread of which among the missions the soldiers were held particularly responsible, was recognized as early as 1786 as a cause of great loss of life in the Dominican missions (Sales, part 1: 87–88), and was without doubt a major cause of the low birth rate as well as of the high death rate in the declining years of Rosario. Troncoso (p. 19), in 1824, declared that Rosario, with good agricultural lands, was one of the most opulent missions, but that the "frightful mortality which its sons have suffered from very active *gálico* has caused its almost total ruin. Nevertheless, it still maintains 130 to 150 inhabitants, most of them sick."

During the first twenty years the food must have been almost always adequate for the population, especially as the diet of the Indians was simple. According to Rojo (pp. 7–8), the Indians of the Dominican missions were fed corn mush (*atole*) on the six workdays, and on Sunday were given meat, and a dish of corn and beans called *pozole*. They must have consumed all the corn and a good part of the meat and beans raised at the mission. The remainder of the meat and beans, and all the wheat, were eaten by the soldiers and padres, granting that the gente de razón of those days had approximately the same diet as their descendants of the present day.

In very good years, Rosario sometimes had a surplus of food, as for example in 1797, when mention is made of seed contributed by it to the contemplated new mission of Santa Catalina (above, p. 36). Rosario, in fact, was the most productive storehouse of all the Dominican foundations (see table 1), yet even here there were bad years when the crops and livestock could not possibly have supported the population. Such years were 1782, 1800, and 1801 (see table 1), probably owing to epidemics rather than to climatic reasons. In these years of crop failure, direct recourse could always be had to an ever-plentiful supply of the wild food in the surrounding country, which previously had been the exclusive means of support of the entire Indian population. Though the cultivated land averaged less than one acre per capita for the Rosario Indians, the wild lands, with their many food-producing plants and animals, averaged two square miles for each man, woman, and child. Even in good years, according to Señora Ortíz, parties would be sent out regularly, one party to gather pitahaya fruit or mescal, another to hunt rabbits or deer, and another to collect clams and mussels at the seashore, and all that was gathered would be carried to the mission and deposited in the courtyard for the padre to distribute or to store. Such a supplementary source of food was probably of more importance at other, less favored missions like San Fernando with its circumscribed valley (Sauer-Meigs: 290–293).

At San Fernando a good part of the population lived in rancherías scattered at long intervals over the wild lands rather than at the central mission, returning to the mission on set days to hear Mass (Arch. Cal., S. P., Miss., 1 : 14). At Rosario, the greater number of the Indians may well have lived in the mission itself, where there was plenty of food and where there are, at least at the second mission, traces of a considerable village. That there were permanent rancherías about Rosario is indicated by the fact that in the *Book of Burials* of Rosario, where the birthplaces were also indicated, the same localities are mentioned year after year. The ten rancherías mentioned in the first four years include the three in the valley which have already been identified (above, p. 49) and in addition the rancherías of Socorro, Santo Domingo, Fiel, Domingo, Agustín, Cava, and Macopá.

Socorro, still known by that name, is the lower end of a broad valley on the coast twenty miles north of Rosario. On a low terrace at the southern side of the valley is one of the largest shell mounds that the writer has seen on the Pacific Coast of the Dominican area, one hundred fifty yards in diameter and one foot deep near the center (pl. 3*b*). Santo Domingo is probably to be identified with the ranchería now known as Santo Dominguito, in the Arroyo of San Juan de Dios (Señor Espinosa). Socorro and Santo Domingo, with the three rancherías of the valley, are the only ones listed in the first burial year, 1775, probably because of their greater accessibility, Socorro being on the main road to the north and Santo Domingo very close to the subjugated territory of San Fernando Mission.

The other five rancherías were probably given the names of their *capitanes,* to judge from the entries in the burial book. None of the five is now known. All but that of Cava seem to have been small, perhaps of only one or two families. One of them may have been half a dozen miles above the mission, at the confluence of Rosario Valley and Agua-gito Valley, where there is said to have been a ranchería. Another may have been at the formerly used caves of Aguagito, farther up the latter valley, where some indisputable Indian shell heaps are found at a distance of twenty miles from the sea. The rancherías cannot generally be recognized from shell heaps alone because of the great number and widespread distributions of these middens, probably of various ages, north and south of Rosario Valley.

From the few rancherías the location of which we know, we can form a rough idea of the limits of the territory tributary to Rosario, which must have included about seven hundred square miles, as shown on the map. Some idea of the relative importance of the rancherías can be gained from the number of burials recorded from each. For the first four years these were approximately as follows:

Santo Domingo	55	Santo Tomás	15
Santa Rosa	31	Fiel	7
Socorro	29	Domingo	7
Cava	28	Macopá	5
Rosario	26	Agustín	1

In addition, ten persons from San Fernando Mission and two from Santa María Mission were buried at Rosario in this period, perhaps some of those who had assisted in the original foundation, as it was customary for a few "tame" Indians from established missions to form a nucleus for a new establishment. There was a certain amount of movement from one mission to another by individuals, too, though it was not permitted indiscriminately (Arch. Cal., P. S. P., 1:265). If an Indian of San Fernando was very bad he was sent to Rosario, and vice versa, to be whipped by command of some other padre than that of his own mission.[9]

The Indians were treated like medieval serfs inseparable from a particular piece of land. The serfs were required each year to turn over a certain part of their harvests to their lord, but the Mission Indians

---

[9] According to Señora Ortíz, who, incidentally, described the whippings so graphically and shudderingly, as they had been described to her by her grandmother, that it is hard to doubt her. That floggings were numerous and many of them severe under the Dominican régime is also stated by Rojo (pp. 8–9), who says that for failure to perform the daily stint of work the punishment, "which was rarely lacking" at the close of the day, consisted of from twelve to twenty-five blows, the Indian being lashed to a whipping post called "picota," which stood at each mission for this purpose. This gives weight to the theory that the severity of the Dominicans caused "much dissatisfaction" to the Indians, in spite of good Father Zephyrin's opinion that they were not unduly severe (Engelhardt, 1908, 1:524). We even have the detailed account by a San Miguel Indian of the severity of the beatings, which led to his running away (Rojo:11).

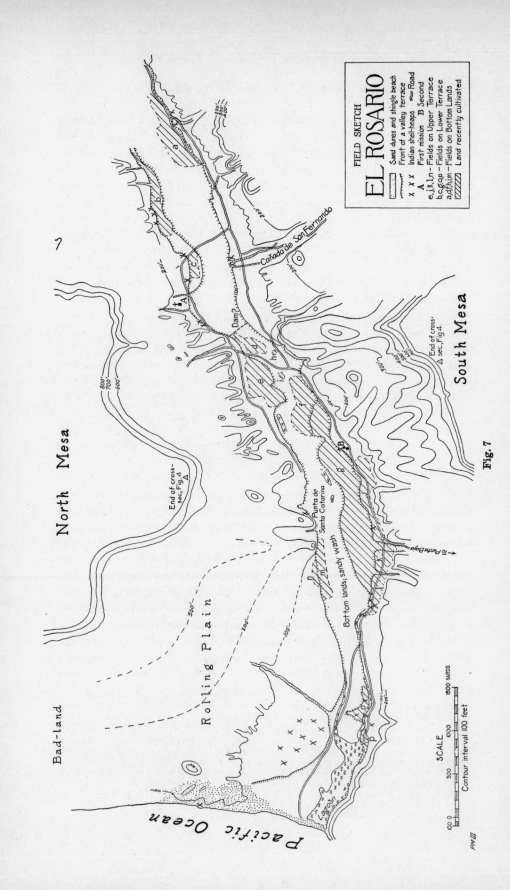

FIELD SKETCH
EL ROSARIO

Sand dunes and shingle beach
Front of a valley terrace
x x x   Indian shell-heaps
A   First mission   B Second
e,j,k,l,n – Fields on Upper Terrace
b,c,g,o,p – Fields on Lower Terrace
a,d,f,h,m – Fields on Bottom Lands
Land recently cultivated
Road

Fig. 7

never had anything of their own to turn over, since they cultivated the common fields, the harvests from which were placed entirely in the hands of the padres, to be distributed later as needed: a sort of paternalistic communism that cannot have given the wards much incentive for hard work. The central building of the mission, including within one enclosure church, dwelling quarters, workshops, storehouses, and defenses, reminds us of another medieval European institution, the self-contained monastery, which in fact suggested the plan of the mission. In spite of its many inherited features, however, the mission system remains an institution unique according to its purpose—the taming and organizing of a frontier wild in land and people.

COMMUNICATIONS

Communication of Rosario with the neighboring missions of San Fernando de Velicatá to the southeast and Santo Domingo to the north was by means of a trail (or camino), traversable only by man and animals.[10] The trail to San Fernando, as described by Negrete on a trip through the Peninsula in 1853, left Rosario Valley opposite the original mission and went up by the Cañada de San Fernando, passed a place called India Flaca, another farther on called Santa Úrsula (a sheep ranch of San Fernando), and arrived at Velicatá four leagues beyond (Negrete: 348). This trail, substantially the same as that used even before the entry of the Dominicans into Baja California (above, p. 12), is still in use for all horseback travel between San Fernando and Rosario, as it is much shorter than the modern wagon road. To the Rosario Mission this southern trail was the most important of all, for it connected with Loreto, the capital of the whole Peninsular mission network, from which issued general orders to the missions, and through which passed nearly all mail and supplies from the Mexican mainland.

The sea route to the northwestern Dominican missions was so roundabout that it was rarely used. That Rosario had occasional direct contact with sea-going vessels is suggested by the statement of Captain Morrell that on April 6, 1825, he reached St. Francis Bay,[11] and that about eight miles north-northeast from the anchorage was the town and mission of Rosario, to which a good road led from the head of the bay. Water and wood, he said, were scarce here, though vessels could procure cattle, sheep, deer, hogs, potatoes, and vegetables at most moderate prices (Morrell: 196–197). The somewhat ambiguous description apparently applies to Rosario Bay, a broad *ensenada* south of Rosario Valley formed by the southward extension of Punta Baja. The point

---

[10] The statement that travel was done without carts is based upon personal knowledge of the trails used and upon the authority of natives of Rosario. The roughness of the land continues southward, and according to Baegert (quoted in Hittell, 1:286) there were no wheeled carriages of any kind used among the Jesuit missions.

[11] Doubtless so called from the Bahía de San Francisco of Viscaino, though the original is some distance to the southward.

gives good protection against the usual coast wind (though not against the southeasterly winter storms) and the bay provides safe anchorage in from five to six fathoms (United States Hydrographic Office, 1880:11). There the mission probably added to its income by selling supplies to vessels, as well as by catching the valuable sea otters which, Morrell found, at the time of his arrival had been nearly extirpated.

The mission camino to the north of Rosario, as traced by Negrete (pp. 349–350), followed almost the present route as far as Socorro. North of Socorro Valley (pl. 3*b*), the dunes have drifted more than a mile inland, in line with the straight, northwest-trending stretch of beach along San Quintín Bay, the northwest winds parallel with the beach having had here an unusually favorable opportunity to pile up sand. It was customary for travelers to skirt these soft dunes for half a dozen miles along the hard sand beach exposed at low tide from Socorro to San Simón, a ranch near the coast south of San Quintín. As late as 1889 the Dominican Father, James Newell, on a preaching tour among the old coastal mission towns, drove along this low-tide road in a buckboard as a matter of course,[12] though the present wagon road makes a long inland detour around the dunes. Even now horsemen avoid the detour by traveling along the beach.

[12] Personal conversation with the writer. It may be of interest to note that it was Father Newell who collected the mission libros, as well as other property from the Lower California missions, and deposited them at the old Dominican monastery at Benicia. Hunt (p. 39) gives a brief account of this journey.

VI. SANTO DOMINGO

SAN QUINTÍN BAY: VOLCANOES, SALT, AND NUTRIAS

The sand barrier at Socorro formed a natural boundary between the respective spheres of influence of Rosario and Santo Domingo. The terrace widens out north of Socorro until it becomes a broad plain, the Llano de San Quintín, three miles wide at San Simón Valley, expanding a few miles farther north to its maximum width of nine and one-half miles, and including a total area of more than one hundred square miles.

This coastal plain, the most extensive in the Dominican area, was made possible through a remarkable group of recent, well-preserved cinder cones which border the coast (pl. 4a) near San Quintín Bay. Two of the cones, three miles from shore, form San Martín Island. The others occur on the mainland near the coast in two groups—a smaller, lower group two miles north of San Quintín Bay, and a larger, higher group between the bay and the ocean. San Quintín Bay, one of the most protected harbors on the Pacific coast of Lower California, was formed by the latter group of volcanoes. The hard basaltic rock (mostly trachyte: Browne, 1869a:635) of the bay group, exposed in places on the open coast by marine erosion, appears also to have been an important agency in protecting the soft sediments of San Quintín Plain against wave attacks. Without this stout shield the broad plain would by now doubtless have been reduced to a narrow terrace like the one to the south. The resistance of the volcano cluster is strikingly indicated on the map by the bold seaward thrust of this part of the coast.

Volcanic action is probably also the explanation of the surface accumulation of salt in a unique series of salinas or salt lagoons, at or a little below sea level, extending for a dozen miles north of the Five Hills. The salt comes to the surface in the form of brine—far heavier than sea water—from warm springs (doubtless partly solfataric) which bubble up in the salinas. In the basins, which are cut off from direct communication with the sea by sand hills, evaporation from the surface of the salinas, aided by aridity or a fresh wind from the sea, causes precipitation of the salt. Since very early times men have used this salt, scraping it from the bottom of the shallow lagoons into heaps where it is allowed to dry before being taken away (pl. 4b). Local tradition says that the Indians were forced by the frailes of Santo Domingo to wade about in the water in order to work the salinas, and that they often suffered painfully swollen legs in consequence. Probably most of the Dominican foundations were supplied with salt from this source, though until 1828 it does not seem to have been produced for purposes of sale. After that date a tax of four *reales* on each fanega was levied to help support the troops (Echeandía, MS).

Vessels came from long distances for this valued commodity, which was lacking on the coasts to the north. Echeandía (MS) stated that "the

Anglo-Americans from the Sandwich Islands regularly extract all they want," and after the levy of the tax they often came and got salt without being seen, as there was nobody staying at San Quintín. In 1829 the Russian brigantine "Baycal" was permitted, at the request of the Governor of the Russian Establishments, to take salt, and took on 2780 *quintales* (140 tons) of it, certainly enough to supply all the Russian settlements on the northwest coast of America.

The men of the "Baycal" also took advantage of the opportunity to carry on their accustomed occupation of sea-otter hunting, and with the aid of two *cayucos* they obtained in and about San Quintín Bay thirty-eight *nutria*[13] skins, half of which were turned over to the Mexicans for the benefit of the national treasury and later sold in San Diego for 296 pesos, 4 reales—cheaply enough in comparison with the prices sometimes received.[14] Nutrias had formerly been much more plentiful, for in 1804 Captain O'Cain, of Boston, with forty Indians and fifteen canoes on board his frigate, spent some time with headquarters at the Port of San Quintín and got about twelve hundred nutria skins, "not counting *lobos del mar* (seals)," according to Borica, who adds that "on the whole coast from el Rosario to Santo Domingo they do not leave a nutria" (Arch. Cal., P. R., 9:47–48, 118–119, 143–145). According to Bancroft (1886, 1:525–526), it was this successful expedition of O'Cain's that led the Russians to invade the hunting waters from Fort Ross south. For a long time numbers of the Northwest Indians were brought annually with their canoes to catch nutrias, even to Guadalupe Island (Browne, 1869*b*: 149), the southern limit of this animal (Scammon: 168), where the Jesuits had hunted them as early as 1737 (Nelson: 111, quoting Venegas).

The Dominican missions, and especially Santo Domingo, added somewhat to their income by the sale of nutria skins, especially by secret sales to foreign vessels. Sales states that in his time the nutria skins were regularly sold to the royal commissioners who came around to the missions at 6, 8, or 10 *pesos fuertes* apiece, although in China and Japan they were valued so highly that more than 100 pesos fuertes were sometimes paid for a single skin (Sales, part 1:26–27).

The native Indian caught the nutrias in a very original way. Kneeling in a small canoe made of bundles of dry tule tied together, and barely large enough to support one man, the Indian would venture upon the sea until he saw a mother nutria with her young floating upon the water. The mother, on sighting the canoe, would dive, leaving the little one behind. To one paw of this little one the Indian would tie a mescal-fiber cord with two hooks near the end. Retiring to a distance, he would jerk

13 Name of inland "beaver," but along the coast used to designate sea otter.

14 Meares (1790), in the last page of his Appendix, states that the valuation of a sea-otter skin as set by the Associated Merchants of London and India was one hundred Spanish dollars. Scammon (p. 174) says the skins averaged about $50 gold in price. Dixon (p. 316) says they sold at Canton in 1786 at from $60 for first-class skins to $10 for fifth-class skins. Murr (p. 409) describes nutria skins as resembling the finest black velvet.

the cord until the little one cried with pain, when the mother would return and try to free it. If the hunter was lucky, she would become entangled in the hooks and he would paddle up and dispatch her with a club. Arrows were not used, for fear of injuring the skin. This was a tedious operation and fraught with considerable danger of upsetting and drowning. Occasionally, nutrias might be caught while sleeping on the water, or when they came ashore. In pre-mission days the nutria skins were used by the Indians for making "half-cloaks," but later they were turned over to the frailes in exchange for wheat, tobacco, sashes, and some little piece of clothing; "and I think," says Sales, "that if all the Missions were supplied with this sort of goods, Nutrias would never be lacking" (*ibid.*: 28–32).

This small-scale nutria catching, which probably would never have exterminated the sea otters, apparently was continued until contact with O'Cain taught the Lower Californians the large-scale Russian methods. Even the *bidarkas* used by the Indians and Russians of the Northwest seem to have been imitated by the Santo Domingo "nutrieros," who called them cayucos, described by Rojo (p. 102) as boats made of a wooden frame with a rawhide covering, in which the nutrieros navigated along the coast and far out to sea. As late as 1835 a party of eight nutrieros is mentioned on the road from the Mission to the San Ramón ranch (*ibid.*: 101). Systematic hunting has nearly exterminated the sea otter from the Lower California coast, though one is occasionally caught napping on the beach, and even as late as 1919 seven skins, valued at $802, were recorded in the export statistics of the United States Consulate at Ensenada.

THE FIRST MISSION

Santo Domingo Mission was twenty miles distant from the Bay, doubtless because there was no permanent supply of fresh water anywhere on the entire plain or its margins. From the Port a road runs north to the arroyo of the Santo Domingo River (Negrete: 350) where it emerges from its cañon and flows along the north side of the valley to the sea. The south side of the cañon mouth is composed of a steep rhyolitic knob (Red Rock) 350 feet high (pl. 4c), at the foot of which was built the original Santo Domingo Mission. At first, according to local tradition, a large cave on the north side of Red Rock was used instead of a building for the church services, and the adobe buildings were built on the west side somewhat later. Of the latter structures nothing now remains but a fragment of adobe foundation.

The broad San Ramón Valley, stretching five and one-half miles to the sea west of this mission, has much good silty and sandy loam. The climate is too arid for dependence upon local rainfall (which at San Quintín averaged 5.1 inches annually for the period 1907–1911: Böse and Wittich, pl. 111), and the Santo Domingo River, though often rushing to the sea in an impassable torrent during winter storms, generally is

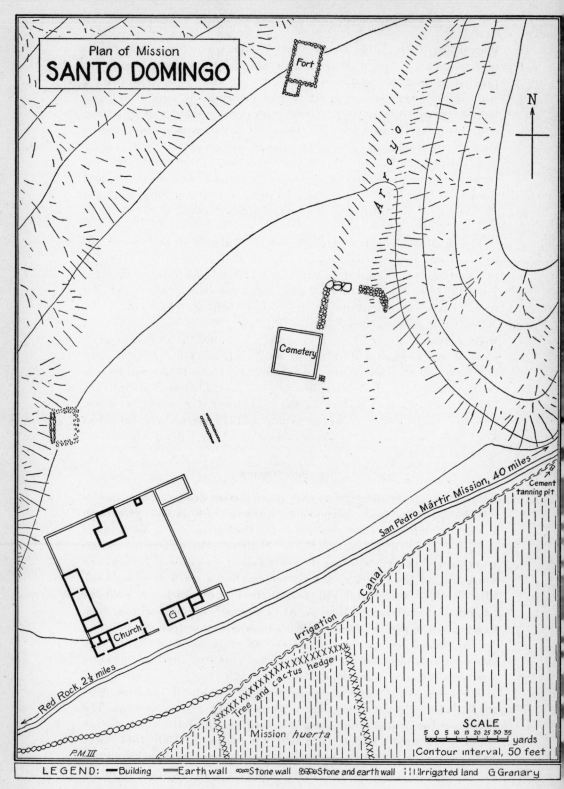

Plan of Mission
SANTO DOMINGO

Fort

N

Arroyo

Cemetery

San Pedro Mártir Mission, 40 miles

Cement tanning pit

Canal

Irrigation

Tree and cactus hedge

Mission *huerta*

Red Rock, 2¼ miles

Church

G

P.M.III

SCALE
5 0 5 10 15 20 25 30 35 yards
Contour interval, 50 feet

LEGEND: ━━Building ═══Earth wall ∞∞∞Stone wall ⊗⊗⊗Stone and earth wall ⋮⋮⋮Irrigated land G Granary

Fig. 8

so dried up in the summer that not even a trickle of water flows as far as Red Rock, making irrigation without storage impracticable in the season when it is most needed.[15] Some of the valley was cultivated under the padres, especially the land in the very mouth of the cañon, and perhaps also part of the land now included in the Hamilton Ranch near the mission (fig. 9). It is likely, also, that land farther up the Santo Domingo Cañon where the water supply is more permanent was cultivated from an early date.

THE SECOND MISSION—SITE

A glance at figure 9 reveals the limited amount of land in the cañon suitable for cultivation. The greater part of the cañon floor consists of sandy bottom lands, with the arroyo meandering through them, and no good valley terraces except fragments of a low, sandy loam terrace. Santo Domingo Cañon runs through resistant rhyolitic rock and other lavas, through which the Santo Domingo River has been able to incise only a narrow gorge. The sides of the cañon rise steeply (at angles between thirty and forty degrees) from the cañon floor to high mesas six hundred to nine hundred feet above, apparently remnants of cut marine terraces, leaving the cañon floor only three hundred to five hundred yards wide in most places (fig. 9).

The greatest width of the floor, one thousand yards, is at a place two miles above Red Rock where two side ravines face each other on opposite sides of the main cañon, forming a widening or node in it. The northern, larger ravine (which I shall here call the "mission ravine") has built up a steep alluvial cone, its base flattening out at the edge of the valley into a gentle fan which extends as a valley terrace halfway across the cañon floor for some distance downstream and for a lesser distance upstream. Upon this terrace, the only one of large extent for a distance of six miles above the cañon mouth, was built the second and final Santo Domingo Mission, at one side of the mouth of the ravine (pl. 5).

BUILDINGS

The main buildings of the Santo Domingo Mission are better preserved than those of the other missions, because they were kept roofed and protected from erosion until about a dozen years ago. The roofs are now lacking, though the church, the only mission building now in use in the Dominican area, is used as a pigpen, while the swallows have used the doorways and windows for their adobe nests.

The courtyard is a quadrangle, smaller than that of the first Rosario Mission, being only 64 by 58 yards (fig. 8). The church, too, is smaller,

---

[15] The only prosperous agricultural ranch in the San Ramón Valley is that of Hattie Hamilton (formerly known as the Young ranch), where fruit and vegetables of almost all sorts flourish amazingly; but this place is chiefly irrigated with water pumped from wells. The Colonia Guerrero, a state agricultural enterprise in the valley, depending upon water from the Santo Domingo River, seems to be in a rather miserable condition, because, according to the colonists, there is barely enough water in the river for one inadequate irrigation in the spring.

17 by 9 yards. With other, adjoining buildings, it occupies the entire front or arroyo-facing side of the quadrangle. Details of construction worth noting are: foundations of angular stones from the adjacent hillsides, roughly fitted together so as to present a fairly smooth outer face; adobe walls three feet thick, containing many large rock fragments; plaster inside and out; heavy wooden door lintels and inset shelves; at least one building (adjoining the church) with gable roof; and a buttress of roughly fitted rocks to prop the western gable.

Above the cemetery is a massive stone-and-adobe embankment six feet high and up to ten feet thick which appears to have served as a diversion dam for storm waters descending the ravine, since it lies athwart the inactive channel. There is also a system of irrigation canals, or *acequias*, which have been well preserved, partly because of continuous use and upkeep since the mission days. The acequia running along the north side of the cañon, traceable for more than two miles, is still used for irrigating the land in front of the mission, while the one by the south side, somewhat less than a mile long, stops some distance up the cañon and is no longer in use. In places, as at "D" in figure 9, the longer acequia is carefully lined with large flat stones, while at other places it appears to be simply cut in the ground. According to local tradition, there was formerly a low adobe dam across the arroyo near the present upper ends of the acequias. A careful investigation in this vicinity revealed, one hundred fifty yards upstream from a large confluent cañon (see fig. 9), rocks at the edge of the cañon floor plastered over with dried mud, very likely all that remains of a dam washed out by winter floods.[16]

A great *horno* (oven) probably used for burning lime, at "E" on figure 2, consists of a cylinder eight feet thick, well baked on the inside, strengthened by heavy adobe and stone buttresses on the outside. Two small openings in the base of the wall on opposite sides provide for a draft, and adobe "andirons" around the edge of the floor allow space for a draft under the material being burned. Across the acequia from the point of hills east of the mission, is a pair of small cement-lined pits 3 feet deep, one of them 4 by 4 feet and the other 2½ by 4 feet. These were doubtless used in mission days for the purpose ascribed by local tradition, namely, the tanning of leather.

FIELDS AND CROPS

The extent of cultivated fields can be determined with much accuracy. The largest field, outlined by the stone wall on the valley terrace in front of the mission (field "a" of fig. 9), covers 89 acres. The huerta, situated by the canal in front of the mission, is recognizable by fruit trees planted

---

16 It is interesting to note that the dam site selected by the padres was nearly the same as that which has recently been chosen for the same purpose by Mexican government engineers. The projected dam is to be a short distance upstream from the mission dam, where the cañon walls are only one hundred fifty yards apart at the base. It is expected that enough water will be obtained to irrigate San Ramón Valley and much of San Quintín Plain.

by the padres and still growing. The remnants include hedges of prickly pear (*nopales*), which were used at many of the missions not only for their fruit (*tuna*) but also to serve as practically impassable spiny barriers (at Santo Domingo probably to help protect the orchard against depredations); fig trees, now top-heavy and sprawling with their trunks on the ground but still bearing black figs; pear trees; and pomegranate trees. The last olive tree is said to have been cut down about 1916, but its stump is still pointed out. There must also have been a vineyard, for in 1780 sixty grapevines were reported (Croix, MS), and in 1786 an estado listed eleven *tinajas* (140 gallons) of wine (Arch. Cal., S. P., 1:43). Altogether, the irrigated land planted to field crops (fields "a," "b," and "c") included only 120 acres.

This area is much less than that which would have been necessary to raise the amounts of crops recorded in the best years. In 1800, the most successful year on record, the crops and the acreage needed for each on the basis of the yields previously noted (above, p. 53), were as follows: wheat, 2600 bushels, 144 acres; corn, 1300 bushels, 54 acres; beans, 260 bushels, 17 acres; total, 215 acres. Furthermore, the area under cultivation was reported as 20 fanegas (148 acres) in 1780 (Croix, MS). The 75-odd acres now under cultivation at the mouth of the cañon were probably not cultivated by the padres after the abandonment of the first mission site. Another patch of land a mile above the dam site, at a place known as San Miguel, was apparently cultivated in mission days, for it still contains sections of a stone-lined acequia said to have been constructed by the padres, and this probably accounts for the extra area under cultivation in 1780. More important, the *Asistencia* of San Telmo had begun to produce by 1800, as will be discussed later.

This harvest of 4160 bushels of field crops is considerably above the average for the mission. In the eight years for which we have records, from 1784 to 1800, inclusive (table 1), the crops averaged only half that amount, 2100 bushels: wheat, the most important, 1500; corn next, 575; and beans reported for only half the years, with crops ranging from 21 to 260 bushels. In two years 52 and 57 bushels of garbanzos and peas were harvested. Barley was not listed here at all until 1830, though at Rosario it had been raised from the beginning.

VEGETATION AND HERDS

In the period within which Rosario had an average of 800 sheep, Santo Domingo had an average of fewer than 200. Cattle at the latter mission, however, averaged 225 for the same period, as compared with Rosario's 200. It is perhaps impossible to account for these differences. Santo Domingo may simply have taken longer to get established in its production along some lines, a theory borne out by the figures in table 1, which show that at the end of the century Santo Domingo was still on the upward trend in production, and that Rosario had definitely reached the peak and was declining.

The quantity of forage in the bottom lands was less than at Rosario. *Romerillo,* willow, and large sagebrush predominate. *Rhus laurina,* a large bush of value for fuel, is common, especially toward the edges of the bottom lands. At some places above the mission is found a little mesquite (*Prosopis glandulosa*), the foliage of which makes good stock-feed, and the bark, good tanning material. It is a marginal intrusion, from the east, of Lower Sonoran life into an area predominantly Upper Sonoran. The valley terrace, too limited to be of much significance as grazing land, tends to be dominated by an association of the small green weed *Ericameria cuneata,* jojoba, and tall sagebrush.

In the surrounding country the high mesa-tops are covered with a modified mescal chamiso association, less xerophytic in character than that by Rosario, with predominance of mescal, *biznaga* (*Echinocactus*) of a low, treacherous form, and a good deal of bunch grass. Dense *Adenostoma* chaparral, five feet high, controls the north-facing brows of the high mesas. Farther down the north slopes coastal sagebrush prevails, with California sagebrush making its appearance as the chief species, together with dwarf buckeye. The drier slopes have a "dry mescal chamiso" like that in the Rosario country, with pitahaya, the most important Indian food cactus, more abundant, and with occasional thickets of small-leaved rose (*Rosa minutifolia*), a peculiar little species frequently mentioned by the early explorers as "Rosa de Castilla." On the San Quintín Plain, San Ramón Valley, and Camalú Mesa (a low mesa on the north side of San Ramón Valley), coastal chamiso prevails, with individual species, often in pure stands, varying greatly from place to place, but with mescal on the whole rather scarce. Perhaps, as was suggested for San Fernando (Sauer-Meigs: 274), Indian food demands have thinned out the mescal. Certainly the San Quintín area was originally one of the most densely settled parts of Lower California.

POPULATION

In pre-mission days there were at least three rancherías around San Quintín Bay (above, p. 18). Judging from plentiful shell middens, there must have been another at San Ramón, beside the permanent fresh-water lagoon that terminates the Santo Domingo River. A few miles north, at the mouth of an arroyo on the north side of Camalú Valley, lay another ranchería. At San Miguel, above the dam, are more shells indicating Indian occupation. Unfortunately, the mission libros give us very little idea of the place of nativity of the neophytes. In the burial book the only mention of a ranchería in the Santo Domingo area, aside from Santo Domingo itself, is of San Telmo, where a burial was recorded in 1777. San Telmo, reached thus early by the missionaries, is a valley and arroyo fifteen miles to the north of Santo Domingo. Apparently an important ranchería of the mission, it later became elevated to the rank of a regular *visita,* as will be shown presently.

In spite of every evidence that the population in the area subsidiary to Santo Domingo was large, the growth of the mission was very slow. In striking contrast to Rosario, where 565 baptisms took place in its first two years of existence, Santo Domingo made two converts the first year, and three the next (fig. 24). At one stage, Fray Miguel Hidalgo, recently assigned to the mission, had to report that "of the three baptized heathen, the two older ones ran away and have not been brought back" (Arch. Cal., P. S. P., 1:275). The books for the first two years show the startling condition of five baptisms (including the two runaways) and six burials, which is explained by the presence of already baptized Indians contributed by other missions. In the first six years of the mission, the nativity of the Indians buried at Santo Domingo was as follows: San Borja Mission, 10; San Fernando Mission, 3; Viñadaco (Rosario), 1; Santo Domingo, 6; San Telmo, 1; birthplace not given, 12. In the fourth year, 56 were baptized, the most for any year until thirteen years later, when, in 1791, 95 entered the fold. On the whole, the progress of the mission, though slow, was more lasting than at Rosario. Owing to the lateness of conversions, the early epidemics did less harm than they might otherwise have done, and even the great smallpox outbreak, which struck this mission in 1781, carried off only forty persons. While baptizing activity at both missions stopped abruptly in 1823, that at Santo Domingo was resumed four years later and continued steadily until 1839, with 45 new Christians in the twelve years, while Rosario had five.

The period of principal missionary activity, when baptism of heathen and their accompanying children was a large item in the books, ended in 1796. After that time, new baptisms were in large measure of párvulos, infants of Mission Indians, as the following figures, roughly tabulated from the *Libro de Bautizmos*, show:

Year	1775	1776	1777	1778	1780	1785	1791	1796	1797	1801	1802	1805
Adults	2	....	15	33	3	15	23	13	1	1	....	2
Children	....	1	2	9	2	12	27	....	....	....	....	....
Párvulos	....	2	9	13	11	4	43	11	8	6	10	7

Consistent excess of deaths over births began with the end of the period of active conversion (fig. 24). An epidemic in 1796 seems to have been the critical factor in turning the tide. The year before marked the high point in the population of the mission, when the neophytes must have numbered at least 350 (fig. 24). The highest census which has been handed down was that of 1800: 315.[17] In 1824, the population of Santo Domingo was estimated by Troncoso as more than 300, while that of Rosario was between 130 and 150, though the former also was being

---

[17] This figure is from an estado by Arrillaga, May 21, 1801, in Bandini, MS. Bancroft gives 257 for that year (N. Mex. States and Tex., following p. 740) but, as he copied Bandini in the figures for the other missions, he must have made the mistake of repeating the Rosario numbers for Santo Domingo.

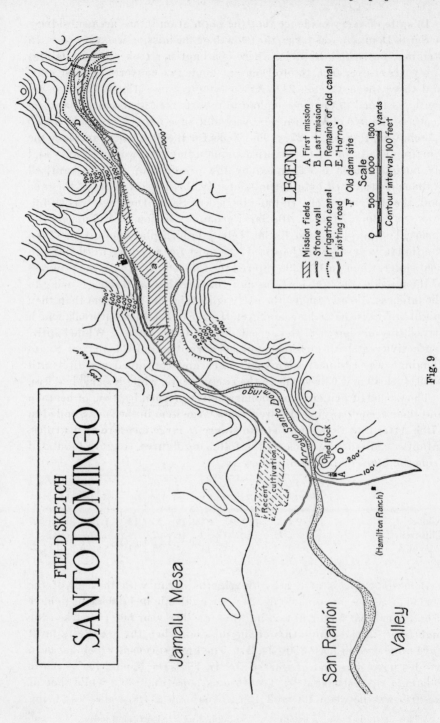

FIELD SKETCH
SANTO DOMINGO

Jamalu Mesa

San Ramón

Valley

LEGEND

Mission fields　　A First mission
Stone wall　　　　B Last mission
Irrigation canal　　D Remains of old canal
Existing road　　　E "Horno"
　　　　　　　　　F Old dam site

Scale
0　500　1000　1500　yards
Contour interval, 100 feet

Arroyo Santo Domingo

Recent
cultivation

Red Rock

(Hamilton Ranch)

Fig. 9

ruined by syphilis (Troncoso: 19–20). This high late figure for Santo Domingo resulted partly from the fact that some or all of the San Pedro Mártir Mission population had been added to that of Santo Domingo (see below, pp. 148, 149).

VII. SAN TELMO ASISTENCIA

CONCERNING THE ESTABLISHMENT at San Telmo we have little information. According to Engelhardt, an establishment equipped as a mission was built at San Telmo in the years 1798–1800, with a chapel, all the workshops necessary for a mission, a granary, a house for the Fathers, a house for cowherds, a corral of adobe posts for the wild (range?) cattle, and a dam and water ditch to irrigate the land. In addition, the water pool was surrounded by adobe pillars to keep the cattle from the water (Engelhardt, 1908:557).

It might well be believed that such extensive works could only be intended to serve as an actual mission. In fact, Gabb, passing San Telmo in 1867, spoke of a near-by "deserted and ruined mission" (Browne, 1869*b*: 111). Had it really been a mission, however, and founded by 1800, it would have been mentioned as such in some of the extant records. Also, the ruins of the Santo Domingo Mission would not now be the best preserved of any in the Dominican area if it had been abandoned in 1800 in favor of San Telmo. In the writer's opinion, San Telmo was operated concurrently with the Santo Domingo Mission and its population was reckoned as belonging to the latter. In other words, it was an *asistencia,* visita, or chapel of Santo Domingo. Finally, we have the statement of Negrete (p. 350) that there was at San Telmo a chapel, a word he did not use in describing the missions.

THE NATURAL LANDSCAPE

The San Telmo site was in many ways superior to that of Santo Domingo, for it had a permanent flow of water, with little seasonal fluctuation, and lands for agriculture and grazing more extensive and more conveniently situated than those at Santo Domingo.

For the first ten miles after its emergence from the mountains, the arroyo runs in a broad smooth valley or plain, known at present as San Telmo Valley, described by Crespi on his famous 1769 expedition as "land as level as the palm of the hand" (Bolton, 1927: 84). At its lower or western end, the valley suddenly narrows into a pass two hundred yards wide, with granite here making its appearance on the south side of the pass as well as on the north side (see fig. 10). Just east of the pass, water begins to appear at the surface in the valley, forming sedge-filled, marshy land. The location of this pass is accurately described by Crespi, who says that near it is the *Poza de San Telmo* (above, p. 10), at which he camped in 1769 after descending the dry valley (Bolton, 1927:85). Junípero Serra, in June of the same year, camped at this pool for two days, and made a thorough examination of it and the surrounding country. His description was taken over almost *in toto* by Crespi. He found the Poza to be about 150 varas long and 20 varas wide, and of a great but unknown depth. An Indian, a good diver, plunged into the pool right at the bank, and "after having been a long time under the water he came up in the same place, and said he could not reach the bottom."[18] The Poza de San Telmo is an impressive pond, in the pass, but so closely rimmed by tall tules that the water can hardly be seen except from the higher slopes at the sides of the pass (pl. 6*b*). As Serra justly observed,

All this blessing of water would be useless, or would cost much work and skill to utilize it for the irrigation of part or all of this beautiful plain (on account of being in the low part of it, although not much below) if divine providence had not arranged that on the west side of the pool there is another beautiful plain in which the same pool runs and spreads, the water occupying land capable for six *fanegas* of planting, a luxuriant place of *tules*. This land thus covered with water is followed by such a plain of good pasture land, that when all could be improved it would without doubt hold at the most 20 *fanegas* of seeding [about 150 acres].[19]

Serra believed that with little difficulty the water could be dammed up and the whole piece irrigated.

It was in this 150-acre "plain" below the Poza that the Dominicans built the chapel of San Telmo. The only breaks in the wall are the narrow eastern inlet and the even narrower western outlet (fig. 10; pl. 6*a*). The latter, like the former, is confined between granite walls, and is continued seaward by a precipitous cañon barely 75 yards wide at the bottom. The arroyo hugs the north side of the basin (fig. 10), and all the basin floor is south of a line drawn between the two passes.

SAN TELMO ARRIBA

At present, the northern half of the basin floor is occupied by the arroyo, here expanded into the semi-marsh of tule, sedge, brush, and willows observed by Serra. The southern half is of dry sandy loam, well adapted to cultivation. Overlooking this good land, about the middle of its south edge on a small alluvial fan that projects into the basin from a side ravine, are the barely discernible remains of the adobe-walled San Telmo Chapel. Near the present village is an orchard of fig, peach, apricot, and especially pear trees, the fruit of which is famous locally for its unusually fine flavor. The trees mark the location of the orchards of the chapel, for some of the pear trees are said to have been planted by the frailes.

The orchard is still watered from an old acequia massively constructed of rocks. The acequia comes through the upper pass, not from the famous Poza, but from a shallow lagoon at the west end of the valley of San Telmo. This lagoon has a somewhat higher elevation than the Poza, and consequently is better suited for irrigation. No dam is necessary, and the writer observed no trace of a dam nor any evidence that the Poza itself was used for irrigation.

From the height of the remaining part of the irrigation canal it is apparent that nearly all the good land in the basin could have been irrigated. Even so, the total cultivated land in the basin could not have ex-

---

[18] Serra, 16:638. Cañizares (MS) said that the Poza appeared to be about 24 *codos* (36 feet) deep.

[19] Serra, *loc. cit.* (Translation not mine.)

ceeded sixty acres (see fig. 10)—at first glance an unimpressive area, but half as much as the total estimated for the parent mission of Santo Domingo (above, p. 69). The marshy meadows of the basin, and the broad stretches of the valley, "well-covered with grass" (Bolton, 1927 : 85), were suited to the support of large herds of cattle and sheep, while the hills to the south, with a mescal chamiso association, and the gentle side valley north of the Poza (pl. 6*b*), could have supported additional sheep and cattle. When Gabb passed San Telmo in April, 1867, long after the time of the frailes, he was impressed by its prosperous appearance, remarking that "large herds of sleek, nice-looking cows were grazing on the flats and lying under the shade of the trees, while several flocks of sheep could be seen dotting the hillsides, or huddling together in some shady spot. . . ." (Browne, 1869*b* : 111).

SAN TELMO ABAJO

Investigations on the ground disclosed the remains of an adobe dam across the arroyo two and one-half miles downstream from the lower pass of San Telmo. Between the dam and San Telmo, a belt of hard rock, mostly acidic lavas similar to those of Santo Domingo, forms a barrier of rough hilly land, through which the cañon winds (see fig. 10). At several spots in the arroyo channel, water appears in marshes or deep pools. Below the dam, the arroyo leaves the hard rock and enters a region of low marine terraces (San Telmo Mesa), two hundred feet above sea level at their upper margin. The arroyo cuts through the terrace zone in a broad flat-bottomed valley a mile wide at one place and ends in a lagoon by the coast. The dam of the asistencia was constructed at a narrow point in the cañon just above where the cañon emerges from the hill belt and widens into the valley in the mesa land. The locality of the dam is known as San Telmo Abajo (Lower San Telmo).[20] From the south end of the dam the remains of an old stone acequia can be traced along the upper margin of the terrace. The larger, upper part, about sixty acres, may be conservatively taken as the land cultivated at San Telmo Abajo. Water enough to irrigate this land is now obtained from a ditch which "takes out" from a marshy place in the arroyo nearly a mile above the dam. Water runs the year round.

At present, wheat and barley are raised at San Telmo Abajo without irrigation; corn and beans require a little. This is the southern limit of regularly practiced dry farming in the coastal mesa lands, though to the north it is common. Rainfall measured by an American rancher (Mr. Christman) twelve miles to the northwest averaged only 5.3 inches annually for the nine-year period 1919–1928. The ranchers think that dry farming is possible because of the heavy fogs which blow in from the sea almost daily in the evening and persist until well into the next morning.

---

[20] More commonly, at present, spoken of as "Legaspe," from the name of the settler who has occupied the site for the last twenty years.

PRODUCTION

In summer, the air at San Telmo Arriba is drier and warmer than that at San Telmo Abajo, owing to the distance from the sea and the existence of an intervening range of hills. The following statement may be taken as typical of the foggy coastal desert. Simultaneous observations taken at 11 A.M., July 25 and 26, 1927, with a clear sky, showed the temperature at the seacoast to be 72°, at San Telmo Abajo 84°, and at San Telmo Arriba 91°, a difference of 12° and 7° respectively between these places, as a result of the winds from the Pacific. With water enough for irrigation and a more favorable climate, then, San Telmo Arriba was the logical site for orchards.

According to a description by Shaler first published in 1808, Santo Domingo was the best of the Lower California missions, with an annual yield of some 1500 fanegas (3900 bushels) of wheat, and other crops in proportion, and with herds of several thousand head of cattle (Cleland: 477). These amounts are so much larger than any others recorded for Santo Domingo that, granting their accuracy, we can conclude that San Telmo was then adding its products to those of the mother mission.

COMMUNICATIONS

Santo Domingo area.—In view of the advantages of water and land at San Telmo, the question might be asked, "Why was the Santo Domingo Mission not transferred to San Telmo?" The answer is doubtless that San Telmo is too far from Rosario. It was one of the functions of the missions to serve as convenient stopping places along the route to California, and the distance between Rosario and Santo Domingo, sixty-four miles, was already greater than that between any other two adjacent missions of the western route. Travelers must have taken two days for the trip between the two missions, camping overnight at Socorro, as is the custom with horse-drawn wagons today. Santo Domingo continued to be important as a stopping place and strategic center, even when excelled by San Telmo as a food producer.

Santo Domingo Mission lay not merely on the north-south trail; it was also the terminus of the shortest road, a day's travel, from San Pedro Mártir to the coast, and thus had the advantages of a crossroads location.

Northern lands.—The trail to the north left San Telmo by the valley opposite the Poza (Negrete: 351; Browne, 1869b: 111, 141) and thence followed nearly in the footsteps of Crespi (Bolton, 1927: 86). Four leagues north of San Telmo was the Valley of San Rafael, ending at the present Colnett Bay. In 1849 it had a ranch with fifteen people (only twelve at San Telmo at the same time), irrigated land (Castro, 2: 368), and a few cattle (Browne: 141). Beyond San Rafael, after traversing some four leagues of fairly smooth old inner terrace, the camino crossed a rough little range and reached El Salado, a name for which Gabb, the geologist, could find no explanation (Browne: 111), though the keen-

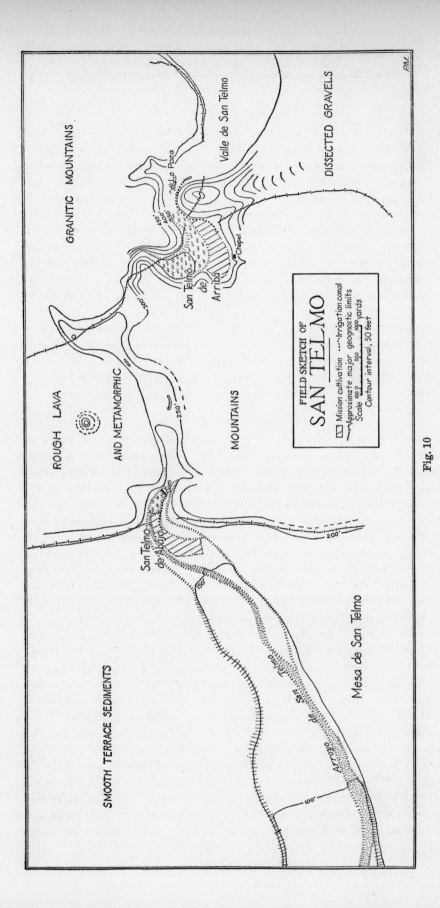

GRANITIC MOUNTAINS

DISSECTED GRAVELS

Valle de San Telmo

La Poza

450
400
350

San Telmo de Arriba

Chapel

500

ROUGH LAVA

AND METAMORPHIC

250'

MOUNTAINS

FIELD SKETCH OF
SAN TELMO

▨ Mission cultivation ····Irrigation canal
--- Approximate major geognostic limits
Scale 100 0 500 1000 yards
Contour interval, 50 feet

200'

San Telmo
de Abajo

150'

SMOOTH TERRACE SEDIMENTS

Arroyo de San Telmo

100'

Mesa de San Telmo

Fig. 10

eyed Crespi noted the characteristics which gave rise to it when he described El Salado (his San Bernabé) as a "valley which has a large, very green plain, and a large pond of salty water, although it has some that is fresh and palatable. It appears that the entire plain is full of alkali" (Bolton, 1927 : 88–89). At the time of the writer's visit in 1926, there was no pond nor any evidence that there had been one for several years, though there was a marshy area. As long ago as 1849, Castro (2 : 369) noted no lake, but described El Salado simply as a swamp in alkaline land, with good lands for cultivation in its vicinity. Hawks, the same year, observed that there was a ranch here, used only for grazing (Browne : 141).

By means of the northward extension of influence made possible by San Telmo, the total area tributary to the Santo Domingo Mission, as approximately outlined on the folded map, must have been some eleven hundred square miles. As always, these total-area figures, which show three or four square miles per capita for the Santo Domingo population, mean little. It was the small, desirable nuclei—Santo Domingo and San Telmo together, for example, had less than half a square mile of crop lands—that chiefly justified the establishment of the mission.

VIII. SAN VICENTE

SAN VICENTE BASIN

EL SALADO is at the southern edge of a plain which extends north fifteen miles to beyond San Vicente, with a width of about eight miles (pl. 6c). The plain is smoothest in the southern part and much dissected by stream erosion toward the north. Its surface is interrupted in several places by isolated granitic hills, or even rough, granitic, mountain clusters. It is surrounded by hard-rock mountains, chiefly granite (some of it partly metamorphosed) to the east and southeast, and acidic lavas (with some younger basalt on the west slopes) to the west, and is thus a basin floor. The writer proposes the name "San Vicente Basin" for the entire mountain-rimmed plain. The southern, unbroken part of the plain is known as the "San Antonio Plain."

The plain is made up in large measure of gravel, sand, and silt, only slightly consolidated here and there by occasional caliche deposits. Evidence that much of the basin floor was laid under water is found in the levelness of the plain and the sharpness of the angle which it makes with the adjacent mountains in many places (pl. 6c).

The level floor of the basin continues seaward unbroken through two narrow cañons which open through the southwestern part of the mountain rim, one of them draining the El Salado area (see folded map), the other, San Antonio Cañon, draining a lesser marsh several miles farther west. A few miles downstream the two cañons unite and lead to the sea near San Antonio del Mar.

North of El Salado Arroyo, another arroyo enters the basin at its eastern edge, flows across it, incised two hundred feet below the level of the basin floor, and cuts through the western mountains to the sea; this is the San Vicente Arroyo. It was better adapted for a mission than the El Salado Arroyo because of its permanent supply of good water, together with good land suitably situated for irrigation. The mission established on its banks was successful; it was, in fact, the only one of the five missions the location of which was never changed.

THE MILITARY CENTER OF THE FRONTERA

For military and administrative purposes, San Vicente was particularly important. From the date of its foundation in 1780 until 1849 it was in fact the "center of the frontier missions," as Troncoso (p. 20) called it in 1824. Castro (2:369) speaks of it as the old capital of the Frontera, where as a rule the military commander resided; Rojo (p. 1) speaks of it as the "Comandante Principal de San Vicente"; and Shaler (1805) excludes it from classification as a presidio only on the ground that it was commanded by an ensign instead of by a lieutenant (Cleland: 475). The existence of a military center in La Frontera was a practical necessity, for the head of authority at the Loreto Presidio, seven hundred fifty miles distant, could hardly have coped with the frequent emergencies.

Strategically, San Vicente was better adapted as the chief stronghold of the Frontera than any other mission center. It was centrally situated in relation to the five "Pacific missions," yet at the same time it lay opposite the part of the frontier most exposed to Indian attacks. The dangerous direction was the east, where, from San Pedro Mártir north, there were numbers of wild Indians against whom protection was more than once necessary. The Arroyo of San Vicente led from the heart of this unsubdued country to San Vicente, providing a natural avenue for Indian attacks. During the seventeen years before the establishment of Santa Catalina, San Vicente was fearful even of attacks by the Río Colorado Indians (above, p. 24), for the San Vicente Arroyo lay on a direct route from the Colorado region by way of the Portezuelo of Santa Catalina. After the foundation of Santa Catalina, San Vicente continued to be important as the base of support for this exposed mission.

Although it formed the nucleus of the "army" of the Frontera, the military force at San Vicente was very small, as the following table of scattered enumerations of soldiers stationed at various missions shows:

	1777*	1783†	1787‡	1804§	1824‖	1840¶
Rosario	....	5	5	....	....	....
Santo Domingo	....	6	5	....	....	....
San Vicente	....	10	8	....	8 or 10	....
San Miguel	....	....	13	....		....
Santa Catalina	....	....	....	12(about)	....	....
Guadalupe	....	....	....		....	17
The whole Frontera	17 to 27	21	31	....	....	....

* See above, p. 23.   § Arch. Cal., P. R., 9: 157.
† Bancroft, 1884*b*, 1: 723 ff.   ‖ Troncoso, 1849, 20.
‡ Sales, statistical table.   ¶ Rojo, 35.

The total force of the Frontera subject to the commands of the officer at San Vicente was only two or three dozen men. Yet such was their hardihood and loyalty, together with their advantage of mounts and superior arms, that they were able to keep order in the area most of the time. Rojo (pp. 1–6), in an excellent discussion of the escolta of the Frontera, asserts that, ably led by Lieutenant Ruiz, it often saved Lower California civilization from ruin at the hands of the Indians.

POPULATION

The maximum population recorded was 317 Indians, in 1787, seven years after its founding. The greatest influx of converts seems to have been from 1782 to 1785 (just after the great epidemic), when the population increased from 83 to 257. Unfortunately, the *Libro de Entierros* gives only meager data. It does show, at any rate, that the two great epidemic years were 1782 and 1805 (as at the other missions), and that in 1782, 27 per cent of the population was buried.

LOCAL SITE AND BUILDINGS

The settlement was situated near the western edge of San Vicente Basin. At the upper bend the arroyo expands from a ribbon of sandy bottom lands a little more than one hundred yards wide to a broad flat or plain a mile long and eight hundred yards wide at the widest place—an expanse at present of useless sandy wash covering about two hundred seventy-five acres (see fig. 12). On the inside of the bend a remnant of the basin materials projects from the northeast as a gently sloping spur, skirted by a nearly level platform. The platform is bordered on the southeast by the arroyo and on the south and west by a stretch of low smooth land. It was on this platform, eight or ten feet above the arroyo level, and extending up the slope of the spur, that the San Vicente Mission was built.

The most striking feature of the plan of the San Vicente Mission (fig. 11) was its size. San Vicente was the largest of the Dominican establishments, in spite of the fact that its population was not exceptionally numerous. The arrangement of the buildings shown in the plan suggests reasons for this size. Within the bounding wall, "three varas high with towers" (Sales, part 3 : 70), which follows the irregularities of the edge of the natural platform, the buildings, instead of being nearly all assembled about one central court, are grouped in two unconnected quadrangles of comparable size. One of these quadrangles, deployed along the forward southern edge of the platform, was unquestionably the main religious center, with a church 22 varas by 6¾ varas, mentioned by Engelhardt as having been in existence in 1793 (Engelhardt, 1908, 1 : 558), the cells of the padres, sleeping quarters of Indians, and probably some storehouses. The second quadrangle, at the very base of the spur, is not so well preserved. Probably it served as the headquarters for the escolta.

VALLEY-FLOOR EROSION AND TERRACES

Along the southwestern foot of the mission platform and dominated by the church and its quadrangle lay the principal cultivated field of the mission. This field ("A," fig. 12) occupies the bottom of a short side valley that opens upon the expanded San Vicente Arroyo from the north. The side-valley floor, of poorly sorted loam and angular rock fragments, sandiest near the San Vicente Arroyo, stretches unbroken to the edge of the arroyo, where it breaks off in an abrupt three-foot drop. South of the sandy wash another valley ("South Valley," with fields "E" and "F") with cultivable land slightly above the arroyo level joins the San Vicente Valley, and at several places both up- and downstream along the San Vicente Arroyo small areas of low terrace at comparable elevations are likewise to be seen. All these low-lying marginal areas, which make up the greater part of the cultivable land at present, represent fragments of what was once the unbroken floor of the San Vicente Valley. Erosion by the main river has washed out the central part of

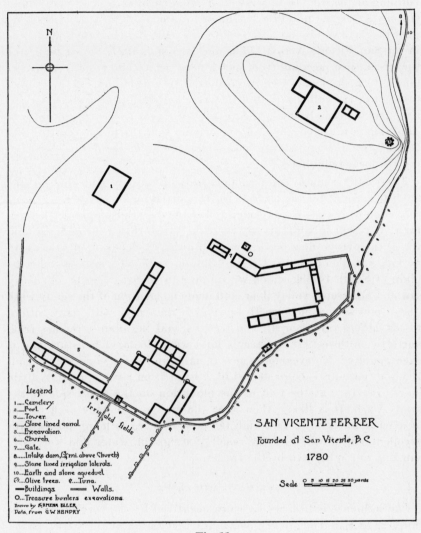

Legend

1....Cemetery.
2....Fort.
3....Tower.
4....Stone lined canal.
5....Excavation.
6....Church.
7....Gate.
8....Intake dam, (⅝ mi. above Church)
9....Stone lined irrigation laterals.
10....Earth and stone aqueduct.
⊘...Olive trees.   ¢...Tuna.
━━━Buildings.   ═══Walls.
O...Treasure hunters excavations.
Drawn by KAMENA ELLER
Data from G W HENDRY

SAN VICENTE FERRER

Founded at San Vicente, B.C.

1780

Scale 0 5 10 15 20 25 30 yards

Fig. 11

the floor and created the present sandy arroyo, which extends continuously to the sea. Thus, the history of the lower terrace of Rosario is here repeated, with the difference that at San Vicente the narrower valley has been more completely denuded of its floor terrace.

The initial cause of the erosion that produced the valley floor terraces can be pretty closely conjectured. The removal of vegetation by livestock would have affected side valleys as well as the main San Vicente Valley, but we find that only the latter has been trenched. There is no evidence of a secular climatic change within the last several hundred years. However, the region is one of seasonal rainfall which converts the San Vicente Arroyo from a dry sandy bed in summer, with a little water running at the surface in a few spots, to a rushing river during winter storms. After the middle of summer, occasional heavy thunderstorms near the headwaters in the interior cause a second, lesser period of flood in the San Vicente Arroyo. Thus, on August 1, 1927, the writer found the stream just receding from such a flood, which had risen from a mere trickle to a sheet of water two hundred feet wide and a foot deep. A resident of the valley said that the river had been up for about a week, and that it normally rose in August every year. No extraordinary assumption is involved, then, in considering that the terrace cutting was begun by an unusually large flood originating inland and thus not affecting the local tributaries.

There still remains land enough in definitely recognizable mission fields to account for the largest crops reported for the mission, yet some reduction of the fields has certainly occurred since Spanish settlement, for the present inhabitants say that some trees that grew on good land where the arroyo now is were washed away by floods. It is also worth noting that the observant Crespi (Bolton, 1927 : 89), in describing the plain of Santa Isabel, which we suppose to be San Vicente, obviously saw an undissected valley floor, and made no mention of the sandy wash that is now so conspicuous. He speaks of "an arroyo with many cottonwoods, alders [sycamores], and willows, and the plain stretches from north to southwest. It has arable land with plenty of moisture and is even marshy." No sycamores now remain, and there is only one small group of cottonwoods, protected by a bend from river erosion. A little marsh remains, at the foot of the mountain on the south side of the sandy wash. It is likely, then, that the arroyo trenching occurred in or after mission days. Two high terraces, covered in many places with excellent soil, are beyond the reach of irrigation water and were presumably not cultivated by the frailes.

CLIMATE AND CROPS

Ocean influence is in large measure negatived by the barrier of mountains, as at San Telmo. The prevailing vegetation of the slopes in the vicinity of the mission, while predominantly of a coastal sagebrush formation (*Artemisia californica* and *Adenostoma,* especially), lacks the mescal of the coast, and includes a liberal sprinkling of Lower Sonoran *Yucca.* South-facing slopes are often a mass of cactus. Vidrío is now growing only on and beside the ruins of the mission. Crops of wheat have been raised successfully on the highest terrace, and even today are raised to a limited extent on the intermediate terrace, without irrigation.

The water for irrigation came from the San Vicente River. From a diversion dam located by Professor Hendry three-quarters of a mile above the church, solidly constructed, stone-rimmed canals lead along both sides of the valley. The total cultivated area in mission days was probably 208 acres.

Here again the existing fields, without the addition of any of the land destroyed by widening of the arroyo, are more than sufficient to produce the largest crops reported for the mission. In the best year recorded, 1800, the crops were: corn, 1040 bushels; wheat, 910 bushels; beans, 260 bushels; requiring, on the basis of yields heretofore used (above, p. 53), 111 acres (see table 1). This accounts for only half of the cultivated mission lands, and it may be explained by assuming that larger crops were harvested in some years of which we have no record, and that the yields on the San Vicente soil, which is in large measure of granitic origin, were not so high as those of the missions to the south. On the average, the crops at San Vicente were about 1000 bushels of corn, 600 of wheat, 50 of beans (reported for only about half the years), and no barley. Of the last-named, 65 bushels were harvested in 1782, and no more were recorded until 1801. With so little barley and so much corn, and with plenty of land and water for irrigation, it appears unlikely that dry farming was attempted in mission days.

OUTER LANDS AND HERDS

At the beginning of the century, when Rosario's production was low, San Vicente's production of crops was holding well up to the average, and its herds were reaching their largest size. The herd of cattle and flock of sheep, of 750 and 1150 head respectively, in 1800, were larger even than those of Santo Domingo, though in previous years cattle had numbered about 200 and sheep 500. Goats ranged in number from 27 to 347, and beasts of burden from 46 in 1782 to 215 in 1801 (table 1). The San Vicente area was rather well supplied with grazing lands, though stretches of it were not available because of deficiency in drinking water. Thus, the many square miles of level land included in the upper San Antonio Plain were without water except at the southern edge, where the upper ends of the San Antonio and El Salado cañons originate in swampy areas. At present, cattle in this plain are dependent upon water raised from a deep well by a windmill.

The limits of the total area within the jurisdiction of the San Vicente Mission can be determined only roughly. Father Luis Sales and the other missionaries at San Vicente made no attempt to record the native rancherías of the Indians confined at the mission. Certainly the entire San Vicente Basin must have been subject to the mission, with El Salado as the southern edge of the level lands. To the north, San Vicente territory probably included the valley of San Jacinto, for not only is the latter nearer to San Vicente than to Santo Tomás (eight and fifteen miles, respectively), the next mission north, but it was apparently visited by Sales, the San Vicente missionary, who tells of finding dead and sick

Indians in a cave at a place called San Jacinto in the epidemic of 1781 (Sales, part 3 : 68). To the east, Valle Trinidad was definitely outside of San Vicente's sphere; the Indians of that valley were from the first recognized as subject to Santa Catalina (Arrillaga, 1796 : 10). With the boundaries suggested, we can assign to San Vicente the comparatively small territory of five hundred square miles.

The area thus approximately defined was, as usual, available for scattered grazing, and almost all parts of it supplied food-producing plants to supplement the Indians' diet. The mescal abounds within two to five miles of the coast, and, farther inland, food plants include jojoba, several types of fruit-bearing cactus, and yucca, the date-like fruit of which is edible. Certain parts of the area were useful to the mission community in other distinctive ways. The mountains west of the San Vicente Basin support stands of coniferous trees, forming the southernmost mainland occurrence of those curious little patches of vestigial conifers scattered along the Pacific in California. The varieties here are a pine (*Pinus muricata*, according to Sudworth : 27) and a cypress (probably *Cupressus forbesii*). Negrete (p. 351) mentions that there were some pines in the sierra between El Salado and San Vicente. They can be seen from the west along the summit of the northern part of the San Antonio Ridge, and at one point they even descend to the San Vicente Cañon.

THE MISSION RANCH

Across the San Vicente Cañon from the mouth of the Arroyo Guadalupe, which enters on the north side, are the remains of an adobe building, known to some of the inhabitants of San Vicente as "the Mission Ranch," with irrigation canals that are in many parts stone-lined. The adobe building itself has massive walls thirty to thirty-four inches thick, which have crumbled to mere mounds except where one room, kept roofed until more recently, still has walls ten feet high. In addition to its moderate agricultural value, the ranch had a strategic location for stock raising and travel.

COASTAL LANDS

After winding westward for two and one-half miles through metamorphic mountains, rising sometimes in brilliant red cones, San Isidro Cañon enters the San Isidro Mesa, a coastal terrace at least two miles wide along the river. Mescals thrive on the foggy, wind-swept mesa. Where the mesa reaches the coast it forms cliffs, mostly of loosely consolidated gravel and sand, in places several scores of feet in height (pl. 7*a*). North and south from San Isidro Arroyo the mesa extends for many miles, continually narrowing, and with at least two higher terraces cut to the rear of it. In places the basal formations are a very hard conglomerate or an even harder basalt (pl. 7*b*). The hard rock, attacked by the waves, forms sea stacks, caves, and ledges, to which countless mussels and abalones attach themselves, while the more detached stacks are the resting places of sea lions. On the cliff tops for miles along the coast, numerous large heaps of abalone and mussel shells, with bits of broken pottery, show the importance of these foods to the Indians. Four and one-half miles south of the San Isidro Arroyo a steep slope near the coast contains a ledge-like cave, thirty-five feet long and from six to twelve feet deep, the floor of which, covered several feet deep with shells, has been raised to within three or four feet of the smoke-blackened ceiling. The mouth of the cave is nearly closed with the shell débris, so that the cave is practically invisible, even from a short distance. A great apron of shells extends for fifty feet down from the mouth of the cave. All in all, there must have been a considerable Indian population along the coast available for the San Vicente mission.

The mission was probably too far from the coast—ten miles—to have depended much upon sea food. The most inland shell heap observed by the writer along the San Isidro Cañon was of mussels, three and one-half miles from the coast, on the 80-foot terrace (see fig. 12), though on the upper San Antonio Plain clam deposits have been made as much as eight miles inland, at the head of the San Antonio Cañon.

COMMUNICATIONS

The main lines of travel in all directions from the mission followed for a distance the valleys which there converge. The San Vicente Valley itself provided not only a path to the ocean, but also, upstream, a route to Santa Catalina by way of the Valley of San Pablo, as described by Arrillaga (1796:46). South Valley provided the exit for the main camino to the south, with an early branch to Valle Trinidad across country by way of Los Coches. The camino to the north followed the side valley for three miles and then forked, giving a choice of two roads to the Santo Tomás Mission. According to the meager early accounts, these two roads must have approximated those now in use.

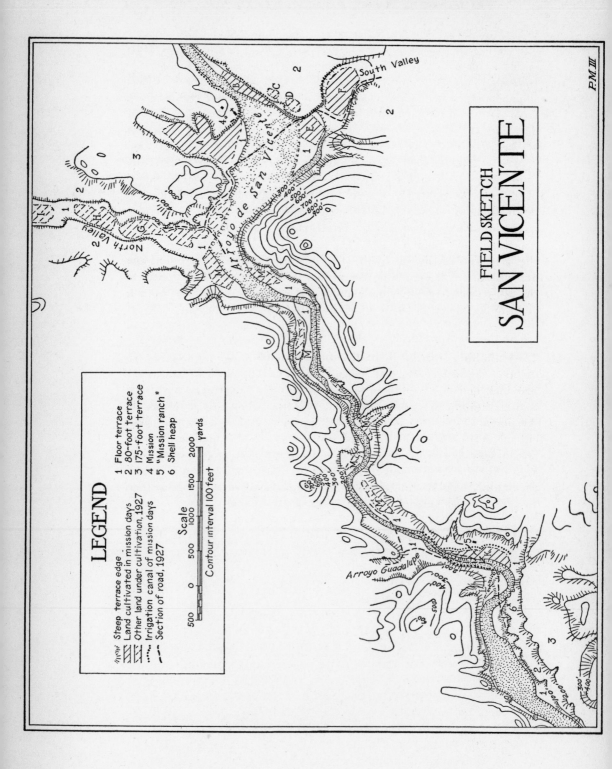

FIELD SKETCH
SAN VICENTE

P.M.III

LEGEND

Steep terrace edge
Land cultivated in mission days
Other land under cultivation, 1927
Irrigation canal of mission days
Section of road, 1927

1 Floor terrace
2 80-foot Terrace
3 175-foot terrace
4 Mission
5 "Mission ranch"
6 Shell heap

Scale

500   0   500   1000   1500   2000
                                    yards

Contour interval 100 feet

South Valley

North Valley

Arroyo de San Vicente

Arroyo Guadalupe

IX. SANTO TOMÁS

Two or three small springs in the midst of an extensive valley determined the site of the Mission of Santo Tomás. Though the water from the springs is only sufficient to irrigate a few score acres of land, the site has been one of lasting attraction, and there is still a little village there. The mission maintained a priest until 1849, ten years later than any other Dominican foundation (Engelhardt, 1929 : 667, 683, 685, 687; Browne, 1896*b* : 141; Rojo, 1879 : 31, 33), and upon his departure Santo Tomás became a military colony, replacing San Vicente as the capital of the area from Tijuana to Santa Gertrudis (Negrete :352).

THE NATURAL LANDSCAPE

The alluvial valley floor, a veritable plain, stretches east and west for ten miles, with an average width of about a mile. Mountain walls, mostly of resistant intrusives and metamorphics, rise in a continuous barrier along the sides to elevations of from 500 to 2000 feet above the floor. Toward the west the sides of the valley gradually converge into the outlet, Santo Tomás Cañon, a hundred yards wide, winding twelve miles westward to the sea, and dropping three hundred fifty feet.

Santo Tomás has the customary foggy desert climate of the northwestern part of the Peninsula; in eight consecutive days of observations by the writer at the head of Santo Tomás Cañon, from July 7 to July 15, 1926, high fog drifted in on five nights, borne by the usual northwest wind. It always cleared overhead before 9 A.M. The clearing began in the east, the eastern edge of the fog retreating seaward by evaporation. Daytime temperatures commonly rose above 80° F, and at the time of greatest heat, dust whirls several hundred feet high often developed on the northwestern part of the smooth valley floor. At night, however, temperatures regularly dropped below 60° F, and dew, sometimes heavy, was noticed on four nights. By the coast at the mouth of Santo Tomás Cañon, on July 10, a typical day, the high fog remained overhead continuously, though only two miles inland the sky was clear. Chilly, overcast summer days are characteristic of the Pacific coast of all the Dominican area.

In the Santo Tomás Cañon the fog-loving vidrío extends inland from the coast only a mile and a half, and the mescal a quarter-mile farther. Beyond, the cañon sides support a growth of low chamiso, while the floor, in addition to grass, and *Rhus laurina* and other shrubs, contains groves and scattered trees of sycamore, willow, and live oak, the last-named not found near the missions south of Santo Tomás. At the head of the cañon, with abundant surface water, is found an especially dense gallery forest (pl. 8*a*). East of the cañon the trees spread out in the lower part of Santo Tomás Valley, the live oaks adhering to the base of the north-facing valley side (pl. 8*b*), and the willows, mingled with

cottonwoods and elders, occupying the arroyos and moist lands of the
valley floor. The great live-oak and cottonwood trees were remarked by
Serra in 1769 (Serra : 642). The general impression of the valley in summer, neglecting the checkerboard of fields, is one of a brown plain inter-
woven with green ribbons of *romerillo*-filled arroyos, with a marked
increase in general greenness toward the tree-filled outlet.

The luxuriance of trees at the lower end of the valley results from the
abundance of arroyo water at that point. In most of the valley the ar-

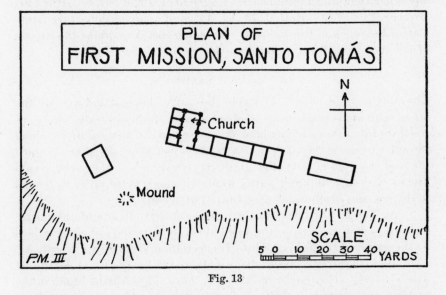

PLAN OF
FIRST MISSION, SANTO TOMÁS

Church

N

Mound

P.M. III

SCALE
5 0   10   20   30   40
YARDS

Fig. 13

royo channels, generally at least two in number, are dry at the surface
except in the winter rainy season;[21] but toward the lower end the water
rises and flows as a perennial stream, forming a permanently swampy
area (see fig. 14). Ordinarily, it is said, the swamp drains through the
cañon outlet and flows as a stream all the way to the coast, but in the
summer of 1926 there was surface water in the cañon only for a mile
or two at the upper and lower ends. At the coast the arroyo ends in a
lagoon, like most of the westward-flowing streams of the Peninsula. The
stream of water at the western end of Santo Tomás Valley, easily the
largest perennial flow of water anywhere in the valley or its margins,
was the basis for the original location of the mission buildings.

THE FIRST MISSION

The ruins of the first mission lie on a small fan on the north side of the
valley overlooking the stream and marsh. So far as can be seen, the usual
quadrangle of buildings was never completed, though outlines of a 70-
yard line of rooms are traceable, parallel with the valley (pl. 8*b;* fig. 13).
The valley-mouth mission was of transient importance. To be sure, the

---

[21] In 1926 the inhabitants stated that water had not flowed the whole length of
the valley for five years because of an unusually dry period.

moist lowland below the mission was well suited to the raising of corn, and the corn crop of 1794, presumably on this land (for the new mission was not built until June, 1794), was the largest on record for any mission except Rosario (see table 1). But the unhealthful conditions also associated with the marsh led to the abandonment of the site three years after it was first developed (above, p. 28).

THE MISSION SPRINGS AND THE SECOND MISSION

The famous "mission springs" are four miles east of the valley outlet and half a mile out in the plain from the southern edge of the valley, opposite a sharp bend in the mountain border. They are marked today by two large sycamore trees, said by tradition to have sprouted from two posts set by the padres on either side of the outlet of the middle spring. Two springs, about one hundred twenty-five yards apart, were flowing in 1926. These are doubtless the two originally described springs, which Serra (p. 642) puts "a little more than a hundred paces" apart. A third little hollow, thirty or forty yards farther up the valley, was said to have contained another spring up to 1921, when it dried up, a statement supported by the evidence of a stone irrigation canal leading from the hollow. Crespi had noted only two of the springs in 1769 (above, p. 29); Negrete (p. 352), in 1853, found all three flowing. While the third spring thus does dry up at times, the other two have apparently been steadily flowing since their first discovery by the white man in 1769; the largest spring, according to Serra's estimate, had a flow of "more than a Naranja" and the other had less, compared with the "more than a Buey of water" in the stream at the mouth of the valley (Serra, p. 642). At the present time, the water is entirely consumed in supporting the little orchards, vineyards, and corn patches of the seven or eight families of the town of Santo Tomás, and according to the still visible remains of the old stone-lined acequia of the padres, nearly a mile long, the land irrigated from the springs in mission days (field "A," fig. 14) was only sixty-five acres.

The mission was built near the arroyo a thousand yards below the springs. Reconstruction of its plan in the field is now impossible, for its ruins have been nearly or quite plowed under. The flat, earth-covered roof of the church and details of the final structure as rebuilt from 1799 to 1801 are listed by Engelhardt (1929:625–626). The heavy timbers appear to have been brought all the way from the sierra near Santa Catalina. Negrete (p. 352) stated that the mission did not have a tile floor and that the bells were hung on two little posts above the door.

FIELDS AND CROPS

Part of the mission orchard still continues to grow and produce fruit (pl. 9a). The orchard in mission days included at least 100 olive trees, 100 pomegranate trees, more than 2000 grapevines, and 3 or 4 peach trees, for these were observed by Negrete (p. 352) still standing in 1853.

He reported that more than 5000 grapevines, and all the apple trees and other fruit trees, had been lost, and that the olive trees bade fair to go the same way because the branches had been much broken down by persons attempting to obtain the olives, which were "as good as those of Seville." Wine is still a major product of Santo Tomás.

Besides the fruit, Negrete found wheat, corn, barley, beans, and vegetables being raised at Santo Tomás, all with irrigation. Apparently even here, dry farming was not being practiced, and therefore probably had not been at the time of the mission. Yet the crops must have covered much more than the sixty-five acres irrigated by the three springs, as the following tabulation of the best recorded year, 1800, with acreages based upon previously given estimates of yields (above, p. 53), shows:

	Wheat	Corn	Barley	Beans	Total
Bushels harvested (table 1)....	1,560	1,300	1,040	130	4,030
Acreage	87	54	42	9	192

The conclusion follows that cultivation of the land at the lower end of the valley near the permanent stream was continued even after the original mission buildings had been abandoned for the later mission. This would add one hundred fifty acres of irrigable land, which is the area now under cultivation there (fields "B, C, D, E, F, G, H, I, J, and K"). With a total of more than two hundred acres of irrigable land, the grain fields and orchard can be well accounted for without assuming that dry farming was resorted to in the valley.

Climatically, dry farming is possible in Santo Tomás Valley. Figure 14 shows about seven hundred fifty acres of land that have been cultivated in recent years without the aid of irrigation. The only thoroughly successful non-irrigated grain here is barley, which can be depended upon to make a good crop nearly every year. The fact that the drought-resistant barley was not more important in the mission harvests is one reason for believing that all the mission crops were raised by irrigation.

Only small amounts of the valley floor have been converted into un-cultivable sandy wastes by arroyo widening (fig. 14), though parts are roughened by old channels, and lateral erosion is progressing.

HERDS AND OUTLYING RANCHES

Though little of the plain was available for agriculture, it helped to support the great herds of the mission most of the year. The surrounding grazing lands, which Crespi (Bolton, 1927 : 92) and Serra (p. 642) had observed in April and June to be green with grass, made their contribution; and the small springs here and there in the surrounding mountains increased the grazing area available.

The old estados show that the Santo Tomás herds were greater than those of the missions to the south. In 1801, just ten years after its foundation, Santo Tomás had 1200 cattle and 2646 sheep (see table 1). The valley, with its uncertain rainfall, could not have supported such a large number of livestock. Some of them were doubtless cared for from near-by centers. Thus La Grulla, five miles north of the valley, with rolling, grassy land and steady springs, could easily have supported many hundred head of cattle.[22] It was classified by Castro (p. 370) in 1849 as a ranchería, where grain and grapes were being produced, and where cattle had been raised.

Another mission ranch, of which no mention has been found by the writer, has been identified by him with the site at which Sales had intended to locate the Santo Tomás Mission after the rejection of the La Grulla site (above, pp. 26, 27). It is in the Santo Tomás Cañon, four and one-half miles below the lower end of the valley, at a place where the cañon expands to a width of about two hundred fifty yards for a distance of nearly half a mile. The widening is floored with a fine sandy loam, much of which has been removed by lateral cutting by the river, leaving the remainder as low marginal floor terraces with a sandy wash in between. Very possibly the dissection of the valley floor resulted from the removal of trees and development of trails in mission days. A small permanent spring issues from the north side of the cañon and empties into an old stone reservoir. From both sides of the reservoir, stone irrigation ditches lead along the side of the valley, lined part of the way by thickets of huge tunas. At present, most of the water escapes from the reservoir and forms a swampy pool just below it. Across the cañon from the spring, nestling close against the southern slope, are the ruins of an adobe building.

The major subsistence areas of the Santo Tomás livestock were two great plains of more humid climate many miles to the north. One of these was the Valley of San Rafael, the other, the Ensenada Plain. Negotiations for the former were carried on in 1796 by the padres of Santo Tomás with Governor Borica (Arch. Cal., P. R., 6:704–705; 5:745, 756), who wished to facilitate a supply of meat for the proposed new establishments on the Río Colorado, and permitted them to take eight hundred cattle to San Rafael Valley in order to start a cattle ranch (*ibid.*, 6:397–398). In return for this privilege, the padres were required to sell livestock at listed prices to the escoltas and to the contemplated Colorado establishment, treat the Indians of the valley with love and charity, guard the cattle adequately, and raise no more than were needed, for fear that the remainder might fall into the hands of the Colorado Indians. In June, 1798, the padres accepted the valley for a ranch of "ganado mayor y menor" (Arch. Arzob., 1:187). It was probably at this time that the rapid increase of the herds began, reaching the large number reported in 1801. The valley is well suited to grazing, and at present supports hundreds of cattle. It is a basin about 18 miles long and 6 wide, situated 2600 feet above sea level, and 25 miles northeast of Santo Tomás between the granite fore-ranges of the Sierra Juarez and the rough metamorphic mountains east of Ensenada. The animal prod-

[22] Negrete (p. 353) found 650 head of livestock at La Grulla.

ucts of the valley were thus definitely assigned to Santo Tomás, but the Indian population was divided with Santa Catalina. The settlement of La Huerta was therefore a ranchería of Santa Catalina, according to the present La Huerta Indians, while Los Álamos on Sangre de Cristo Arroyo in the southern end of the valley, was a Santo Tomás ranchería.

Similarly, the Ensenada Plain (pl. 9*b*) is situated about midway between the missions of Santo Tomás and San Miguel. San Miguel had plenty of excellent grazing land for all its needs close at hand and did not attempt to use the plain. In 1804, with the consent of both missions, the northern half of the Ensenada Plain, 5000 varas north to El Carmen Arroyo and 10,000 varas south to Maneadero Paraje, was granted by Arrillaga to the Ensign José Manuel Ruiz for cattle raising.[23] The southern half, known as "Maneadero Valley," was retained by Santo Tomás. According to Pattie (whose numbers are invariably exaggerated), in 1828 the plain was covered with horses and cattle belonging to the mission (Santo Tomás). Wild oats[24] and clover grew knee-high (in April; Pattie: 226).

The total territory subject to Santo Tomás, as sketched on the folded map, was about 1050 square miles. The average rainfall at Ensenada (9.91 inches for the 26-year period, 1894–1921)[25] is at least twice as great as that of San Quintín,[26] with a consequent superiority in forage over the neighboring mission to the south. Todos Santos Bay, like San Quintín Bay, had some rancherías of Indians along its margins. Crespi (Bolton, 1927: 99) mentioned seeing one village here, at the foot of the hills at the north end of the Ensenada Plain. Numerous large deposits of shell fragments and rock chips indicate the former existence of at least occasional rancherías at the southern end of the plain, on and near Cerro Banda, the long mountain that forms the southern edge of Ensenada Plain and Bay.

POPULATION

With all its natural resources, Santo Tomás had a population but little larger than that of the average Dominican mission. The largest population reported in any available estado was 262, in 1800 (see table 2), though Troncoso (p. 20) in 1824 gave it as more than four hundred, the largest of any of the Five Missions. Within five days after the original founding, some children and twenty adults had been baptized (Arch. Cal., S. P. Sac., 5: 846–847), and at the end of the first eight months the number had increased to ninety-six (see table 2). The first recruits probably came from Indians already living in Santo Tomás Valley. Apparently, Indians lived in the middle part of the plain, in the vicinity of the

---

[23] Copy of this and other grants exhibited by David Goldbaum, Ensenada.

[24] One of the earliest notices of wild oats on the Pacific Coast which the writer has seen.

[25] Böse and Wittich, pl. 111, to 1911; since then, record of David Goldbaum.

[26] Above, p. 65. During the four years of the San Quintín record, the average of 5.1 inches compared with 11.6 inches at Ensenada for the same years.

mission springs, while many others lived round about (above, p. 28), in addition to the previously noted rancherías at La Grulla and the shores of the Ensenada. Other parts of the seacoast, too, supported Indians, as shown by the plentiful shell heaps and mescal pits on both sides of the mouth of Santo Tomás Cañon, and by the shell deposits on many parts of the marine terraces near San José a few miles farther south. With its crops and herds, Santo Tomás probably produced enough food for its Indian population without recourse to the wild food. Pattie (p. 226) makes the interesting statement that in 1828 thirty beeves were slaughtered weekly for the sustenance of the mission, though in the same breath he declares that the population of the mission was one thousand. If his beef figures are as exaggerated as his population figures (which are more than double those of Troncoso's report of four years earlier), the actual slaughter would have been twelve weekly, representing, at the rate of increase assumed for Rosario (above, p. 55), the product of a herd of about fifteen hundred cattle, a reasonable number.

HARBORS AND SEA TRADE

The coasts were useful to Santo Tomás, not only for the Indian population attracted by the shellfish, but also for the trade carried on through Santo Tomás Bay and Todos Santos Bay or the Ensenada. The former, situated just north of the mouth of Santo Tomás Cañon, is a deep bight between two steep lava ridges, of which the northern one, Santo Tomás Point, projecting into the ocean with a slight southern hook, gives splendid shelter from the prevailing northwesterly winds.

The only report we have of a vessel in Santo Tomás Bay in mission times is by Rojo (pp. 96–102), who says that in December, 1835, a ship with cannibalistic Indians, believed to have come from the northwest, arrived in the Bay, and the Tomaseños hurried to the shore with fruits and beef to trade as usual. The Tomaseños were disappointed, a party from the ship having merely landed in a small boat, partly eaten an Indian who lived on the beach by gathering clams and abalones, and hurried back to the ship. The intimation is that trading with vessels at this bay was a customary practice, and that this particular event was mentioned because of the attending extraordinary circumstances. Certainly the bay, hidden among its hills and far from the main highway, yet only a few hours' ride from the mission, provided an ideal port for illicit trade with foreign vessels.

The chief port through which the mission traded, however, was the great Ensenada de Todos Santos (pl. 9b). Though somewhat less secure for small boats than San Quintín Bay, the other major port, it had, according to Shaler's report based on his voyage of 1805, a scanty supply of wood and water, while San Quintín had neither (Cleland: 479). At first glance the Ensenada appears to afford little shelter from the prevailing winds, for its major outline is an angular embayment of the

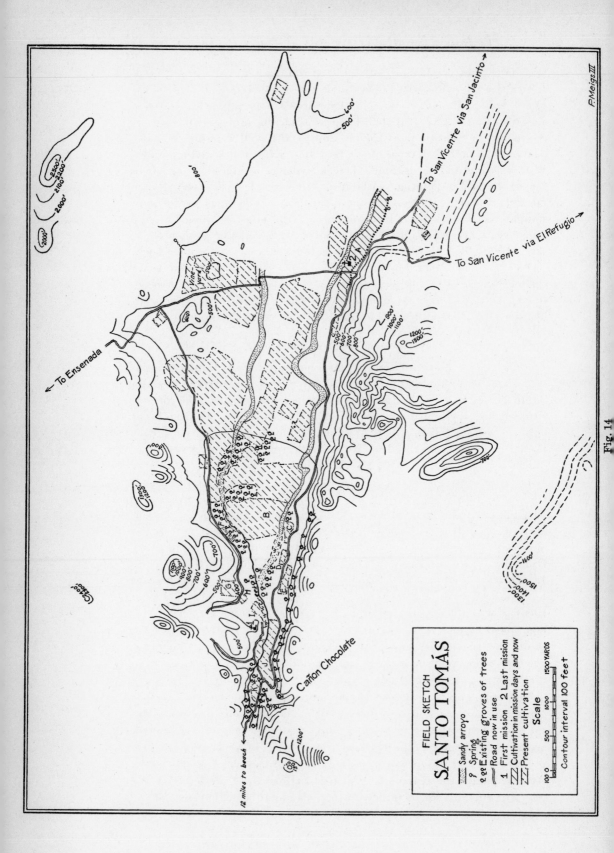

FIELD SKETCH
SANTO TOMÁS

Sandy arroyo
Spring
Existing groves of trees
Road now in use
1 First mission   2 Last mission
Cultivation in mission days and now
Present cultivation

Scale

100 0   500   1000   1500 YARDS

Contour interval 100 feet

To Ensenada

To San Vicente via San Jacinto
To San Vicente via El Refugio

Cañon Chocolate

12 miles to beach

Viñe yard

P. Meigs III

Fig. 14

coast, ten miles broad, with rather straight sides trending north of west and open to the most exposed quarter. The northeast corner, however, is formed by a short cross-range which projects southwestward into the bay for half a mile, terminates in Ensenada Point, and provides a small protected anchorage in from three to five fathoms of water (United States Hydrographic Office, 1880 : 5). Here at the north end of the bay, as at Santo Tomás Bay, and for the same reasons, was the principal landing of the port (Negrete : 354), now the town of Ensenada, the capital of the Northern District of Lower California from 1882 to 1915 and the largest town within the former Dominican area. During the southeast storms of winter, anchorage was made in the southeast part of the bay proteced by Cerro Banda.[27]

The statement is commonly made that the trade along the Lower Californian coast in mission days was contraband and clandestine, because of the restriction imposed by Spain in an attempt to obtain all the trade for her own ships, and that after freedom had been gained in the war of independence, trade greatly increased (e.g., Browne, 1869*b* : 42). Definite occurrences of trading which have been recorded were carried out openly and with the knowledge of the civil authorities. Commonly the vessels, especially the "whalers from Boston" and other parts of the world which were stationed along the coast until they had completed cargoes of oil (Rojo : 96), would stop at a port simply to obtain food and water for their current operations. One such vessel, the "Resolution," an English whaler, Captain John Locke, anchored in the Ensenada in 1795,[28] and took on provisions that were supplied freely by the padres of Santo Tomás and San Miguel. The supplies provided were: 3 head of cattle, 6 steers, 40 *arrobas* of flour, 24 chickens, 6 arrobas of onions, some *calabazas,* 15 fanegas of maize, 6 fanegas of beans, 4 fanegas of salt (Arch. Cal., P. S. P., 13 : 585–590). This adds chickens and onions to the list of known products of these missions. The transaction was reported to the Governor and even to the Viceroy, who responded with a warning to give foreign vessels only such aid as was necessary, without letting them reconnoiter the land (*ibid.*, pp. 147–151, 389–390). Shaler, in 1805, thought that the missions in touch with Todos Santos and San Quintín bays were too poor to be depended upon for much in the way of supplies (Cleland : 479).

An entirely different class of commerce arose with merchantmen who visited the coast for the express purpose of profiting by trade, not simply of getting provisions. Such a vessel, the "Dromio," of Boston, was said by Taylor (Browne, 1869*b* : 42) to have arrived at the Ensenada de Todos Santos on January 4, 1809. It remained there trading for thirty-four days (hardly clandestine), met many Indians but few Spaniards, and obtained 1700 "fur-otter" skins in exchange for most of the rem-

[27] Thus, on December 6, 1798, an American vessel was anchored here.—Arch. Cal., P. R., 5:776–777.

[28] Bancroft, 1884*b*, 1:731; Arch. Cal., P. S. P., 13:147–151, 389–390.

nants of its cargo. At the average price of $50 for sea-otter skins, this means that the countryside may have had an income of $85,000 worth of goods in a little more than a month from nutria skins alone. A more prosaic and probably more steady source of income was mentioned by Pattie (p. 225) for the mission of Santo Tomás—"the hides and tallow they sell to vessels that visit their coast, in exchange for such goods as they need." Payment in kind was the common practice, because, Rojo says (p. 94), of the local high prices. He mentions clothes, rice, sugar, and tobacco as some of the items taken by the ranchers in exchange for their goods. Even an approximate estimate of the actual amount or proportion of the total coastal trade that went to the missions is impossible. We can only say that at first and well into the nineteenth century most of the business was in their hands, while later, and especially after the Revolution, more and more of it was carried on by private individuals.

X. SAN MIGUEL

THE TRAYS: DISTINCTIVE LAND-FORMS

THE MISSION OF SAN MIGUEL, a mile and a half from the coast and thirty miles by road northwest of Ensenada, is surrounded by about one hundred square miles of a type of landscape found nowhere else in the Dominican area. The distinctive feature of this landscape is an elevated elongated flat, known locally as a mesa, but differing from a mesa in being bordered partly or entirely by higher rims of basaltic lavas. For lack of any known existing distinctive name, the descriptive term "tray" is here used to designate this land form.

Many of the trays are extensive. The floors are commonly so level, however, that slope is hardly perceptible, the gentle inclination of two degrees, one degree, or even less being determinable only with instruments (pl. 10a). Poor surface drainage is the rule, with extensive development of gritty clay loam, and with eroded channels or arroyos entirely lacking except here and there at a sharp notch in the basalt rim where a channel, heading only a short distance back in the flat, drains outward, changing to a steep gash where it cuts through the rim and drops to a lower level beyond (pl. 10a). The rim itself is of varying height, though commonly it rises above the plain only a few score feet. In the profile of one tray the west rim is fifty feet above the floor. The outer edge of this rim, however, drops eight hundred feet, with a slope of thirty-four degrees, interrupted midway by a great step, also of lava. Such a steep drop, though not always associated with a step, is characteristic. The drop may end in a valley, a marine terrace, or another tray. Lack of uniformity in elevation of the trays is striking, the seven observed by the writer ranging from six hundred to thirteen hundred feet above sea level. Rather close agreement is found in the trends of the long, straight rims. All those observed were aligned in approximately a north-south direction. The five most typical trays trended between N 18° W and N 10° E.

The trays are apparently fault features. The straight stretches of the rims, their general alignment in a north-south direction parallel with the coast in this locality, and their variation in elevation are general characters that suggest the possibility of a system of fractures. Detailed examination at several points supports the theory. The profile of the west slope of the rim of one tray shows at the lower cliff's base a series of undrained depressions which are unquestionably sag ponds. They are frequently separated from one another by well-developed slice blocks and kernbut ridges. The terrace-like break halfway down the slope is undoubtedly a faulted step. Other forms—facets—which may indicate faulting are observable along the inner edge of the east rim of a tray in the El Tigre area, where the low basalt rim, rising only twenty-five feet above the plain, has been dissected transversely into gentle ridges terminated by oversteepenings, aligned in a west of north direction.

CLIMATE AND VEGETATION

The tray flats have been important to the successive groups of people into whose hands they have passed, partly because of the climate of the area, which is humid enough to permit the regular raising of wheat—practiced now by Russian settlers without irrigation. There is mention of the sowing of wheat and barley on the "mesas del Tigre" by the San Miguel Indians in 1840 (Rojo: 38). The natural vegetation is grass, which was observed by Crespi (Bolton, 1927: 105, 108) on the mesas both north and south of San Miguel, long before white men disturbed the normal cover. At present wild oats is also an important element. The rims of the trays support a coastal sagebrush formation. The nearest systematic rainfall observations have been made in the hill land a few miles east of the tray area, at Matajanal (elevation about 900 feet). In the 1926–1927 season the rainfall was 22 inches; in 1927–1928, 12.35 inches; and the average, according to Mr. Tom Grove, the observer, is from five to six inches above that of Ensenada. This places the flats toward the moist limit within the warm steppe climate, *BSh* of Köppen (1923). Most of the land above 1300 feet elevation, including some of the tray rims, appears to fall, on the one hand, within the warm Mediterranean climate, *Csa* of Köppen, for it supports dense, tall chaparral of *Adenostoma,* live oaks on slopes definitely out of reach of the water table of the valley bottoms, and even, above 1750 feet on some of the mountains overlooking the west edge of Guadalupe Valley, groves of cypress. On the other hand, a strip of low marine terraces, mostly narrow, which borders the tray area and the ocean, belongs distinctly to the foggy coastal desert climate, *BWhn,* for the vegetation is here a mescal chamiso, with mescal, siempre vive, and vidrío conspicuous. Other important elements in the vegetation of the area are the groves of sycamores and live oaks that occupy many patches of valley floor and other depressions where the water table is within easy reach of roots.

SAN MIGUEL VALLEY

San Miguel Valley is a deep east-west gash through the tray area with a level floor some four hundred yards wide. Half a dozen miles east of its mouth on the coast, it terminates in a narrow gorge above a sweeping bend. A perennial stream meanders through the valley, its volume augmented at one point by warm springs bubbling up in the arroyo. This San Miguel River is the lowest part of the long, intermittent stream known near its head in San Rafael Valley as Arroyo San Rafael, in its middle, most important stretch as Río Guadalupe, and in its next lower section, as Arroyo Santa Rosa. The river ends at the coast in a lagoon, sometimes shut off from the sea by a sand bank, sometimes breaking through the bank on the south.

LAND USE AND RANCHERÍAS OF THE INDIANS

San Miguel Valley, the site of the mission, was in pre-mission days a principal center for Indians. A living Indian informant states that the locality was known as *Ja-kwatl-jap* (*ja*=water; *jap*=hot), from the warm springs in the valley. The first explorers to reach this valley (Crespi's "San Juan Bautista") found it well populated, with many little Indian houses, appearing like a town (Bolton, 1927:105). Food abounded on all sides: mescal at the mouth of the valley and north and south near the coast, acorns farther inland, and plentiful fish and shell-fish along the shore. According to Indians now living some miles inland at San José and Rincón de los Encinos, sea fishing was carried on in the ocean here with hook and line from carefully made tule balsas. In the lagoon, which even now abounds with mullet, fish were regularly caught with long nets of mescal. Sales (part 3:83) stated that the "estero" supplied with fish all persons living on the plain.

While fishing and navigation were carried on by the local residents only, Indians from the interior would come down every winter to get shellfish. The existing shell heaps bear out this statement, for the largest ones occur on the terraces just north and south of the junction of valley mouth and seacoast, where doubtless the visitors carried their mussels and clams for immediate eating and for drying. A rather large accumulation of shells, also the work of transients, is found at the summit of the high southern cliff of the valley, at an elevation of seven hundred feet. Down in the valley the principal shell heaps are found a mile or more from the coast. The deposits include pottery fragments as well as the usual rock chips that occur in all the heaps. They probably mark the location of permanent dwellings. Possibly the Indians could even obtain salt locally, for at present the lowest sag pond on the north side of the valley contains a pool of water which shows a deposit of low-grade salt around the edge.

At La Salina, three miles south of San Miguel Valley, an important source of good salt was available. In dry years at present, so much salt accumulates that people are said to carry it away by the cartload. This may have been the source of the salt sold to the "Resolution" at Ensenada (above, p. 97), though mission records mention only the San Quintín salt.

At Matajanal and El Tigre, mortars are found worn in the bedrock on a ridge. Acorns and *chía* (*Salvia columbariae*) seeds from the slopes and valleys, and prickly-pear seeds and (in mission times) wild oats from the trays, were commonly available grist, according to the natives. Mr. Grove and others in a position to speak from observation say that the Indians liked to camp on ridge tops or other commanding points while away from home, and this would explain the locations of some of the shell heaps.

Concerning the locations of rancherías of the mission, we have evidence from primitive Indians still living in the area. In a visit to San Miguel in 1856, A. S. Taylor (May 18, 1860) was informed that rancherías of the mission were Otat, Hawaii, Ekquall, in the mountains; Hassasei and Inomassi on the sea beach; Nellmole and Mattawotis. The modern Indians, still speaking their original language, do not recognize any of these names. "Ekquall" is probably to be identified with "Kwatl," a family name; this ranchería may well have been that now known as San José, a few miles east of San Miguel Valley in a tributary valley (see folded map) which has been called the home of the *Kwatl cumiyai* (coastal Kwatl). Three Indian families still live here, their culture much modified by European contact, though they still eat acorn mush, the old women (of at least one family) live in a primitive little stone hut (pl. 10c),[29] the children speak only the original language, and basketry is still made. Mr. Grove reported another ranchería at Los Alisos, on the Río Guadalupe just south of Matajanal, as being in existence as late as 1891. Just north of the eastern end of San Miguel Valley the Mesa del Baile, so called because Indians used to hold fiestas there, is said to have had another ranchería, on its summit. Along the coast, Serra (pp. 71–72) came upon a populous ranchería at El Sausal de Comacho, just south of the tray area, well within the territory of San Miguel. It was a permanent settlement, for its inhabitants fished with balsas, and the modern Indians say that only those living on the immediate coast knew how to make these little tule craft. Another ranchería that may have belonged to San Miguel was come upon by Crespi (Bolton, 1927:99) at Ensenada (known, present Indians say, as *Pa-tai: pa*=man, and *tai*=large).

HERDS

In spite of their good pastures, the trays do not appear to have been much used for general grazing purposes, because of surface-water deficiency. At present, even in the spring, herds of horses are almost the only livestock to be seen there, except at occasional places where wells have been drilled. While only limited numbers of this type of livestock can have been of much use to the mission, it is interesting to note that Pattie (p. 226), in 1828, was particularly impressed at this mission by the numbers of horses and mules. An estado for 1800 lists 328 horses, mules, and burros, the largest number reported for any Dominican mission (see table 1). By 1801 there were 1600 cattle and 2104 sheep (see table 1). Some of these doubtless grazed in the Descanso area, but others used the lowlands along the Guadalupe-San Miguel River. As early as 1796 it was reported that cattle of the San Miguel Mission grazed at San Marcos, in the lower end of Guadalupe Valley (see folded map; Arrillaga, 1796, September 26). Negrete (p. 354) stated that there was a ranch of the mission at Santa Rosa, a deep river basin, with more than a square mile of grazing land, midway between San Miguel and Guada-

---

[29] The more usual type of hut was of brush.

lupe (see folded map). Farther downstream, the eastern half of San Miguel Valley provided more than another square mile of good grazing land, supplemented by side valleys. The first post-mission ranch,

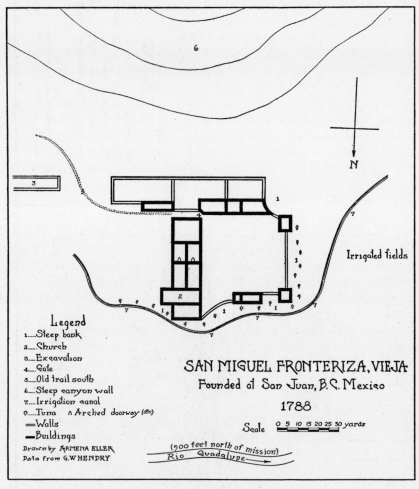

Fig. 15

still known as "Rancho Viejo," had its headquarters there, at the big bend of the valley about four miles east of the mission.

MISSION BUILDINGS AND COMMUNICATIONS

The trays also facilitated travel. The principal road to the south from San Miguel Valley led across the trays to Santa Rosa Valley, and thence to El Tigre Arroyo (Negrete: 354). A branch connected Santa Rosa Valley with Guadalupe Valley. The hardest part of the route was the steep descent from the trays into San Miguel Valley. To one traveling north on the old road across the gentle plains, the sudden view of this mission valley seven hundred feet below him is impressive.

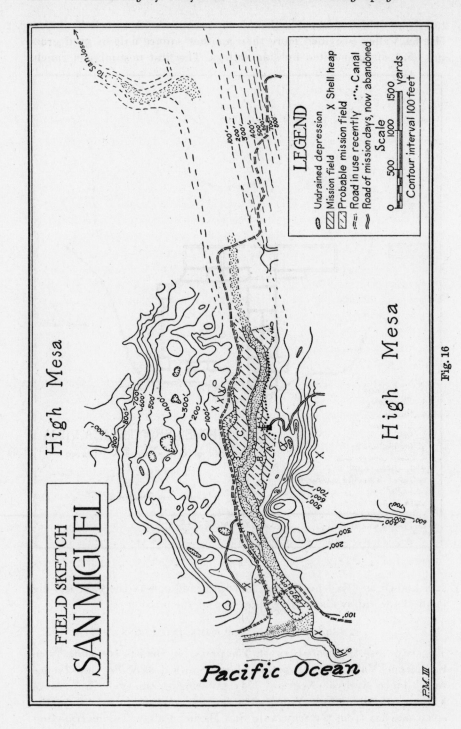

Fig. 16

The mission itself was two and one-half miles west of the place where the road started its laborious descent into the valley, and a mile and a half from the coast. The buildings occupy the lower part of the sag-pond area on the south side of the valley (pl. 10*b*), a small platform forty feet above the valley floor. The buildings were constructed in the midst of Indian shell mounds; a deep pit which has been dug in the church shows a layer of shells three feet below the floorings. The general plan of the buildings is a good example of the central court type, with an open court fifty yards wide and sixty long.

FIELDS AND CROPS

Along the foot of the mission wound an irrigation canal. It can be traced along the south side of the valley for twelve hundred yards, ending just below the mission (see fig. 16). At present, a narrow strip of vidrío-covered sandy silt valley-floor terrace, of twenty acres (field "A," fig. 16), is the only land that could have been watered from the existing canal. Between this field and the sandy arroyo is a lower 35-acre piece of land (field "B") of similar soil but not irrigable because it is badly sliced up by floodwaters from the arroyo. North of the arroyo, plot "C," fifty-five acres, similar to "B," but less dissected, is sometimes cultivated today. It is certain that much or most of the irrigated land of the mission was washed away by floods (above, p. 37) about 1815. At the yields used heretofore (above, p. 53), it would have required 110 acres of land to raise the crops of 1800: 1170 bushels of wheat, 520 of corn, 541 of barley, and 42 bushels of beans and *garbanzos* (table 1). No trace of an orchard has been found near the mission.

POPULATION

In population, San Miguel had a good start and grew well up to the average. Sales (part 3: 82) stated that in the first half-year of operations 123 heathen were baptized. By the end of 1787 there were 137 (*ibid.*, statistical table). The number gradually increased, reaching 224 in 1800; the highest number was recorded by Troncoso in 1824—between 350 and 400 souls (see table 1). These figures include Indians obtained in the Descanso area, some of whom were brought into the fold in the very first year of the mission (*ibid.*: 82). After the washout in the San Miguel Valley the emphasis definitely shifted to Descanso.

XI. DESCANSO AND THE NORTHERN BORDER

EXISTING RECORDS OF DESCANSO

THE LITERATURE CONTAINS only meager references to Descanso. The only statistics available for it are of doubtful accuracy, given by Lassepas (p. 105), who said that in 1855 it had a population of twenty-four. It is likely that most references to San Miguel after 1830 actually referred to Descanso, for the latter was sometimes called *San Miguel Nuevo* (Negrete: 354), and the original *Misión Vieja de San Miguel* took a subordinate position about that date (above, p. 37). Thus, the figures given by Lassepas (p. 105) for San Miguel in 1834 probably applied to Descanso and the San Marcos cattle ranch as well as to the old San Miguel. They include 254 Indians, 3500 cattle, 1500 sheep, 50 horses, 10 mules, 32 *suertes* of cultivated land, and crops of 240 *fanegas* of wheat, 7 of corn, and 315 of barley. As Father Ahumada has stated that there was *tierra de humedad* at Descanso, and as wheat and barley were raised *de humedad* in some abundance in the Arroyo del Mogano (Troncoso: 21 ff.) just to the north, the foregoing list would represent crops raised (without irrigation) at Descanso, floods having destroyed much of the irrigable land at Misión Vieja. Rojo (pp. 78–79) agreed that Descanso had more and better agricultural lands than San Miguel. Negrete (p. 354) mentioned its good crop lands and the church built by Caballero, the ruins of which, in use as a sheep pen in 1853, were on the gentle slope of a low hill. Further details concerning this mission are based perforce upon field work.

DESCANSO VALLEY AND ITS CHANGING FLOOR

The westward-trending Descanso Valley (fig. 18) emerges four miles from the sea out of a narrow basalt-walled gorge surmounted by high mesas. West of the gorge the mesa tops recede, and for two miles the valley floor has a width of one hundred fifty yards. Farther west, the mesas on the south side break down into basalt hills, terminated by two or three levels of marine terrace along the coast, and on the north side smooth hills of soft sedimentary rocks appear. Here the valley, for its last two miles, broadens to an average width of six hundred yards. This western section contains the chief cultivable lands of the valley, and was chosen for the fields of the mission. The level floor of the valley is surfaced with a sandy silt loam, varying considerably in texture.

The change of the Descanso River from an aggrading to a degrading stream apparently occurred after European occupation, as a result of removal of the vegetation preparatory to cultivation of the soil. Before the establishment of the mission, the valley was "grown with tule and a thick wood of very tall saplings." Crespi thought that by clearing away the trees the valley might serve as a town site (Bolton, 1927: p. 108). The arroyo has of late years been rapidly widening at the time of winter floods, although for most of the year it contains a small permanent creek only in its lower part, emptying into the usual lagoon. In February, 1927, there was a seven-day rain, which caused eight acres of plowed land of the valley floor to be swept away. The striking arroyo lobe cut by this flood in the silt valley floor was mapped (fig. 18) and photographed (pl. 11a) in May, 1927. At the same time on the floor of the lobe the flood dumped quantities of gravel. In this way the valley floor is being attacked at its upper end. Eventually all that will remain of it will be a marginal remnant, which will then be a lateral terrace. In great part, above the lobe, this condition already exists.

Whether or not the arroyo cutting began in mission days is hard to say. Probably most of it has occurred since that time. Three and one-half miles up the valley, a section of sandy arroyo that was estimated by David Goldbaum to have been only about fifteen feet wide in 1894 is now more than one hundred yards wide.

FIELDS

The total amount of formerly cultivated valley floor in the lower two miles of the valley is 175 acres (fig. 18). Of this, probably at least the 120 acres of the largest continuous fields ("A," "B," "C") north of the arroyo, nearest the mission, were cultivated in mission days. In addition, the 35 acres ("D") in the floor of a wide, gently sloping tributary valley, or dale, entering the main valley on the north side a mile from the coast, may also have been a mission field. Small alluvial fans occupy the margins of the dale at places, and gullying is now progressing in its bottom and sides (fig. 18). Some of the gullying, perhaps all, originated where the surface vegetation had been removed by cattle trails. The locality is heavily overgrazed. One remarkable gully, followed by the writer for more than a mile along the bottom of the dale, has been cut as a deep, narrow, steep-walled gash into the clay loam fill. Just above its junction with another long gully (fig. 18), it is 30 feet deep and only 11 feet wide at the top; three hundred yards farther up, the gash is 41 feet deep and 21 feet wide at the top. Yet the entire vertical incision has been made without any change in the local base level of erosion, for the gully grows shallower toward its lower end and disappears entirely as it reaches the edge of Descanso Valley, where its channel is dissipated on the more gently sloping undisturbed silty floor, without reaching the Descanso Arroyo.

CLIMATE

The climate of Descanso permits dry farming; barley and beans are raised successfully on the floor of the valley and the dale at the present time. The winter rainfall is aided by the low rate of evaporation in summer, resulting from the moisture-laden sea breezes which blow almost constantly during the day. Thus, on a characteristic day, May 31, 1927, at a point in the valley near the south side 1400 yards from the coast, the temperature ranged between 48° F and 64° F; the relative humidity from 8 A.M. to 4 P.M., observed hourly, ranged between 74 per cent and 84 per cent; and the wind blew from the west until late afternoon. From a calm in the early morning, the sea breeze set in before 8 A.M. and increased steadily to its maximum violence at about 2 P.M., becoming calm again by 6 P.M., and changing into a gentle land breeze in the night. High fog, which had disappeared about 8 A.M., began to form again by 3 P.M., and by 7 P.M. completely covered the sky. A light dew formed in the morning, and again the next morning. The temperature, 62° F at 8 A.M.,

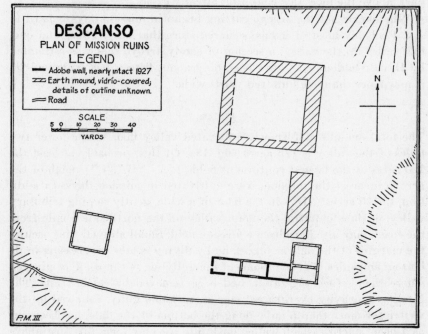

Fig. 17

attained its maximum of 64° F before 11 A.M., and began to drop before 1 P.M., reaching 55° F by 8 P.M.—the morning maximum is characteristic of the Lower California coast. Vidrío grows luxuriantly here, as might be expected, especially on areas which are hardened by trampling. On plowed land which had been left unplanted for a season, wild mustard was twelve feet high in places in May, 1927, forming almost impenetrable thickets.

BUILDINGS

At the northern edge of the valley floor, on the larger of the low platforms that extend from the valley side, are the remains of the Descanso Mission (pl. 11*b*). The ruins show the outlines of adobe buildings grouped about a court, with thick plastered walls and, here and there, fragments of red tiles. Reconstruction of the plan (fig. 17) must be highly tentative, because of the excessive disintegration of the buildings—a result of making the adobe bricks of coarse material, lacking in cohesion and including many midden shells.

Another ruin at Descanso lies across the valley near the top of the 150-foot slope of the southern valley side (pl. 11*b;* fig. 18). From its strategic position, having within its view the whole valley and commanding the approaches from the south, as well as from its outlines, this structure appears to have been a fort or guardhouse. This agrees with tradition in the valley. A stone foundation wall outlines a court about 33 by 37 yards. Within the court, near the northwest corner, but not a part of the main wall, are the dim outlines of a building about 12 yards square, of massive adobe foundations, subdivided into at least two rooms. The whole plan is unlike that of any of the other missions.

LA VIÑA ORCHARD

Still other evidence of mission development at Descanso is the mission orchard, which is three and one-half miles up the valley from the coast at a place now known as "La Viña" (fig. 18). The reason for this apparently inconvenient location was the nearness of the mission site to the cool foggy coast. The missions farther south of San Miguel did not need to be thus divorced from their orchards, for all of them with the exception of Rosario were placed on sheltered sites away from the coast. The name, La Viña, is derived from a huge grapevine, with a trunk twelve inches in diameter four feet above the ground in 1927, and a branch spread fifty feet in diameter (said to have been much greater before its years of neglect). The vidrío, which covers the ruins of the mission, is lacking at La Viña, but live oaks thrive there, as they do not so close to the coast as is the mission.

The mission orchard covers about twenty acres ("E") of a narrow terrace on the southern side of the valley at and near the mouth of a short tributary cañon. The terrace is skirted by a lower strip of sandy land ("F") now in large part overgrown with vegetation, which in turn borders the bare, gravelly main arroyo. The orchard terrace has been seriously reduced by lateral stream erosions. The side cañon, filled with live oaks, has a permanent spring of good water, which was diverted into a reservoir, twenty-five feet square, still remaining. From the reservoir the water was led eastward along the orchard for at least five hundred yards by an irrigation ditch (fig. 18).

OUTLYING LANDSCAPES

The tray landscape extends north of Descanso Valley for only a few miles, keeping at a distance of about four miles from the coast. Between it and the coast, for about five miles north from Descanso, the landscape is one of low, rounded, rather flat-topped hills, evidently a marine terrace. Cliffs have been etched along the coast into striking patterns and caves (pl. 12*a*) much like those of La Jolla north of San Diego. Most of

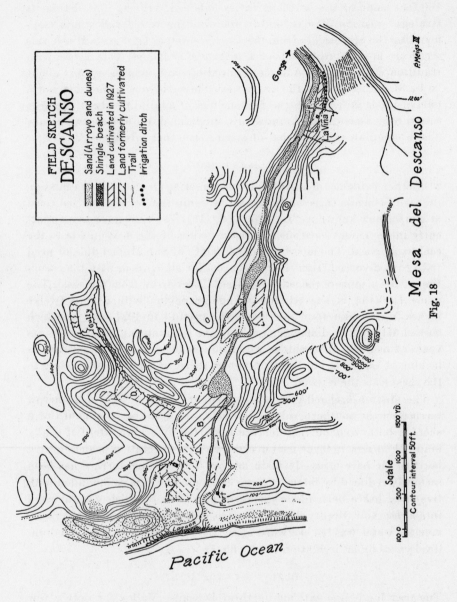

Fig. 18

Pacific Ocean

Mesa del Descanso

FIELD SKETCH
DESCANSO

Sand (Arroyo and dunes)
Shingle beach
Land cultivated in 1927
Land formerly cultivated
Trail
Irrigation ditch

Scale

100 0   500   1000   1500 YD.

Contour interval 50 ft.

the cañon slopes and the flatter summits are inactive and closely covered with grass, which must have been an important resource for the mission herds and flocks.

This grassy rolling area, three or four hundred feet in elevation, is bordered on the west by a low, narrow marine terrace, averaging one hundred feet high and two hundred yards wide, which runs continuously along the coast. The surface of this terrace is sharply broken here and there by recent cañons and areas of deep badland erosion (pl. 12b). The badland gullies are limited to an upper layer of unconsolidated material (derived at least in part from the higher land to the east), through which they have cut downward to a uniform floor level on the top of underlying harder sandstone. That some at least of these results of erosion antedated the mission is indicated by Crespi (Bolton, 1927: 110), who remarked that at this locality in 1769 "there were many cañons to cross, they being ravines of pure earth which must have been formed by the water that flows in the rainy season to the sea."

The area of rolling sedimentary land is traversed by one large valley, trending in a west-southwest direction to reach the coast two and one-half miles north of Descanso Valley. This is Médano Valley, so called from a great strip of sand dunes (*médanos*) which runs along the coast for at least a mile north of Descanso Valley. Médano Valley, described by Crespi (*loc. cit.*) as "a very wide green valley, with less brush than the one before [Descanso]," is three-quarters of a mile wide, with a small stream of water ending at the beach in the usual lagoon. This valley for a while lay at the northern limit of the Dominican realm.

THE DOMINICAN-FRANCISCAN BOUNDARY

The original definition of the boundary between Franciscan and Dominican territory in California, arrived at by mutual agreement in 1772 (above, p. 3) and officially accepted by the Council of the Indies in 1775 (Chapman, 1916: 118, note 59), was expressed by the latter in somewhat ambiguous terms. The Dominicans were to proceed *hasta llegar a los confines de la Misión de S^n. Diego en su Puerto, poniendo la última en el Arroyo de S^n. Juan Bautista* [San Miguel Mission] *q^e. finalizaría cinco leguas mas adelante de una Punta que saliendo de la Sierra Madre, termina antes de llegar á la Playa, donde podrían torcer al Leste con poca inclinación al Les-Nordeste con q^e. salían al fin del Golfo Califórnico y Río Colorado.* Five leagues (thirteen miles in an air line) north-northwest of San Miguel Mission, a high peak known as Mount Médano (3 miles north of Médano Valley) rises to a height of 2400 feet two and one-half miles from the coast, terminating a conspicuous east-west ridge (pl. 13a). To the east, the ridge includes two other prominent peaks: a slightly lower sharp peak which the natives call El Coronel and, still farther to the east, a higher mountain, Cerro Santo Domingo, labeled on the United States Hydrographic Survey map simply "cone," 3782 feet high. From its distance from San Miguel and its conspicuousness, rising abruptly above the rolling Médano lands, this mountain range must have been the one originally selected to separate Lower from Upper California, and Mount Médano must have been the Punta which, "coming from the Sierra Madre, ends before reaching the coast."

The Médano Range, as we may call it, constitutes the best natural boundary line between north and south. Nevertheless, among the half-dozen boundaries that have been mapped from time to time (Hendry, 1926, fig. 1), not one followed this natural line of demarcation. The vagueness of the original description of the boundary had something to do with the uncertainty surrounding it. Thus, the Conde and Disturnell "international boundaries" of 1845 and 1847 begin at the "Arroyo de San Juan Bautista," doubtless based upon one interpretation of the original concordat.

The first official marking of the boundary on the ground was done in 1773 by the Franciscan padre, Francisco Palóu, on a trip north to San Diego. According to his own account (Palóu, 1874, 1:256–260), he erected a large cross of sycamore wood on a high rock close to the road, to serve as a marker. However,

The holy Cross was not placed on the new point of the Sierra Madre which ends before reaching the coast, as is indicated in the Agreement, because said point is more than 3 leagues from the public highway, but at the end of said sierra, which we religious who made the examination, and the soldiers with the sergeant who knew said road, judged to be parallel with the said point 5 leagues distant from the said Arroyo de San Juan Bautista, and about 15 from the port of San Diego, so that where the Cross marks the dividing line a downward course begins to a very high elevation in the land below[30] until the road is about to reach the place called De los Médanos, where we made a stop on the 20th (August).—Bolton's translation, cited in Hendry, 1926: 6.

While this description is vague in certain respects (how, for example, can one point be parallel with another?), Hendry (1926:7), who made a special search for the marker, is doubtless correct in locating it as overlooking Médano Valley on the south side, though in respect of the exact rock which Palóu used there is room for argument.[31] The boundary marked by Palóu was three miles south of Mount Médano, and left the attractive Médano Valley on the Franciscan side of the line. Perhaps Palóu was subconsciously biased in favor of his own order when he selected the site for the cross.

Although historically interesting, Palóu's boundary was of little significance in the development of Lower California. Fifteen years after its

---

[30] A poor translation of the original *"empieza a bajar hasta una cuesta muy empinada de tierra baja,"* which the present writer would translate "it begins to drop down to a very steep slope of the land below." The "cuesta" is the steep slope of the valley side, down which the trail drops to the valley floor.

[31] In believing one particular rock to be Palóu's rock, Hendry *(loc. cit.)* states as evidence that a prominent rocky dome "directly east" is the "new point of the Sierra Madre" described by Palóu. Instrumental observations show it to be N 40° E from Hendry's rock.

marking, the boundary was shifted fourteen miles north from Médano Valley to the Arroyo del Rosarito (Rosarito Creek), where it remained until the present international boundary was agreed upon, and must therefore be considered the real northern boundary of the Dominican territory. Negrete (p. 354), on his way north from Descanso, stated that he crossed the *"Arroyo del rancho del Rosarito,"* which "was the dividing line between Alta and Baja California, before the treaties of peace with North America." This fact, which must have been known to other Lower Californians besides Negrete, was apparently not communicated to the commissioners of the United States when they agreed to place the boundary as far north as it exists, nor to any historians or geographers subsequent to Negrete. The Rosarito Creek boundary was apparently the one used on the 1846 Mitchell map (Hendry, 1926, fig. 1).

Father Sales, the Dominican, was responsible for the shift of this southern Franciscan territory to the Dominican side of the line, and the abandonment of Palóu's old marker. Shortly after the founding of the San Miguel Mission in 1788, Sales found a small village of Indians about halfway between San Miguel and San Diego. After communicating with them for two months, he annexed them to San Miguel, in view of which action the Governor gave the land to that mission.[32]

FRONTIER LANDS: ROSARIO PLAIN, MÉDANO VALLEY

The best lands thus acquired by San Miguel were Médano Valley and an extensive coastal plain of a dozen square miles, the Rosario Plain, which is traversed by Rosarito Creek. A smaller arroyo just north in the plain, the Arroyo Rosario, is sometimes confused with the Arroyo Rosarito, so that it is impossible to tell which is meant in some statements and maps. El Rosario is mentioned by a soldier in 1795, in connection with "a great plain, with abundant pastures and water," between the rancherías of La Punta and El Miligo de Gentiles (Arch. Cal., P. S. P., 13:585–590), the latter perhaps the village brought into the fold by Sales. Castro (2:372), in 1849, described Rosario as a ranch with a population of ten, with level land and pasture, but few cultivable lands.

Doubtless the whole plain, both north and south of the Rosarito boundary, was used as a stock ranch by the mission, for it was too distant to have been shared with San Diego. Although it may well have supported large herds, it is likely that Pattie (p. 227) exaggerated, as usual, when he remarked that at this ranch (his "Buenos Agnos"), belonging to San Miguel Mission, 30,000 sheep were kept in 1828. Exposed to the full sweep of the fog-laden ocean winds, the plain was poorly suited to grain raising.

Another resource was shellfish: clams in the sandy strip bordering the plain, and mussels on basalt points and sea stacks north and south.

---

[32] Sales, part 3:82–83; Hittell (1885), 1:607, quoting Arch. Cal., P. R., 10:4, 8 (not extant), says the dividing line between the two Californias was fixed in 1806 at the *Arroyo de Barrabas ó del Rosario,* 15 or 20 miles south of San Diego.

Indian shell deposits are numerous along the coast, and occur occasionally on the crests of terraces as far as a mile and a half inland. One strip of deposits, with shells, rock chips, charcoal, blackened stones, and charcoal, extends continuously for two miles from the northern edge of the plain, along the top of the cliffs overlooking the beach, with a width of one hundred twenty-five yards. The middens were partly the result of semi-permanent rancherías, such as the one noted by Crespi, and partly the work of Indians from the interior, who came down to the coast to dry clams to take home with them. The following statement of an Indian of mission days indicates that the dried clams were carried at least thirty-five miles inland, to Nejí.

I and two relatives of mine went down from the Sierra of Nejí to the beach of Rosarito, to get clams to eat and to carry back to the sierra as was our custom every year: we did no harm to anyone on the road and on the beach we had no other idea than to get and dry clams to take to our ranchería.—Rojo, p. 9.

The total area subject to the San Miguel-Descanso missions, including the Rosario Plain, Santo Domingo, Guadalupe, and the intervening mostly useless lands, covered about 700 square miles (see folded map).

XII. GUADALUPE

As THE SAN MIGUEL MISSION DECLINED, Descanso well filled its place. Because of Descanso's distance from the San Marcos cattle ranch, however, the building of another mission—Guadalupe—in the fertile San Marcos Valley was a logical development (above, p. 38). Guadalupe Mission was the last and the shortest-lived of them all, and it has been utterly neglected by writers. Thanks to the energy of Mission President Caballero, the industry of the Indians, and the natural resources of the valley, the mission was for a short time prosperous and powerful.

NATURAL LANDSCAPES

Guadalupe Valley, a basin rimmed with granite mountains, lies a dozen miles inland from San Miguel. Its smooth floor, of twenty-five square miles, four times as long as it is wide, slopes gently from northeast to southwest, with an average elevation above sea level of 1100 feet. The margins of the plain are composed of alluvial fans and colluvium of reddish soil swept out from the surrounding mountains, and the middle, somewhat more than half of the total surface of the valley floor, consists of deposits of very sandy but fertile soil, much dissected in places by old channels of the Guadalupe River, which meanders freely over the gentle plain. Except in the rainy season, the river is lost for long stretches beneath the sand of its wide arroyo. The abandoned channels are occupied in places by permanent ponds, evidently cut below the water table. Near the narrowest part of the valley a small isolated platform (*mesita*), some eight acres in extent, rises abruptly twenty feet above the plain, evidently an erosion remnant. Upon this the mission buildings were erected. One mountain west of the valley between San Marcos Pass and San Felipe Cañon is capped above an elevation of 1800 feet with a grove of cypress trees (*Cupressus forbesii*) of the same type as the isolated groves northeast of Ensenada and on San Antonio Mountain south of San Vicente. Arrillaga (1796, September 26) noticed some "pine-wood" belonging to San Miguel Mission when he passed through San Marcos Valley in 1796. To the south, near the great granite landmark known locally as San Antonio Peak, 4432 feet high ("Three Peaks" on the Hydrographic Chart), is found an interesting relict forest of still larger conifers, knobcone pines (*Pinus attenuata*) (pl. 13*b*).

INDIANS: RANCHERÍAS AND REBELLIONS

Besides its advantages of soil, surface, water, and vegetation, Guadalupe had numerous Indians. Originally many must have lived in the main part of the valley, where water was abundant. Although uncertain whether or not there was any general Indian name for the whole valley, the present Indians are sure that the mission and its locality were called "*Ojá cuñúrr*" (*ojá*=cave; *cuñúrr*=painted), from a near-by over-

hanging granite rock (pl. 14*a;* fig. 19). This rock is decorated with
crude hieroglyphs in red, yellow, and white. Probable outlying rancherías of the mission were Agua Escondida, two miles north of the valley
(see fig. 19) at a running arroyo; San José, four and one-half miles
farther; Rincón de los Encinos, at the mouth of a side cañon just south
of the upper end of the valley (pl. 13*b*) ; and San Antonio de Nicuárr,
in the cañon three miles above Rincón. The ranchería at Rincón de los
Encinos seems to have been the largest attached to Guadalupe. According to one estimate, there were 150 huts at Rincón as late as 1900.[33] In

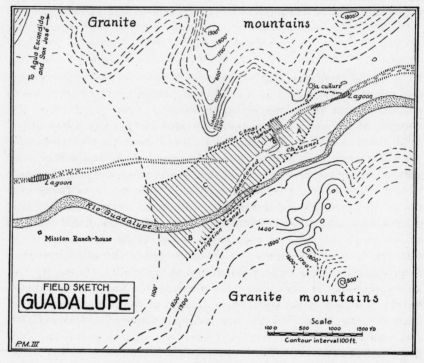

Fig. 19

the absence of any census of mission times we may conservatively estimate the Indian population of the valley and its margins at 400 (Mrs.
Barré said more than 330 in 1885). Most of them must have lived in their
rancherías; there were too many to have lived at the mission.

So many heathen being near at hand, it is unlikely that the mission extended its influence much beyond the limits of the valley. Furthermore,
the Indians to the northeast were of an independent spirit; they resisted
attempts at Christianization, and seemed always ready to attack the
missions. In 1836 there had been an uprising of Jacume (50 miles northeast of Guadalupe, on the present international border) and Yuma Indians against San Diego, which had forced the people at that port to

---

[33] Mr. Barré, who has lived in the valley for more than 40 years.

flee to a whaler for safety. Responding to a hurried call for help from the San Diego presidio, Lieutenant Macedonio Gonzales, commander of the escolta of twenty-five men at San Vicente, hastened to the rescue. On his way north he enlisted the support of "Jatiñil" (Jatñil, of the Mitlkwitl lineage, according to his living descendants), a powerful captain of the Indians of Nejí (30 miles northeast of Guadalupe). On this and other occasions, according to Rojo, the tribe of Jatñil was to the Frontera what Tlaxcala was to Mexico at the time of the Conquest. In 1837 two Colorado Indians, held captives at San Miguel, killed a corporal and escaped. Later in the same year they raised four hundred Yuma and attacked the Guadalupe Mission. After 1836, Guadalupe, on the exposed front, seems to have become the headquarters of the Frontera escolta, but on the day of the Indian attack all but five of the escolta were away. However, the five were prepared, and their defense saved the mission (Rojo:23–31). The Indian troubles seem to have been caused by harsh treatment at the missions.

Rebellion against oppression usually took the form of spontaneous, poorly organized outbursts, but the Indians of Nejí had effective leadership. Jatñil, who had been of great assistance to the missionaries (Rojo: 47, 80), finally became enraged at the forced baptism and "enslavement" of several of the Nejí. In February, 1840, with a number of armed Indians, Jatñil entered the mission and frightened Father Caballero into a flight south without even stopping to collect his cattle.[34] The rancherías at Rincón de los Encinos and San Antonio, under the leadership of Nicuárr, their last Captain, of the Kwatl lineage, were said to have been always friendly to the mission, and enemies of Jatñil.

At San José, Agua Escondida, Rincón de los Encinos, and near Cañon del Burro at the northeast end of the valley, half a dozen Indian families are still living, dependent now upon agriculture and work on neighboring ranches for a livelihood, but conserving their language and some customs (above, p. 102). This condition, quite different from that along the coast, where the few remaining Indians have become almost completely Latinized, prevails throughout the northern interior of the Peninsula, where several native rancherías persist.

MISSION DEVELOPMENTS

According to all reports, there was impressive development at Guadalupe in the brief six years of its existence. Father Caballero, whatever his faults, was said to have been one of the most active of the missionaries (Rojo: 76). Besides fulfilling his duties as President of the Dominican Missions of Lower California, for many years before his death he had sole personal charge of the Frontier area, being, at the same time, the

---

[34] *Ibid.*: 31–57. The account just given, graphically related by Rojo from statements of eyewitnesses, is further corroborated at many points by independent testimony of present occupants of the valley, who knew or are descendants of actors in the scenes described, including Juan Cuñúrr, a Mitlkwitl living at San José, who asserts that he is a great-grandson of Jatñil.

padre of San Miguel, Descanso, Guadalupe, and Santa Catalina (Engelhardt, 1929: 626). His interests included an annual sea-otter hunt, for which he provided the equipment (Rojo: 33).

The mission buildings were at the eastern edge of the low *mesita,* in the middle of the valley nearly half a mile from the nearest mountain border. The adobe walls have been destroyed by casual treasure seekers, the only remaining evidence of their location being a single angle of stone foundations, its two arms sixty and thirty yards in length respectively, close to the edge of the mesita. Within the angle are numerous pieces of red floor tiles. From the south side of the mission, it is said, broad steps led down the embankment to two cement tinajas into which emptied the water from a spring.

Water for irrigation came from lagoons half a mile and more east of the mission. Irrigation canals were built for an estimated distance of about two miles on both sides of the valley. The north acequia watered the mission huerta, a 6-acre plot just north of the mesita, where vegetables and fruits were raised, including at least grapes, pears, and apricots. The rest of the land between the acequias is fertile sandy soil; it included about forty acres just east of the mission and four hundred acres west of the mission (fig. 19). According to Juan Silva, a resident, all the grain of the mission was raised at this place by means of irrigation, though Caballero certainly knew that it could have been raised *de humedad.*[35] Most of the valley was used for livestock, and the herds of cattle were larger there than at any other mission in the Dominican area. In 1840, Caballero's cattle numbered by count 4915 (Rojo :53), a figure which may have included those of San Miguel and Descanso. A dozen years after the abandonment of the mission, Guadalupe Valley supported 3000 cattle and some horses (Negrete, p. 355). The strong association of the San Marcos Valley with cattle is interestingly indicated by the Indian name for San Marcos: *Kwak-ipa-ñurr:* "Painted man-deer" (*kwak*=deer; *ipa*=people; *ñurr*= painted). During the life of the Guadalupe Mission the ranch house was not at San Marcos, but farther up the valley, closer to the mission. The ruins of the mission ranch house, two and one-half miles west of the mission, are still pointed out.

---

[35] Schmieder (1928: 420) states that the present Russian occupants of the valley produce 125,000 bushels of wheat in normal years, by dry farming.

XIII. SANTA CATALINA

THE ÁLAMO PLAIN AND ITS MARGINS

THE SANTA CATALINA MISSION was near the center of the Peninsula, in the spacious Álamo Plain, which stretches more than twenty miles in a northwest-southeast direction with an average width of about ten miles. With an average elevation of 3500 feet, it slopes slightly toward the south, where is the principal outlet, by way of the Valley of San Pablo to the San Vicente River. The plain is interrupted in places by low island mountains (pl. 14b), which coalesce to form a range of low granite mountains on the west, where there is a drop of 1000 feet to the San Rafael Valley. The southern margin of the plain is somewhat elevated above the general level. It contains a confusion of steep, mostly metamorphic mountains which in the south and west extend to the Pacific coastal plains, and in the southeast slope steeply into Valle Trinidad, also 1000 feet below the plain (pl. 15a). To the north the plain rises 1500 feet by a gentle grade to the smooth summit of the granite block of the Sierra Juarez. The gentle southern slope of Sierra Juarez granite is buried to the east by remarkable accumulations of bedded lavas, tuffs, and sediments, forming a line of high mesas all the way to Valle Trinidad, and presenting a steep wall 1000 feet and more in height to the eastern edge of the Álamo Plain (pl. 15b). East of these "Catalina Mesas," as we may call them, a steep slope, a continuation of the eastern slope of the Sierra Juarez, drops to the low desert Laguna Salada Basin, north of the San Felipe Desert and separated from it by east-west mountain spurs.

The slope and the mountains form a tremendous barrier to east-west travel, so that the only two good passes through them have been of importance. One of these, the San Matías Pass, at the eastern end of Valle Trinidad, lies at the southern end of the mesas and just north of the Sierra San Pedro Mártir (pl. 16a), constituting the lowest (elevation about 3000 feet) and best pass across the peninsula. It was marginal to the Santa Catalina area and led to the San Felipe Desert, somewhat south of the Colorado Plains, and therefore was not of so great importance to the mission as the second pass, that of El Portezuelo. This latter pass lies in a gap in the Catalina Mesas three leagues (Arch. Cal., P. S. P., 13: 547–552) east-southeast of Santa Catalina. It was through this gap that the Dominicans at one time hoped to control the Colorado Indians. The gap was the chief avenue of communication between the Colorado-Cocopa Indians and the Álamo Plain Indians, and was an opportune place for raids by the former upon the missions.

Much of the winter precipitation is in the form of snow, which is often six inches deep in the vicinity of the mission. The summer is clear and hot, with rather numerous thunderstorms, though there is a distinct winter maximum in precipitation. The vegetation indicates a warm steppe climate (*BSh* of Köppen), for, though the characteristic cold-

steppe plants of juniper and sagebrush are conspicuous, in places there
is a liberal sprinkling of succulents (biznaga, tuna, small mescal) and
yucca (pl. 16b). Mesquite is plentiful, especially in the lower valleys,
San Rafael and Trinidad. Altogether the plain is well adapted to the
support of large herds of cattle, as had been observed by the original
explorers (above, p. 33). The Sierra Juarez, with a *Csa* climate like that
of the Peninsular sierra of California, has many grassy openings in the
forest that are also suitable for grazing (pl. 17a).

HERDS

In 1801, three years after the establishment of the mission, there were
reported 364 cattle, 205 sheep, 149 horses, 26 mules and asses, and 91
goats; in 1934, according to Lassepas, there were 1000 cattle and 600
sheep (table 1). Stealing by wild Indians from the east probably held
down the number of livestock. Pattie (p. 222), who was forced to stay at
least a week at the mission, went so far as to say that at that time (1828)
Santa Catalina had no livestock: it had all been plundered by wild
Indians from the (eastern) desert.

INDIAN POPULATION AND RANCHERÍAS

According to the enumeration of mission rancherías by the present-day
Indians, corroborated by Arrillaga's original survey, the lands tributary
to Santa Catalina included the whole Álamo Plain and some marginal
lands, from Agua Caliente on the east to the eastern edge of San Rafael
Valley on the west, and from Laguna Hanson in the granite Sierra
Juarez on the north to Valle Trinidad on the south, all inclusive: a total
area of about one thousand square miles. The rancherías of the mission
were located at La Ciénega and El Rincón (Indian name, Ñimai-ja =
water nipple), north of the mission near Cerro de la Ciénega (pl. 15b);
La Huerta and Sangre de Cristo, at the eastern edge of San Rafael Valley; Cerro Colorado, a few miles north of the present Álamo; San Pablo,
just east of Álamo; El Portezuelo; Agua Caliente del Portezuelo; Los
Bateques and Poza de Gonzales, on the road between Santa Catalina
and Valle Trinidad; Agua Caliente at the west end of Valle Trinidad;
and Arroyo Carrisito, emptying into Valle Trinidad on the north, five
miles east of Agua Caliente.

The continuous importance of the watering places at which these rancherías were situated is indicated by the present existence of rancherías
at La Huerta, Agua Caliente de Valle Trinidad and del Portezuelo, and
Santa Catalina, besides ranches at most of the other points, as well as by
the existence of rancherías at almost all the watering places even before
the days of the mission, as recorded in 1796 by Arrillaga.

Most of the available Indians were converted. The maximum recorded
population of Santa Catalina was more than 600, reported for 1824 by
Troncoso—the largest number recorded for any Dominican mission.
As early as 1801 the mission population numbered 223, and as late

as 1834, according to a manuscript leaflet accompanying the other mission libros, there were 239 souls (Lassepas said 250, in the same year; table 2). These are rather large numbers, in view of the hostility of the Indians frequently reported (e.g., Arch. Arzob., 1 : 112, 183). The neighboring eastern tribes of Keliwa and Cocopa were never brought into the mission, and were in fact hostile (Rojo: 47).

To judge from the small crops recorded for 1800 and 1801 (table 1), the Indians must have continued to eat wild plants even after the establishment of the mission. Many important native foods of the area were not found near the coast. These, according to present Indians, include the highly prized, date-like fruit of the "dátil" (yucca); mesquite bean; the boiled flower-bud of the biznaga; tuna seeds, and various other seeds which were ground up into pinole. The delicious roasted head of the mescal was a staple food, as on the coast. The high Sierra Juarez, although not permanently inhabited, was the autumn goal not only of the Santa Catalina Indians, but also of the Cocopa (Kniffen, 1931: 53), for the eastern margins of the Sierra abound in piñon groves, yielding another major food. The Cocopa, though living not very far from Santa Catalina, refused to live at the mission because of the winter cold. It is said that many of the upland Indians were in the habit of going down to spend the winter with relatives in the Cocopa lands in order to escape the cold and rain. One source of friction was the refusal of the padres to let the people go down in winter.

LOCAL SITE AND PLAN OF THE MISSION

At the center of radiating trails was the Santa Catalina Aguage, which had determined the precise location of the mission. The stream originates in a wide plain, the "Mission Plain" of figure 21. It is underlain by granite, which outcrops in small woolsacks here and there, and is dotted by low hills of reddish lava covered with large pebbles of the same material. The surface material of most of the plain is granitic sand. From the lower end of the flat the stream enters a rough granite gorge, through which it flows for a quarter-mile, dropping fifty feet to the second flat, a granite-encircled valley, known as Santa Catalina Valley (pl. 17b). From a marsh at the lower end of the valley the stream again plunges into a granite cañon, dropping one hundred seventy-five feet to the third, southernmost flat, San Miguel Valley, which joins, through a wide gap, the general surface of the Álamo Plain. The original Indian name for Santa Catalina, *Jactobjol*, "place where the water falls over stones," is said by present Indians to refer to the water in the upper end of the lower cañon, just below the marsh.

The mission buildings were on a shelf of one of the gentle red lava knolls overlooking the western edge of the upper flat (pls. 15b, 16b). The rocky knoll supports a growth of large junipers and mescal, and is backed on the west and north by chaparral-covered granite slopes. Crop production was dependent upon local precipitation, for the creek is too far below the level of the fields to have served for irrigation. The Catalina Indians of today say that the padres raised wheat.

Although at first glance it might seem strange that the mission was not built in either of the lower, irrigable valleys, it must be remembered that the mission occupied a highly dangerous frontier, and that its com-

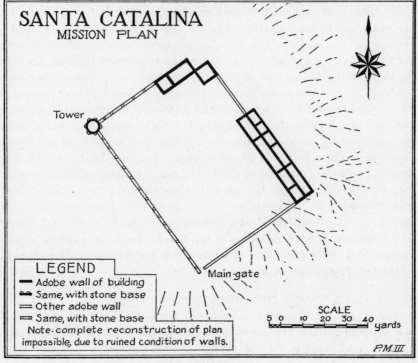

Fig. 20

manding site was well suited for a fort. The destruction of the mission has been so complete that nothing but low mounds of earth remain, in some places still upon a stone foundation (pl. 16b).

INDIAN UPRISINGS

That the military precautions were justified is shown by various references to attacks by Indians. Thus, Troncoso (p. 20), in 1824, said that the mission was fortified because of the repeated assaults of the Indians of the Colorado River. The attack which put an end to the mission occurred in 1840 (Arch. San Diego: 260). An account of the destruction of the mission is related by a living Catalina Indian;[36] according to him, a year or two after Fray Felix left for Guadalupe, one September, when most of the people were away from Santa Catalina getting piñon to the northward along the eastern slope of the Sierra Juarez, the Keliwa came

---

[36] José Domingo Castro, a Pai Pai about sixty years old, born at San Miguel (near Santa Catalina).

and burned the mission. The sacristan and a few old women were there, but they escaped. (A more authentic version states that sixteen of the neophytes were killed in the attack.)[37] Nicuárr, with five hundred of his people, pursued the Keliwa into the San Pedro Mártir Sierra and killed most of them. Other Indians at Santa Catalina said that the uprising which destroyed the mission "was general, including Pai-Pai, Keliwa, Huerteña, Riaño [Colorado], and all. They were without a leader in the attack; all fought like animals. They all hated the frailes: the Indians died when the frailes came. Arroyo Grande was never taken into any mission. It was lucky enough to escape." The Keliwa name for Santa Catalina is *Wa'iú-ichíu* (*wa* = house; *iú* = empty; *ichíu* = burned). The change in settlement of the Keliwa from Arroyo Grande to Arroyo León, where they now live, is estimated by them (in 1929) to have taken place about ninety years ago, and may well have been the result of the passing of the danger of missionization. The Keliwa even now have a warlike reputation; as late as 1911 they took part in the filibustering "revolution" of Lower California, which was suppressed by government troops with considerable bloodshed.

DEVELOPMENTS IN CROP LANDS AND CAÑONS

At the lower end of the Mission Plain the stream drops in a series of little waterfalls into the upper granite cañon. A hundred yards below the falls are the remains of a strong dam, nine feet high, constructed of adobe and red lava. The impounded water was used to irrigate Santa Catalina Valley, beyond the lower end of the short cañon. According to the Indians now living there, the acequia went along the west side of the valley (see fig. 21), which means there must have been about twenty-five acres of irrigable land. The arroyo, with the present stream, runs along the east side of the valley, ending in a swamp in the lower end. From the swamp the water flows into the lower cañon at Jactobjol. A short distance below the swamp is the little irrigable 6-acre flat which, from its size and relation to the swamp, must have been the one noticed by Ruiz in the original exploration (above, p. 33). This little flat was probably the only land cultivated in the early years of the mission. The annual grain crops for 1800 and 1801 were only about 75 bushels, consisting, in 1800, of 16 bushels of wheat and 65 of corn (see table 1), and requiring, on the yield basis previously used, only about four acres of land.

A mile below Jactobjol the lower cañon was dammed for the irrigation of the San Miguel Valley. In 1929 the writer found the remains of three dams here within a stretch of two hundred yards. The southernmost is a low, crude, rock dam, used by the present Indians for irrigating lands in the valley. Fifty yards farther up the cañon, at a place where steep granite walls come close together, leaving only a 50-foot gap in

---

[37] Engelhardt, 1929: 666; quoting Bancroft and Hittell; quoting Arch. San Diego, *loc. cit.*

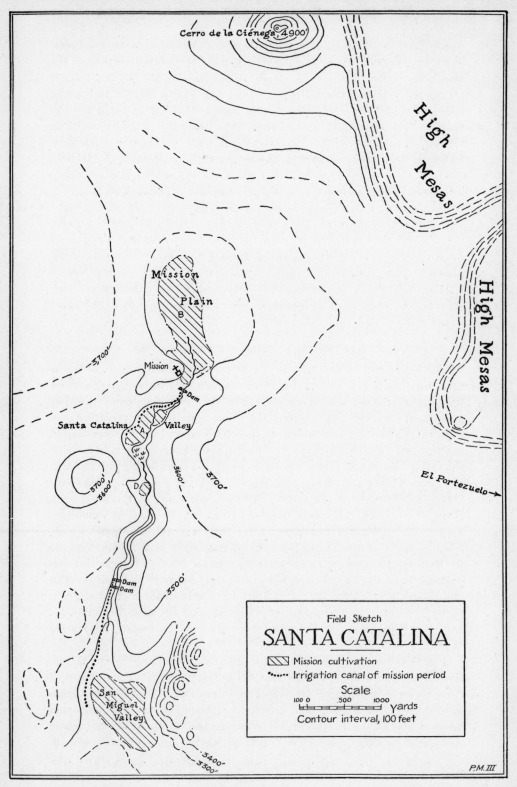

Cerro de la Ciénega, 4900'

High Mesas

High Mesas

Mission Plain

B

3,700'

Mission
D
Dam

Santa Catalina
A
Valley

3700'
3600'

D

3600'

3700'

El Portezuelo →

Dam
Dam

3500'

Field Sketch
SANTA CATALINA
◫ Mission cultivation
•••• Irrigation canal of mission period
Scale
100 0   500   1000
yards
Contour interval, 100 feet

San
Miguel
Valley
C

3400'
3300'

P.M.III

Fig. 21

the cañon bottom, are the remains of a second dam, nearly all washed away. It was made of granite boulders and earth, with the top eight feet above the stream. Still farther up the cañon are the slight remains of a third dam, which apparently was built of earth and was about ten feet high. Upstream from the third dam there are no signs of further works of man. Each dam had its own canal. The canals can be traced leading out from the mouth of the cañon and winding along the side of the ridge west of San Miguel Valley for about half a mile (see fig. 21). About eight feet higher than the modern ditch now in use is the acequia of the middle dam, composed of well-made tiles cemented together. Parallel to it and seven feet higher is the cruder, wider canal of the upper dam, consisting chiefly of a double line of stones four to five feet apart, faithfully following the contour of the hillsides.

Why were two parallel acequias and two separate dams built by the padres? Field inspection indicates that the higher ones are the older, for both dam and ditch are more nearly destroyed than the lower ones. Perhaps floods destroyed the upper, earthen dam, and the new, stronger, stone-and-earth dam was built farther downstream, with a lower height and a lower, smaller ditch. Experience had probably taught that the amount of water available was not so great as had first been planned for. The flow at the upper waterfall (and the flow is only a little less in the lower cañons), carefully estimated by the writer on June 14, 1929, after a winter said to have been unusually dry, was fifteen cubic feet a minute. The storage capacity of the largest dam was estimated at some sixty thousand cubic feet.

The total irrigable land of San Miguel Valley is estimated at 115 acres, and is therefore to be identified with the 10 fanegas of land which Ruiz had expected would form the chief mission field (above, p. 33). This field, added to those already noted above, gives a total of 146 acres of irrigated land for the mission, besides the 150 acres of dry wheat land in the Mission Plain. Santa Catalina was a severe test of the ability of the mission system to get results under adverse human conditions.

SURVIVING INDIANS

The very factors which handicapped and finally destroyed the Santa Catalina Mission—unruliness of the Indians and isolation on a frontier —led to a survival of more of its population in place than at any other mission. In 1929 there were still seven Indian families living here: three in Santa Catalina Valley (pl. 17c), one on the little flat just below Jactobjol, and three in San Miguel Valley. A great contrast to this fairly well settled scene is presented by the lonely, abandoned site of the other "Sierra" mission, San Pedro Mártir.

XIV. SAN PEDRO MÁRTIR

THE SIERRA

SAN PEDRO MÁRTIR MISSION, more than a mile above sea level and about two thousand feet higher than Santa Catalina, was the most elevated mission of either Baja or Alta California. It lay on San Pedro Mártir "Mountain" (a plateau about 25 miles long from north to south and 10 miles from east to west) near the low southwestern margin. Here the forest thins out to a scattering growth of Parry piñon trees (*Pinus quadrifolia*), the chief food piñon of the Indians (Goldman, 1916: 314), surrounded by dense, high chaparral.

The higher part of the San Pedro Mártir plateau, to the north and east of the mission, is covered with forest, predominantly of yellow pine (*Pinus ponderosa*), with some white fir (*Abies concolor*), sugar pine (*Pinus lambertiana*), and cedar (*Libocedrus decurrens*) scattered through it above an elevation of about 7000 feet, and, above 7500 feet, good stands of lodgepole pine (*Pinus contorta*). The last, a representative of the Canadian Life-Zone, has been used by Russell (1926:83) in California as a partial indicator of the *Ds* (microthermal, summer-dry) climate. Together with the known cold winters and deep snow (Nordhoff, p. 119, sets the average snowfall at 6 to 8 feet), it is good evidence of the existence of that type of climate here in the higher parts of the plateau. The yellow-pine and piñon-chaparral growths between 7500 and 5000 feet, including the southern half of the plateau and the site of the mission, indicate *Csa* climate, like that of the Sierra Juarez. The plateau forest, crossed by granite ridges thinly covered with trees, contains a number of grassy, open basins at elevations of from 7000 to 8000 feet (pl. 18*a* and 18*b*). The highest of these basins, Vallecito, as well as the most microthermal forest, occurs near the eastern edge of the plateau, which attains here its greatest elevation, slightly more than 9000 feet.

To the east of this edge the plateau drops by the great escarpment to the lowlying San Felipe Desert. Jutting out from the escarpment and separated by a deep cañon from the main San Pedro Mártir plateau, rises the highest peak of Lower California (pl. 19*a*), Picacho de la Providencia, as it is most commonly known, or Calamahue Mountain, as it was called when mapped for the first time by the U. S. S. "Narragansett" Survey, which gave its elevation as 10,126 feet.[38] Other names given for it are Picacho del Diablo (the name by which it is known locally), Tres Palomas (from its three white peaks), Santa Catalina, and La Encantada. Some maps show two near-by peaks, using two of these names. Although it is a conspicuous landmark from the Gulf side (whence it was first remarked in 1702 by Kino and mapped in 1873–1875 by the

---

[38] United States Hydrographic Office: 127. As the peak has no connection with the original Calamahue, much farther south, it is mapped by the writer as La Povidencia in order to obviate confusion.

"Narragansett"), it is shut off from view to the west by the San Pedro Mártir plateau.

From its eastern edge, the San Pedro Mártir plateau is inclined gently west and south. Most of the streams upon its surface drain westward into the Santo Domingo River, which has, consequently, a dependable flow of water. A steep scarp of 1500 to 3000 feet terminates the northern and western edge of the plateau, marked by cascades in the streams, notably the Falls of San Antonio in the La Grulla Arroyo, the largest stream of the plateau. To the south the plateau gradually merges into the Llanos de Buenos Aires, a part of the San Borja Desert.

OUTLANDS AND RANCHES

According to the Keliwa now living at Arroyo León, the forest-covered plateau was never permanently inhabited by Indians, because of the winter cold. It was, they say, visited annually for piñon by Indians from all sides, who sometimes hunted deer there in the warm season. Arrillaga (1796, August 26–28) in August found traces of some large rancherías along the east base of the sierra at the arroyos of San Elias and "de la Vieja," but the inhabitants were all in the sierra "where they live regularly in summer." The Keliwa even now make autumn expeditions to the northern slopes for piñon, but the mountain is still not permanently inhabited by Indians, even at the site of the San Pedro Mártir Mission. Personal information of the kind that was obtained for Santa Catalina is therefore lacking for San Pedro Mártir, as the present Keliwa say that they know nothing about the mission. There is a bare possibility that there are a few wild Indians still living in the neighborhood, for in 1926 the writer observed, in a mesquite thicket in the San Pedro Mártir Cañon a few miles below the mission, two *metates,* with *manos,* that had evidently been used recently for grinding.

Written data relating to this mission are very scant. Two years after its foundation, Arrillaga (1796, August 22) reported that the mission had a ranch of cattle and horses three and one-half hours away at La Encantada. The name La Encantada is applied at present to one of the grassy basins, at about 7500 feet elevation, northeast of the mission (pl. 18*b*). It is probable that cattle were also raised in some of the other mountain basins such as La Grulla, Santa Rosa, and Santo Tomás, the last being watered by a west-flowing stream parallel with and just south of San Pedro Mártir Arroyo and within the southern margin of the yellow-pine forest (pl. 19*b*). These sierra basins are all used at present for summer grazing. Probably a seasonal migration of the mission herds was the rule, as at present, the cattle being driven down in the autumn to the lower lands near San Isidoro. This place, three hours' trip by trail from the mission, has stone and adobe walls which Señor Murillo, the present occupant of the San Isidoro Ranch, thinks were built by the padres. The trail from the mission to San Isidoro drops down the steep western descent of the plateau. Even figs and apricots thrive here, but

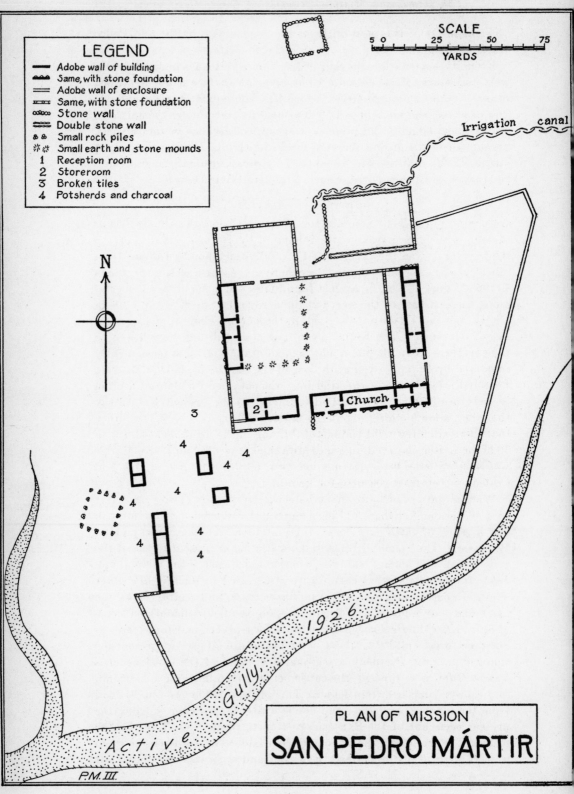

LEGEND
▬▬▬ Adobe wall of building
⌒⌒⌒ Same, with stone foundation
≡≡≡ Adobe wall of enclosure
▦▦▦ Same, with stone foundation
∞∞∞ Stone wall
〰〰 Double stone wall
♨ ♨ Small rock piles
※ ※ Small earth and stone mounds
1 Reception room
2 Storeroom
3 Broken tiles
4 Potsherds and charcoal

N

Irrigation canal

3

2   1   Church

4
4
4   4
4   4
4
4
4
4

Active   Gully, 1926

P.M. III

PLAN OF MISSION
SAN PEDRO MÁRTIR

SCALE
5   0   25   50   75
YARDS

Fig. 22

the climate is too cool for oranges. San Isidoro lay on the main inland trail, between the San Fernando and Santa Catalina missions.

If we assume that the places just mentioned marked the extent of mission lands, the total area subject to the San Pedro Mártir Mission would have been only five hundred square miles. The Indian rancherías reported by Arrillaga and said by the present Keliwa to have existed at the aguages along the east foot of the San Pedro Mártir Sierra no longer exist, which is evidence that they were included in mission territory. If we assume that the originally contemplated site at Cieneguilla (above, p. 30) was also included, the mission lands must have comprised one thousand square miles. In the map of mission lands (see folded map) an area of six hundred square miles, starting just north of San Antonio, has not been assigned to any mission, since there is no record of its missionization.

The chief productive merit of the San Pedro Mártir Mission area was the grazing resource of the grassy mountain meadows and the plentiful forage of the San Isidoro locality. The herds seem to have been well up to the average mission herd, in spite of inroads upon them by Indians (Arch. Cal., P. S. P., 12:316), for in 1801 there were reported 700 cattle, 500 sheep, 150 goats, 50 swine, and 169 horses, mules, and donkeys (table 1).

POPULATION

The population of the mission did not increase so rapidly as the livestock. In 1801, seven years after the foundation, the population numbered only 94 (table 2), though the unrecorded figures of later years may have been greater. There may have been fewer Indians available for this mission than for most, especially as much of the area was without permanent rancherías. Certainly there was trouble with Indians escaping (Arrillaga, 1796, August 6–22, 26, 29). Sergeant Ruiz tells in 1794 of having erected at San Pedro Mártir two bulwarks with cannon embrasures for the better protection of the mission (Arch. Cal., P. S. P., 12:316).

THE MISSION VALLEY AND ITS DEVELOPMENT

There does not seem to have been scarcity of crops. Harvests, though smaller than those at most of the missions in the two years for which we have data, were fully as adequate in proportion to the population. In 1800, the better year, the crops were: corn, 780 bushels; beans, 208 bushels; wheat, 130 bushels. The predominance of corn was even greater the next year, and barley, not reported the first year, was reported in the second year (see table 1). The emphasis on corn is explainable by the limited extent of cultivable land and the need of getting as much food as possible from each acre. The only good crop land within half a dozen miles of the mission was the mission valley.

The small mission valley is closely circumscribed by rocky granitic hills, high on the north and east (as much as 1000 feet higher than the valley floor) and lower on the south and west. A thin stand of Parry piñon and a very dense growth of chaparral, with occasional yuccas, cover most of the slopes. The valley floor is covered with sagebrush, except where the central arroyo of the valley provides a strip of willow thicket. The arroyo separates the valley floor into two flats, the larger being on the north side. Its water does not appear to have been used at

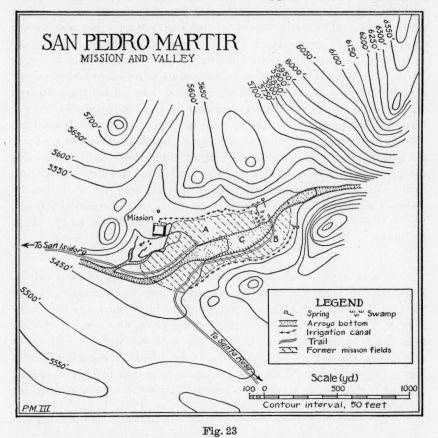

SAN PEDRO MARTIR
MISSION AND VALLEY

LEGEND
Spring   Swamp
Arroyo bottom
Irrigation canal
Trail
Former mission fields

Scale (yd.)
100 0   500   1000
Contour interval, 50 feet

P.M.III

Fig. 23

all for irrigating the fields. Facilities for irrigation were of a type unique among the missions: near the upper end of the valley, on both sides, springs of water break out from the hills a few feet above the valley floor, and from these almost ideally situated springs well-made irrigation ditches lead along each side of the valley for half a mile, so placed as to make possible the irrigation of any part of the flats (see fig. 23). The two flats, constituting all the present cultivable land in the valley, have a combined area of just fifty acres. The crops of 1800, at the yields heretofore used, would have required fifty-three and one-half acres. The steep, fresh cuts in the arroyo walls indicate recent widening, while absolute evidence of valley-floor erosion since the building of the mission is afforded by a 75-yard gap in the lower stone-and-adobe outer wall of the mission, cut by a deep recent gully tributary to the main arroyo (see figs.

22, 23). Even so, San Pedro Mártir had fewer cultivable lands than any other mission, and its little valley must have been most intensively used.

The same care and skill that developed the irrigation system of the valley were also used in the construction of the mission buildings. Extensive ruins show that these were on an alluvial fan emerging from a side cañon at the northwestern edge of the valley (fig. 23). Enough of the walls remain to make possible a fairly complete reconstruction of the plan (fig. 22). Two or three acres of land adjoining the quadrangle on the east and south are enclosed by a strong stone-and-adobe wall, the one which has been breached by the gully as previously noted. Other niceties observed at this sierra mission were floors partly tiled, for remains of 9- by 9- by 1½-inch red bricks are found. Pieces of red roof tiles are fairly abundant.

From all points of view San Pedro Mártir seems to have been a highly developed, picturesque, and unique mission in spite of its isolation.

PART THREE

SUMMATION

XV. FIGURES OF ABORIGINAL POPULATION

BY THE USE OF THE DETAILS given in the previous sections, a rather close estimate of the aboriginal population of the Dominican area can be obtained. The census figures of the missions are of slight value for this purpose, for of the Indians originally within the territory of a mission some were never brought into the fold, because of death from pestilence or because of flight, and those who were brought in were never all on the rolls of the mission at the same time. Pre-mission estimates for some parts of the area are available and supply one basis for calculation.

EARLY ESTIMATES

Velazquez (above, p. 13), in 1770, on a rapid journey from Velicatá to San Diego, saw nineteen rancherías, with an estimated population of 2000, nearly all within future Dominican territory. Arrillaga (1796: 8, 10), in his notably thorough exploration of the Santa Catalina area, reached the conclusion that it contained more than 1000 Indians (above, p. 33), which he said were enough to justify a mission (implying that that was the usual number in a mission area). Even assuming that Velazquez saw nearly all the rancherías in the area through which he passed, the areas of Rosario, Guadalupe, and Santo Domingo (the San Telmo quarter excepted) were not touched by his route. For Rosario, 10 rancherías were reported (above, p. 59); for Guadalupe, seven (see folded map); and for Santo Domingo, seven, including the four noted by early explorers along the coast and three others indicated by shell mounds (above, p. 70). At the rate of 105 souls to a ranchería (the average of Velazquez' report and approximately the average of Arrillaga's; above, p. 33), the areas of these three missions would have included about 1050, 735, and 735 Indians, respectively. In addition, there were at least three rancherías along the eastern base of the Sierra San Pedro Mártir (Arrillaga, 1796, August 26–28), far from the route of Velazquez. These would add approximately 315 Indians to the total, and similarly the total obtained for the original population of the whole Dominican area would be 5835. This figure is certainly too low, for it is based upon the assumption that all the rancherías in the areas of the Missions San Vicente, Santo Tomás, and San Miguel were noted by Velazquez.

MISSION BOOKS

The foregoing estimate of population can be supplemented and checked by the mission records. For Rosario and Santo Domingo especially, continuous records of baptism and burial (fig. 24) are preserved.

The total original population of the Rosario area may be considered as the total number of baptisms during the first twenty years of the mission's life (the period of active recruiting), minus the number of baptisms of infants born at the mission, plus the number of unbaptized runaways from the area, plus the number of deaths, from epidemic, of unbaptized Indians in that period. It is here assumed that birth and death rates among wild Indians were approximately equal. The total number of baptisms for the first twenty years was 1311. In the first six months of the mission (1774), about 10 per cent of the baptisms were of infants. As almost all these children must have been brought to the mission with their parents, we may accept 10 per cent as the approximate maximum proportion of infants to total recruits for later years, and 3½ per cent roughly as the birth rate (for the "infants" were considered to be those three years old or younger; above, p. 56).

These percentages check well with the records of the early years of the mission. Thus, in 1776, 24 of 98 baptisms were of infants (above, p. 57; fig. 24), and 74 of "adults"; 3½ per cent of 540 (the average population of the mission for the year)[1] is 19, the probable increase from births within the mission; 98 minus 19 is 79, the probable number of recruits brought in from outside; 10 per cent of 79 equals 8, the probable number of infants among the newcomers. The discrepancy between the actual (24) and theoretical ($19 + 8 = 27$) number of new infants is thus only 3. By applying the same method to 1777 we arrive at 18 as the theoretical number of mission births, 2 as the theoretical number of imported infants; since actual baptisms of babies numbered 21, the discrepancy between fact and theory is, in this example, 1. In the most successful year, 1775, a little more than 10 per cent of the 419 baptisms were of infants, and of these the number of babies born at the mission must have been about 12 (3½ per cent of that year's average population). For the remaining seventeen years (1778–1794), baptisms totaled 615, of which about half (307), according to a random sampling of the baptismal book, were infants. With an average population for the period of about 350 souls (calculated on the basis of estimated yearly population, fig. 24), the mission would have had in the seventeen years 208 births at the rate of 3½ per cent a year. Adding 41 imported children (10 per cent of total immigrants: 615 — 208), we would find 58 (615 — 249 compared with 308) children unaccounted for, for the period. A complete knowledge of the exact proportion of infants among the baptized and of the true population each year would doubtless reduce the error. Assuming that half of the 58 babies unaccounted for were born at the mission, we get 237 as a close approximation to the number of births at the mission from 1778 to 1794, inclusive.

The total number of births at the mission in the 20-year period (the sum of the four estimates in the paragraph above) was approximately

---

[1] One-half the sum of population at the beginning and the end of the year.

286. Deducting this from 1311 (total number of baptisms) leaves 1025 as the total number of Indians of heathen parentage baptized—a number surprisingly close to the 1050 previously estimated by the "ranchería method." If it needs any change, this "libros" estimate of original population should be higher, for some of the Indians must have died from epidemics without having been baptized, and some may have escaped by flight. These sources of uncertainty are less important for Rosario than for the other missions because two-thirds of the Rosario conversions were made in the first three years of the life of the mission, before the first big epidemic of 1777. Nevertheless, some of the unbaptized Indians must have died in epidemics, for there were about 380 recruits between 1777 and 1794, a period in which there were three epidemics (fig. 24). In the three years 1777–1779, 213 burials, representing 38 per cent of the population, were recorded at the mission. If we consider the average normal annual mortality at the mission to have been about 6 per cent in healthful years (the figure for a year of few burials, 1787), 20 per cent of the mission Indians must have died of the epidemic in 1777–1779, in addition to those that died away from the mission of whose burial there is no record. If the outside death rate, in less crowded quarters but with poorer medical attention, were even half as great in the epidemics as at the mission, some 35 outside Indians would have died in the 1777 epidemic, and as many more in the other epidemics up to 1794. This would raise the final figure of aboriginal population of the Rosario area to 1095 souls, the most accurate estimate obtainable for any of the missions.

The population of the Santo Domingo area cannot be calculated so precisely as that of Rosario, though the baptismal and burial registers of both missions are nearly complete. Conversions were negligible (5) in number at Santo Domingo the first two years. The greater percentage of infants baptized here than at Rosario was doubtless partly a result of the circumstance that there was a greater percentage of women in the mission. At Santo Domingo, furthermore, children four years old or less were generally classified as infants, which would automatically mean that the number of infants among recruits would be one-third greater than in the Rosario classification.

One result of slowness of early recruiting at Santo Domingo must have been that many more Indians died unbaptized in epidemics there than at Rosario. The terrible smallpox epidemic of 1781 exacted a heavy toll at Santo Domingo, carrying off one-third of the mission population. Assuming that tolls outside the mission were half as heavy as within (and with smallpox they may have been even heavier), about 92 unbaptized Indians must have died at the time of that epidemic; for of the 694 baptisms in the active period of conversion (1775–1796; above, p. 71), about 564 were of imported Indians (694 minus 3½ per cent each year of the average population, 175, or 130 mission births); and of these 564, by similar calculation, about 462 were outside the mission until after

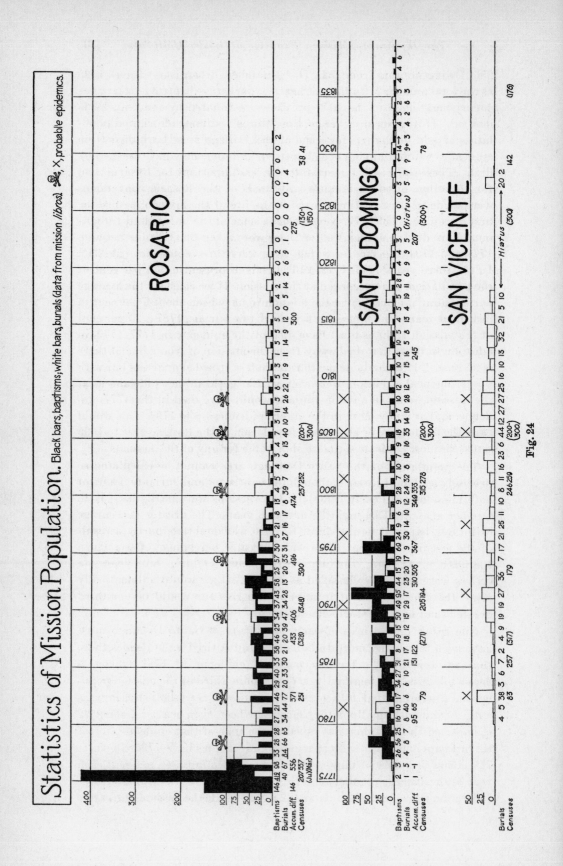

Statistics of Mission Population. Black bars, baptisms; white bars, burials (data from mission *libros*) ☠, probable epidemics.

Fig. 24

1780. The epidemics of 1790 and 1796, similarly, would have killed about 20 more outside Indians. Adding the 112 unbaptized epidemic victims to the 564 wild Indians converted, plus about 25 recruits after 1796, a total figure of 701 original inhabitants of the Santo Domingo area is obtained as a minimum. This figure should be indefinitely increased by the number of Indians who fled from conversion, or who died, without baptism, from *gálico*. In the absence of more evidence, it is reasonably safe to assume a total original population for the Santo Domingo area of about 840 (8 rancherías, including at least one for the San Telmo area, at 105 Indians for each ranchería according to the Velazquez average). This would mean a density of population of three-fourths of a person to the square mile, only half as great as that of the Rosario area.

The technique used in estimating the aboriginal populations of the areas of the first two missions cannot be used for the others, because their baptismal registers are not available. For San Vicente, the burial record gives some basis for a comparison with the other two missions, although there is a hiatus in the book from 1818 to 1826. Aside from these nine blank years, there were 606 burials recorded at the mission. If 15 burials a year were made during the blank period (the average of the number of burials for the year next preceding and the year next following the hiatus), we should add 135 to the 606, with a resulting total of 741 as the probable number of burials performed at San Vicente up to 1829. At Santo Domingo there were approximately 725 burials up to 1829, 15 per cent fewer than the estimated number of aborigines. At Rosario there were about 1211 burials by the same date, 10 per cent more than the estimated number of aborigines. Population conditions at San Vicente resembled those at Santo Domingo rather than those at Rosario in that epidemics seriously reduced the number of wild Indians in the early years of the mission, and even previously. Thus, the smallpox epidemic of 1781 struck San Vicente the year after its foundation and reached its height there in 1782.

With approximately equal numbers of burials in the same period of time, it might be supposed that Santo Domingo and San Vicente had also similar numbers of original heathen; 840 is estimated for Santo Domingo. It is probable, however, that the heathen of San Vicente were more completely gathered into the fold than those of Santo Domingo. If we assume that non-baptized runaways and non-epidemic heathen deaths at Santo Domingo were about equal, there would have been some 70 Indians in the former category in the Santo Domingo area. Deducting that number from 840 (under the supposition that runaways from the San Vicente area were negligible), a final figure of 770 is obtained for the approximate original population of the San Vicente area. This gives a population density figure almost the same as that of Rosario. Why the density should be so much greater at San Vicente than at Santo Domingo is not clear. Possibly the area under control of San Vicente was greater than estimated; or the San Vicente Mission may have drawn upon the Indians in lands subsequently taken over by Santo Domingo or Santo Tomás. The San Vicente territory was slightly more desirable for the aborigine than that of Santo Domingo.

CENSUSES AND OTHER SOURCES

Estimates of aboriginal population for the coastal lands north of San Vicente can be little more than careful guesses, for none of the mission books is available for this area. The ratio of aborigines to later mission population gives one clue. At Rosario, the aboriginal population was just twice as great as the highest official mission census figure. At Santo Domingo the ratio was 2.87 to 1; at San Vicente, 2.46 to 1. The differences in ratio can be accounted for (aside from inaccuracies) by the fact that the Rosario mission population represented a more complete gathering-in of heathen than occurred at any other Dominican establishment, and the Santo Domingo recruiting was the least successful of any except that of San Pedro Mártir.

The fragmentary censuses indicate that conditions at Santo Tomás were comparable to those at San Vicente, in that conversions increased from the beginning at a steady, moderate rate, and that consequently the San Vicente ratio (2½) should be used. Multiplying the highest census estimate (400, in 1824) by 2½, we obtain 1000 for the number of Santo Tomás aborigines. This would give an original population density of one person to the square mile for the Santo Tomás area.

At San Miguel, recruiting started in 1787 with a rush, no doubt because of the large number of Indians present at the mission site, and Father Sales reported the baptism of 123 in the first half-year of the mission. Later, however, progress was unsatisfactory (Sales, part 3:81–82). The average rate of growth at this mission and at San Vicente was probably the same, and we may therefore multiply the highest census figure (224, in 1800) by 2½, obtaining 560 as a preliminary estimate of the aboriginal population in the area of San Miguel. Following the transfer of headquarters from San Miguel to Descanso and the accompanying explorations, many years after 1800 (above, p. 37), we may safely assume an additional aboriginal population equivalent to at least one ranchería, bringing the total number to 665. Possibly this figure should be revised upward, for it is based upon the assumption that the few and scattered censuses that remain for this mission include the maximum population figures. The Troncoso figure for 1824 cannot be depended upon here, for by that time San Miguel recruiting may have begun to overlap into the future Guadalupe area.

No census of the short-lived Guadalupe mission has been handed down. For lack of better evidence, the figure of 735, based upon the estimated number and size of rancherías (above, p. 133), is used as the original number of inhabitants for the Guadalupe area. This agrees roughly with two and one-half times the number of Indians estimated as living in Guadalupe Valley in 1885 (above, p. 116). The population density indicated for the entire San Miguel-Guadalupe area is then two to the square mile, which would mean that this was the most densely settled part of all the Dominican area. This agrees well with the reports of the early explorers, who remarked upon the size and number of villages along this part of the coast. The San Miguel area was in many ways the most favorable for aboriginal occupation, since it included the most humid part of the coast lands, was the best suited for the growth of the plant and animal food of the Indians, and contained plentiful sea food, which was lacking in the interior of the Peninsula.

For Santa Catalina the careful pre-mission estimates of the original population as 1000 (above, p. 133) may be accepted: this indicates a density of one to the square mile for this entire inland area. Owing to the late founding of this mission, only two official censuses are available. These show an increase in population from the fourth to the fifth year from 133 to 223, indicating active growth at that time. A separate sheet preserved with the existing books of the other missions lists 239 individuals of Santa Catalina under date of 1834. Troncoso's 1824 estimate of more than 600 souls (table 2), if accurate, indicates that diseases did not affect this marginal mission so seriously as they affected the coastal missions.

At San Pedro Mártir the mission population was 60 in 1794, 92 in 1800, and 94 in 1801. These are the only definite population figures known. Before 1800 the missionaries had great trouble with runaways (above, p. 129), and in the absence of any subsequent news it may be assumed that the mission went out of existence not long afterward. The San Pedro Mártir area was doubtless less densely settled than the Santa Catalina area, for more than half of the former consisted of highlands without permanent settlements. There were probably at least six rancherías or their equivalent grouped about the margins of the San Pedro Mártir Sierra, three along the eastern base (above, p. 127) and three along the western (at Cieneguilla, San Isidoro, and San Antonio or Santa Cruz), which, at the rate of 105 per ranchería, would very uncertainly indicate an aboriginal population of 630—.63 persons to the square mile, the lowest density for any of the mission areas.

The debatable area of six hundred square miles of unattractive land northwest of the San Pedro Mártir area may have had 300 or 400 Indians not included in any mission territory. Data concerning the district are so uncertain that it will not be included in the summaries. If it was divided up, probably San Vicente and San Pedro Mártir had the greater portion of it, which would mean that the density at San Vicente would have been only one to the square mile, and the density at San Pedro Mártir about the same as already estimated. The population estimate of the area of the latter mission would then have to be increased by about 150.

Summarizing the data for the entire area definitely within the field of the Dominican missionary activities, a figure of 6745 is obtained for the total aboriginal population, with an average density of population of slightly more than one person to the square mile. The following table presents the detailed data in convenient form:

SUMMARY OF ABORIGINAL POPULATION ESTIMATES

Mission	Area (sq. mi.)	Original Population	Density (Persons per sq. mi.)
Rosario	700	1095	1.57
Santo Domingo	1100	840	.77
San Vicente	500	780	1.56
Santo Tomás	1050	1000	.95
San Miguel-Descanso ⎱ Guadalupe ⎰	700	{ 665 735 }	2.
Santa Catalina	1000	1000	1.
San Pedro Mártir	1000	630	.63
Total	5850	6745	1.15
Average	731	843	(density of whole area)

COMPARISONS WITH UPPER CALIFORNIA

A comparison of the aboriginal population densities of Lower and Upper California is interesting. A careful analysis of the latter, giving due consideration to previous estimates, has been made by Kroeber (chap. 57), with the surprising result that he assigns to Upper California, the promised land of the Franciscans, less than one person to the square mile, or less than was assigned to the poor desert-and-steppe land of the Dominicans. Kroeber's results were similar under two different methods of computation. One computation was based upon an admittedly rough estimate of the original population of the Franciscan mission area (following Merriam in method), the estimate being then applied to the rest of the non-desert part of the area. Any error in the mission-land estimate would materially affect the final conclusions. Kroeber suggests that his preliminary figures be checked by an analysis of the baptismal records of the Franciscan missions. The second method of computation was based upon the sum of the estimates of the population of the various Indian groups of the area.

The present writer is inclined to think that Kroeber's estimate is about right, because of the counterbalancing effect of two sets of errors in the first computation. The original population of the mission area of California was probably greater than the 50,000 assigned it by Merriam and Kroeber, for their figure is only twice the *total population of the missions in 1830,* while it has been shown above that the population of the Dominican area was from two to two and one-half times as great as the total of the *maximum population for each of the missions*. The population of the interior of California, however, was probably not so dense as that of the coast, which was included in the mission areas. Certainly the Lower California figures show that the density was greater at coastal missions than at interior missions. The density in the San Miguel-Descanso area, which most nearly resembled the Alta California coastal areas, must have approached three to the square mile, after allowance is made for the inland closely articulated Guadalupe area. This would explain the fact that Kroeber's additive estimate of the mission area population of Alta California was 64,000, and confirm his doubts of the reliability of the multiplicative method (*ibid.:* 885–886).

Granting, then, the correctness of Kroeber's summary figures, the difference in density of population between Upper and Lower California can easily be accounted for when it is remembered that in neither of the Californias did the Indians depend upon agriculture, and that in a gathering economy the suitability of land for crops is of little importance. Grassy land provides for more game, but desert land is conducive to the growth of directly edible vegetation in the form of succulent stems (*mescal*), roots, and seeds. Even more important in the present consideration is the sea food, which favored the greatest densities in Lower California and probably in Upper California. Lower California, being narrow, has more seacoast in proportion to its area than Upper California, a fact which would be enough to account for a slightly greater density in the former even without any additional factor.

POPULATION OF EXTRA-DOMINICAN LANDS

An estimate for the entire aboriginal population of the Pacific-facing slope of Lower California north of the Jesuit area is in order. Just south of the Dominican-developed lands were the lands of the Franciscan Mission of San Fernando, with an area of some 2750 square miles and with a native population of about 2800 (twice the maximum population of the mission).[2] To the north of the Dominican lands and south of the present international boundary lies an area of 2125 square miles (including the non-Dominican part of the Catalina mesas) which we may call the Nejí area. From its similarity to the San Pedro Mártir area, and in the absence of adequate field data, we may assume a density for this northern district of .63 to the square mile, as at San Pedro Mártir. Adding the San Fernando and Nejí figures to the 6745 of the Dominican mission lands (assuming that the 315 persons of the San Pedro Mártir rancherías at the eastern foot of the mountains were just balanced by those of the debatable San Isidoro area), a total figure is obtained of 10,884 persons, in an area (excluding the east sierra slope) of 11,125 square miles. Further research will be necessary to determine the orig-

---

[2] For San Fernando population figures see Sauer and Meigs (pp. 288–289). The maximum population recorded was 1406, probably in 1776, according to Arch. Cal., P. R., 1:62–63.

inal population of the rest of Lower California. The northern part of the
Jesuit area will probably be found to have had a density similar to that
of San Fernando, while the southern, moister, narrower part may have
been somewhat more densely settled. There must have been more than
22,000, the number reported for 1740 (Arch. Cal., S. P., Miss. and Col.,
1:281–323), in the Jesuit area. The Colorado Desert region, with the
driest, hottest climate of all, seems to have been the most densely settled
part of the entire Peninsula because it included agricultural Indians,
in the Colorado delta, and had plentiful sea food available farther south.
Kniffen (p. 51) estimated a minimum original density of Indian population of 46 to the square mile on hundreds of square miles of cultivated
delta overflow lands, mostly in Lower California. Such a density was not
possible among the non-agricultural people among whom the Dominicans
labored.

XVI. A GENERAL VIEW OF THE MISSIONS

AVERAGE MISSION DEVELOPMENT

TAKING INTO CONSIDERATION only the productive potentialities of the Frontera, one might expect that the population would have increased after the introduction of agriculture and stock raising by the missionaries. As a matter of fact, however, the population of the Dominican area was never so large after the establishment of missions as it had been before. At all the missions, so far as we can tell, the death rate exceeded the birth rate almost from the beginning, on account of the unaccustomed diseases and living conditions introduced among the Indians.

The decline was not apparent in the early annual censuses of the missions because new converts were being continually added to the rolls, replacing those who died. Also the total mission population progressively increased with the founding of successive missions. The highest total detailed census figure for the Dominican missions was the last one available: 1568, for the year 1801. Of this total, San Pedro Mártir Mission had 94, and the other six missions averaged 246 each (table 2). Shaler stated that in 1805 each of the seven missions had between 200 and 300 members (Cleland: 473). The highest credible estimate ever given was by Troncoso, for 1824, when he estimated the mission population at more than 2100—an average of more than 300 to a mission (table 2).

The average Dominican mission during its active life may, then, be pictured as a settlement with a population fluctuating around 250. Part of the population lived at the central mission establishment, and part, at least in the early years, was gathered into outlying communities, the rancherías of the missions. An average annual crop of 2000 bushels of grain to each mission was produced (table 1), providing more than a pound of cereal food per day per capita. Corn made up about half the crop, the remainder being wheat and barley, with a few beans. All these were raised on the valley floors by means of irrigation except near the northern border, where some dry farming was practiced. Crops fluctuated greatly from year to year. Thus, at Rosario, in 1785, following a winter of deficient rainfall (Arch. Cal., P. S. P., 13: 333–334), the grain crop totaled 1560 bushels, and the next year, after a rainy winter (Arch. Cal., S. P., Miss. and Col., 1 :92–94), the crop rose to 6328 bushels. Grapes, orchard fruits, and vegetables of unknown quantity were produced, and wine, sometimes of very good quality, was manufactured at most of the missions (Cleland: 477). Approximately two hundred acres of land were under irrigation in each mission valley, though not all that acreage was cultivated each year. The adobe mission buildings, grouped in a close, protective quadrangle, lay in the valley near the edge, on a low terrace. Land at a slightly lower elevation than the buildings contained the irrigated fields. The main valley arroyo was commonly the source of the irrigation water.

On the uncultivated parts of the valley floor, and on the rest of the 750 square miles of land subject to each mission, livestock raising was an important occupation. The herds of a mission averaged 400 cattle, 600 sheep, 150 goats, and a few pigs, besides 100 horses, mules, and burros. So important were the pasture lands that Arrillaga spoke of them as "the principal foundation of the prosperity of the land" (Arch. Cal., P. S. P., 13:333–334). The herds provided not only food, but also the raw materials for the manufacture of two mission products, namely, woolen cloth and leather. The pasture and the herds, like the irrigated crops, were seriously affected by dry seasons. This is illustrated by the drop in number of cattle at Santo Domingo from 130 in 1784 to 39 in 1785, and a rise to 172 the following year (table 1). Even the important supplementary sources of food from the rough parts of the area—the wild plants and seeds—were inadequate after very dry winters, as was observed in 1795 (*ibid.*: 323–326).

An idea of the total production of the missions is given by the figures for the year 1794 (a good year), when the five main coastal missions had not yet entered upon their period of decline. The total crops of the Frontera for that year were as follows:

Corn	9,012 bushels	Barley	1,542 bushels
Wheat	3,219 bushels	Beans	335 bushels

The flocks and herds attained their maximum size later, owing to the better forage in the north. A comparison of total number of livestock in the Frontera for 1794 (including five missions) and 1801 (the last year for which complete figures are available, including seven missions), follows:

	1794	1801
Sheep	2,486	7,255
Cattle	1,666	5,454
Goats	639	940
Hogs	228	140
Horses	472	1,109
Mules	152	266
Asses	7	10

The totals are not of great significance because the Frontera was not operated as a unit. Each mission was in large measure self-reliant and economically independent of the others.

MISSION INDIVIDUALITIES

Each of the mission establishments was in an almost constant state of change, with growth in the first part of the mission's life and deterioration in the last. Furthermore, each of the missions possessed such distinctive traits of nature and of culture that a mere average or summary does not give an adequate, truthful picture of the Dominican Frontera. A brief summary, bringing out the salient characteristics of each, is a necessary supplement.

Rosario.—The most peaceful, stable, and prosperous of the missions seems to have been Rosario, the oldest of them all. Its broad valley produced the largest crops recorded. The Rosario crops of maize, in particular, were sometimes larger than those of all the rest of the Frontera combined, in spite of the frequent fogs in summer. The oasis character of the site and the absence of any other permanent fresh-water supply within twenty miles favored a unified development in this valley. The arroyo was already a center of attraction for the Indians when the mission was founded. This fact doubtless contributed to the phenomenal success of the padres in making so many conversions that at the end of the first year and a half the Rosario population, more than five hundred, exceeded that ever attained by any other Frontera mission with the possible exception of Santa Catalina.

Santo Domingo.—Santo Domingo Mission took ten years to reach a population of one hundred. It was handicapped from the beginning because the chief native population of its area lived along the coast, especially around San Quintín Bay, yet the Santo Domingo River, the only dependable water supply, sank into its sandy arroyo bed more than six miles inland, and twenty miles from San Quintín Bay. The mission had perforce to be situated marginally to the principal aboriginal rancherías. The Santo Domingo Cañon, where the mission was placed so as to be within reach of the water, was narrow, with crop lands limited to the little node by the mission—quite different from the broad Rosario Valley.

The meager central site of Santo Domingo encouraged a dispersion of development. Thus, the subsidiary San Telmo Chapel, fifteen miles northwest of the mission, in more open country, became important as a supplementary farm center. Santo Domingo was the sole Frontera mission consistently reporting wheat crops larger than corn crops. The vicinity of San Quintín Bay constituted another center of activity far from the parent mission. The salt fields just north of the bay not only provided salt for the Frontera missions but also afforded revenue for the support of the troops. Sea otters, killed in and near the bay, were an even more important source of income here, though they were caught in some measure at all the coastal missions. The sea otters caught by the Santo Domingo people were apparently sold for the benefit of that mission, while the sale of those caught by Russians and other outsiders, on shares, contributed to the general administrative fund of the Frontera.

San Vicente.—From the date of its foundation, five years later than Santo Domingo, San Vicente served as the capital of the Frontera. Its central, crossroads location was ideal for the headquarters of the presidial company. The main north-south presidial camino and its most important offshoot toward Santa Catalina intersected at San Vicente. The importance of the Catalina route arose from the fact that it led to an exposed and warlike frontier, and that until the turn of the century it formed the beginning of what was to be the road to the Colorado River.

San Vicente was thus the base for the Santa Catalina "March" and for contemplated future advances northeastward, besides being the most centrally situated of the coastal missions and therefore in a position to send military aid to any part of the Frontera in the shortest possible time.

Santo Tomás.—The advantages of the site at Santo Tomás—only twenty miles from San Vicente—were too great to be passed by. The mission was built in a mile-wide valley. As at San Vicente, a steep belt of mountains shuts off the valley from the direct influence of the sea, here a dozen miles distant. The climate at the seaward end of the valley is more humid than in the middle and eastern part; groves of live oaks appear, the climate being too dry for them at the missions farther south. A less arid climate (*BSh3* of fig. 3) makes its appearance in the coastal mountains between San Vicente and Santo Tomás and widens rapidly northward. A good growth of grass accompanies this belt, which helps to explain the fact that Santo Tomás had much larger herds of livestock than any of the missions to the south. Economically, Santo Tomás was primarily a stock ranch, with the livestock scattered over the grassy lands to the north, particularly in the Maneadero Plain and the San Rafael Valley.

Crops at Santo Tomás differed little from the usual mission crops. In the Dominican area, where irrigation of crops was the rule, humidity of climate had a marked influence upon grazing, but little upon agriculture. The largest crops were in the dry south of the Frontera, the largest herds in the moister north. The level floor of the Santo Tomás Valley included a superabundance of good soil, but most of it lay upstream from and out of reach of permanently flowing arroyo water. Irrigated land at the lower end of the valley was supplemented by a few score acres within reach of the springs in the valley floor four miles above the cañon. These springs, far excelling any water supply at the other missions, watered the flourishing orchard and vineyard of Santo Tomás, and were the determining factor in the final placing of the mission buildings. Besides these favorable natural conditions for production, the prosperity of Santo Tomás was further promoted by the possibilities of sea trade.

San Miguel.—The northernmost of the coastal chain of five missions was San Miguel, forty-five miles north of Santo Tomás. (Descanso, an establishment half a dozen miles north of San Miguel, represented simply a transferred, later center of mission authority following destructive floods at San Miguel.) Lying at the end of the Dominican trail, at the edge of the Frontera, San Miguel was somewhat isolated from the rest of the missions. In its early years at least, it was under the military jurisdiction of the San Diego Presidio, fifty miles away.

San Miguel and Descanso were the most coastal of the missions. They lay one and one-half miles and half a mile, respectively, from the coast, in linear, westward-trending valleys. So windy and foggy were their sites that the orchard and vineyard of at least one of them appear to have been planted several miles up the cañon from the mission center, in a more sheltered, sunnier spot. Proximity to the coast, however, gave the missions the advantage of nearness to the dense native population supported by the plentiful sea food.

Because of its northern position, San Miguel had the most humid climate of all the coastal missions. Climatic conditions here were fully as favorable as those of San Diego, in Alta California. Indeed, at Descanso grain was raised without irrigation, though the usual irrigation was practiced at San Miguel. Pasturage was even better in the San Miguel area. The best grasslands included the level Rosarito coastal plain at the northern limit of the Dominican area, the gently rolling hills which led down from the north to the open Descanso Valley, and the elevated, less accessible flats. It is not surprising that San Miguel surpassed the other coastal missions in number of cattle and horses, and was a close second to Santo Tomás in number of sheep.

Guadalupe.—Between the coastal missions and the far interior missions lay the mission of Guadalupe, fifteen miles east of San Miguel. It was occupied by the Dominicans for only six years and was then abandoned (1840) after an Indian uprising. During its brief and harried existence, however, it held an important position as the headquarters of the Dominican President of Lower California. Guadalupe Valley, the broad, undissected, grassy basin in which the mission was built, had been previously a grazing district for San Miguel, and the Guadalupe Mission continued to specialize in cattle raising. In addition to livestock, the usual irrigated field crops and fruits were developed, watered by a permanent stream and spring.

Santa Catalina.—Santa Catalina was thirty miles northeast of San Vicente, its nearest mission neighbor, and near El Portezuelo, one of the few good passes giving access to the desert lowlands of the Colorado. The original plan of advance to the Colorado, together with the exposure to attacks from desert Indians and the hostile attitude of many of the Indians near Santa Catalina, explains the fort-like character of this mission outpost. The mission quadrangle of Santa Catalina was the only one in the Dominican area not built in a valley: it stood on a small hill in a commanding position overlooking part of the extensive Álamo Plain. The plain, remote from the Pacific Ocean and the Gulf of California, and at an elevation of about 3500 feet, is characterized by a somewhat continental steppe climate. Grazing flourished in mission days, and even some dry farming of wheat seems to have been practiced. A large permanent spring determined the exact location of the mission. Water from the spring, flowing through two small valleys below the general surface of the plain, was dammed in the cañons above the valleys and used for irrigation. Santa Catalina, of course, lacked the supplementary sea food which the coastal missions and even Guadalupe enjoyed.

From the time of its founding until its destruction in an Indian attack in 1840, Santa Catalina seems to have been a large and powerful mission. In 1824 it had the largest population of any Dominican mission—more than 600, according to Troncoso (table 2).

San Pedro Mártir.—This mission was less successful than Santa Catalina. It had an even harder struggle with intractable Indians, and was the first of the Dominican missions to die, sometime between 1805 and 1824. San Pedro Mártir was less vital to the mission system than the other missions. Although it lay opposite a pass to the eastern deserts, the pass was higher, rougher, and less accessible than that of Santa Catalina. Its elevation was greater than that of any other mission of the Peninsula, and the winters were colder. It was the only mission among the conifers, in a humid climate, with a superabundance of running water.

The site was a tiny, mountain-surrounded valley with a floor of only seventy-five acres. From marginal springs a pair of irrigating ditches conducted the water along both sides of the valley at the edges of the fields. The plentiful water of the central arroyo was not needed. Corn was the principal crop. There appears to have been less dependence here upon crops than upon livestock, which was particularly favored by the luxuriant summer pasturage in the forests of the San Pedro Mártir Sierra. The economy of San Pedro Mártir illustrates once again the tendency in the more humid climates to promote stock raising rather than agriculture in the Frontera.

COMMUNICATIONS

Routes and distances.—Although sporadic trading was carried on between the missions and occasional coastwise vessels, the writer has seen no mention of the arrival of any supply ships from the Mexican mainland at any of the ports of the Frontera. Most of the official contacts of the Frontera with the outside were overland, either with Loreto, the capital of Lower California, or with San Diego. Two through trails, roughly parallel with the coast, traversed the Frontera—the Pacific Trail and the Sierra Trail. They intersected just beyond the limits of the Frontera at San Fernando to the south and near Tijuana to the north. The Pacific Trail, the more used of the two, connected the five original missions, taking advantage of the flat coastal terraces. The Sierra Trail, touching only two of the Dominican missions until the founding of Guadalupe, was probably little used as a through route. The interior route was only a little longer than the coastal route—about 295 compared with 280 miles. The average spacing between missions on the coastal route was forty-seven miles: two days of normal travel from one to the next except with respect to Santo Tomás and San Vicente, which were only a day apart. The interior missions, however, even including Guadalupe, averaged seventy-four miles or three days apart. Along both routes there were conveniently spaced watering places for the overnight encampments between missions. The following table of distances between missions along these routes, from north to south, was calculated as closely as possible on personal observations and estimates.[3]

Pacific Trail—   *Miles*

    San Diego to San Miguel.. 55
        (Descanso to San Miguel, 9 miles)
    San Miguel to Santo Tomás.. 55
    Santo Tomás to San Vicente... 24
    San Vicente to Santo Domingo.. 50
    Santo Domingo to Rosario... 60
    Rosario to San Fernando... 36

Sierra Trail—

    San Diego to Guadalupe.. 70
    Guadalupe to Santa Catalina... 70
    Santa Catalina to San Isidoro (by San Pedro Mártir).......... 80
    San Isidoro to San Fernando.. 75

Probably more important than the Sierra Trail were the connecting trails running toward the coast from the interior, generally following arroyo cañons leading down from the highlands. One of the most important of these was the one connecting San Vicente, the headquarters of the Frontera, with Santa Catalina, a distance of thirty-five miles. A second important transverse route was the one following the Santo Domingo River forty miles from San Pedro Mártir to Santo Domingo. The two latter missions seem to have been always in close touch with each other, and the present Santo Domingueños say that upon the abandonment of the sierra mission its population moved down and was added to that of Santo Domingo. The third of the cross routes, which was especially important during the last period of mission development, ran from San Miguel to Guadalupe (20 miles) and to Santa Catalina.

In addition to the main trails, webs of minor trails (only partly shown on the folded map) radiated from each mission, interconnecting the rancherías and other points within a mission area.

Traffic.—The main trails of the Frontera were used for through traffic from the Mexican mainland to Alta California by way of Loreto. Especially when haste was needed, this route, though tedious, was preferred to the uncertain all-sea route; regular mail and special official messages from Loreto or Mexico commonly followed the trails. Occasionally troops, officials, or settlers entered Alta California by the Baja California land route, as had occurred in the original peopling of Los Angeles (Richman: 126). After the destruction of the Colorado River missions in 1781, the Lower California route remained the only land route from Mexico.

---

  [3] It is impossible to use accurately the league distances given in travel accounts, as different individuals seem to have had independent ideas of the length of a league; one man even made irregular estimates in the course of a single journey. A check of known distances given by Arrillaga in his travels of 1796, for example, shows that a league in his notes may be the equivalent of anything from 1.6 to 3.5 miles. Crespi's league was consistently about 2.6 miles (1769); Negrete's, 2.7 miles (1853); Gabb's, usually more than 3 miles (1867).

Main-line traffic originating within the Frontera included the export of mission products, such as hides, sea-otter furs, and wine. Many of these goods went to San Diego. Hayes mentioned frequent notices of hides taken from missions to San Diego (Arch. San Diego, Misc. Papers: 10). Circulation of goods between missions within the Dominican area apparently was not great except at the founding of a new mission, when streams of supplies would go to the new establishment, or in years when crop failures at some missions necessitated contributions from the others. Probably the most frequent users of the mission trails were the troops.

On the whole, each mission was essentially self-reliant, and movement was for the most part limited to individual mission areas. The greater number of the Indians probably passed their lives within the territory of their own mission. In the early years of conversion, the padres and soldiers made frequent journeys from the mission to surrounding rancherías in order to gain neophytes for the mission, and the padres continued to make visits to permanent mission rancherías in fulfillment of their religious duties. Where the population had not all been concentrated at the mission, the Christians of the rancherías went at regular times to the church to hear Mass.

At San Pedro Mártir a seasonal shift of livestock between mountain meadows and lower lands was necessary, and at the other missions there was a movement of cattle to the watered valleys toward the end of the dry summer and a spreading out over the surrounding lands during and following the rainy season. The Indians constantly moved about between each mission and its outlying lands for the purpose of gathering wild plant and animal food.

COMPARISON WITH ADJACENT MISSION SYSTEMS

In 1801, when Dominican and Franciscan developments were of comparable maturity, the seven Frontera missions of the former had an average population of 224, while the twenty-one California missions of the latter averaged 730 souls (Bandini, 1776–1864, June 29, 1802). Among the largest in Alta California, the Mission San Buenaventura in 1816 reported 1328 (Arch. del Obisp. de Mont. and L. A.: 99–119), and San Diego, in 1822, had 1697 (Arch. Arzob., 5, part 2, between pp. 30 and 31). San Buenaventura harvested 19,188 bushels of grain, and San Diego, 10,504. About half the total harvest was wheat, followed by barley, with corn in a poor third place. In the same years "Ventura" had 23,400 head of cattle and 13,144 sheep, while San Diego had 9245 cattle and 19,000 sheep. San Luis Rey had 14,340 cattle and 20,230 sheep in 1822. The best Dominican developments seem pitifully small by contrast; the entire production of crops and livestock of the Frontera for the best years was less than that of a single Alta California mission.

The production in the Jesuit foundations to the south varied little from that in the Dominican, according to a late report (Sales, 1794, statistical table), though wheat was more important than corn, because of inadequate water (Clavigero: 8–9). In 1768, the average enrollment of the thirteen existing missions (not counting the Loreto presidio) was 507; and of the three northernmost permanent ones, which had in large part escaped the epidemics of 1742, 1744, and 1748, the population was: San Ignacio, 750; Santa Gertrudis, 1000; and San Francisco de Borja, 1500 (Engelhardt, 1929: 271, 342). The similar adjacent Franciscan Mission, San Fernando de Velicatá, had about 1400 in 1776 (above, p. 141 n.). Thus, even the San Borja Desert missions were better populated than the Dominican foundations.

Why were the Dominican establishments the smallest and poorest ones of the Californias? So far as production is concerned, differences in the natural milieu were of primary importance, particularly climatic differences. Since both Dominican and Jesuit areas were in large part arid where not mountainous, and crops were consequently raised by means of irrigation, amount of water and cultivable land were exceedingly important in determining the size of crops. Although detailed studies of the Jesuit valleys have not been made, it is likely that they varied little in extent from the Dominican ones; water, it is true, was less abundant, at least in the San Borja Desert. Some of the Alta California valleys were no larger than those of Baja California; many, however, were even larger than Guadalupe Valley. Moreover, because of the more humid climate, nearly all the good soil of Alta California could be put into crops, even in the valleys and plains out of reach of irrigation. A foretaste of the lands *de humedad* of the north was experienced in that part of the San Miguel area of Baja California where the thorny vegetation of Lower California gives way to stretches of good grassland in Alta California, much better suited to grazing. The predominance of the small grains in the Franciscan harvests indicates dry farming; even in Alta California, the coincidence of the dry and the hot season makes corn-growing without irrigation unsatisfactory. In every respect, the Franciscans never had cause to regret leaving Baja California to the Dominicans.

The differences in population among the missions are not all explainable by the same reasons as differences in production. While greater abundance of food in a moister climate may have permitted a somewhat denser native population to subsist in parts of Alta California, it has been shown that the differences in population between Alta and Baja California were not great. Certainly the Jesuit area was not superior to the Dominican. Yet the missions of the San Borja Desert, in the driest district of all, had populations of more than 1000 each, compared with the 250 in the missions of the moister Frontera. The explanation is simple: the Jesuits had more individual tributary territory than the Dominicans, and consequently more available Indians. The 730 square miles of each Dominican mission compare with about 4000 square miles each for San Ignacio, Santa Gertrudis, and San Borja, and 2750 for San

Fernando de Velicatá. The Franciscan missions of Alta California had an average territory roughly estimated at 1500 square miles. The Frontera had the additional handicap of comparative isolation from Mexico and the outside world, with contact only by the hard trail to Loreto.

OUTSIDE INCOME

The Dominican missions were barely self-supporting. The only support received from outside the area, aside from the small but necessary body of government soldiers, was that given by a share in the Pious Fund. From this the necessary vestments and sacred vessels, and an additional sum of $1000, were given to each new mission. In addition, it provided traveling expenses and an annual payment (*sínodo*) of $350 for each missionary, which was made mostly in the form of goods needed at the mission (*ibid.:* 511, 663). The sínodo added certainly not more than 10 per cent to the annual income derived from the crops and herds.

XVII. THE PASSING OF MISSION CULTURE

LIFE-CYCLES OF THE MISSIONS

THE FRAGMENTARY POPULATION FIGURES show that each Dominican mission, if not brought to an untimely and violent end, lasted about fifty years with enough neophytes to carry on the usual mission work. The mission's life was ordinarily most vigorous in the first twenty years, since throughout those years it received a continual injection of fresh neophytes. There followed a period of slow, steady decline, with burials consistently more numerous than baptisms. By the end of the first fifty years the loss of population had become so great that the activities of the mission were seriously handicapped.

Since each mission passed through a roughly similar decline, it was natural that the youngest missions should outlive the oldest. Rosario, the oldest mission, was the first to reach senility. Its 50-year period had been passed by 1824, when Troncoso (p. 19) reported it as having only from 130 to 150 inhabitants (fewer than at any other mission), most of them sick with gálico. Its period of active conversion, with baptisms predominating over burials, lasted just twenty years—through 1794. The biggest crops of the mission had been those of 1793. Short-time fluctuations within this 20-year period were violent, as figure 24 shows. A large population growth marked the first three years; six years of declining population followed, between the epidemic years of 1777 and 1782; from then until 1795, at the end of the conversion period, growth was steady except in two years. During the entire life of the mission, as shown in the burial book, periods of great mortality, evidently epidemics, occurred roughly at five-year intervals. The peaks of these epidemics came in 1777, 1782, 1789, 1794, 1800, 1805, 1808, and 1818 (fig. 24).

That years of numerous burials were really times of epidemics is proved by the fact that in each such year excessive deaths appeared simultaneously in at least two adjacent missions, and that every epidemic except those of 1800 and possibly 1818 swept through all four of the missions the records of which are available—San Fernando de Velicatá (Sauer and Meigs: 288), Rosario, Santo Domingo, and San Vicente. The epidemics did not always begin nor reach their height in exactly the same year at every mission, no doubt because of the infrequency of contact among the various missions. The difference in date of epidemics is enough to prove that they originated in the south and spread northward. The epidemic of 1800 started at San Fernando, spread north to Rosario, then to Santo Domingo, but did not reach San Vicente. Of the eight epidemics, six definitely moved from south to north, one appeared at all four missions in the same year (1805), and of one, the weakest of all (1818), available information is inconclusive. A study of the records of the Jesuit foundations, in the south, should shed further light upon this matter.

At Santo Domingo the period of active conversion covered twenty-two years, ending with 1796. The turning point here, as at Rosario, was marked by an epidemic. At Santo Domingo, too, this period included fluctuations in population, more numerous but less violent than at Rosario, and with a gradual rise to the maximum of 1795. The ensuing period of decline was similar to that at Rosario except that, just preceding 1824, a group of San Pedro Mártir Indians (above, p. 73) was added to the Santo Domingo population. This late ingathering of recruits would account for the fact that Santo Domingo in 1824 still had a population estimated at more than 300. Gálico was ruining the mission even then (*loc. cit.*), and in 1830 the population numbered only 78 (table 2).

Lacking the books of vital statistics, it is not possible to discuss in much detail the fluctuations in the development of the other missions. The censuses indicate that population at these missions reached its peak at some time in the blank period between 1801 and 1824. San Vicente, founded five years later than Santo Domingo, still had a population of about 300 in 1824 and 142 in 1829 (table 2). Santo Tomás, eleven years younger than San Vicente, seems to have been near its peak in 1824, when its population was reported as more than 400 (table 2). Both Santo Tomás, in 1835, and San Miguel, in 1834, were reported by Lassepas as having 254 inhabitants (table 2), though one of these figures (probably for Santo Tomás) is doubtless in error. These missions seem to have had the normal fifty years before senility set in. By 1834 San Miguel and Santa Catalina were the only missions that were still producing good-sized crops and herds (table 1); the others were definitely decadent.

The interior missions met violent ends. San Pedro Mártir, after an obscure existence of less than thirty years, was extinguished and its population was transferred to Santo Domingo. Santa Catalina and Guadalupe, the two youngest missions, were still full of vitality when they were destroyed by Indian attacks in 1840, though Santa Catalina was definitely in the period of decline (population more than 600 in 1824; 250 in 1834). Santa Catalina had lived for forty-two years; Guadalupe, for only six.

In 1849, the last year in which any Dominican minister remained in the Frontera, an account of the low estate to which the missions had fallen was provided through a trip made by Castro,[4] and it was supplemented four years later by a tour by Negrete (pp. 349–355). Rosario, with a population in 1849 of 25 (12 in 1853, 7 of whom were Indians), had about twenty-five acres under cultivation, besides some activity in gathering sea food and hunting nutrias. Santo Domingo, with 25 inhabitants in 1849, had 30 Indians in 1853. San Vicente, with 7 persons in 1849, had "some Indians" in 1853, besides 15 *personas de razón*. Santo Tomás, with a new colony of 60 in 1849, had only 1 Indian in 1853,

---

[4] Doc. Orig. para la Hist. de la B. Cfa., 2: 367–372. The population figures of Castro usually do not distinguish between Indians and *personas de razón*.

though a special census in 1851 showed 73 Indians, including 5 non-Christians (Doc. Orig., 2: 157–163). San Miguel had 40 inhabitants, mostly Indians, in 1849—the largest population of any coastal mission that year. Four years later, the mission had only 1 inhabitant. Descanso had 25 persons in 1849, though four years later it was occupied only by its owner. None of the old mission rancherías of the coastal region were in existence in 1849, except La Grulla, which was reported as a ranchería and ranch, with 40 souls. The total Indian population remaining in the coastal mission lands in 1849 must have been approximately 100, and some of these may have been immigrants from the interior. In addition, there remained several hundred Indians in the old areas of Guadalupe (above, p. 116) and Santa Catalina,[5] though the missions of course no longer existed.

All the missions had been sold or granted to private individuals before 1859, and probably by 1855. Guadalupe was sold in 1845 (Lassepas: 143); San Vicente and evidently Santo Tomás had been sold by 1849, (Doc. Orig., 2:368–369), and Rosario, Santo Domingo, and Descanso sometime before 1853 (Negrete: 349–354); Santa Catalina was sold in 1855,[6] and San Pedro Mártir and San Miguel sometime before 1859 (Lassepas: 142–143). The decree for colonization of all the former mission lands was not made until 1851, but all the missions had been discontinued and a new culture period initiated before that date.

CAUSES OF THE DECLINE

The fundamental cause for the deterioration of the missions was the spread among the Indians of diseases introduced into Baja California from outside, in the form of frequent, severe epidemics of smallpox and other ailments, and in the ceaseless attack of syphilis. The last-named disease seems to have wrought little havoc among the Dominican missions until near the close of the eighteenth century, for Arrillaga reported in 1795 that there was no gálico in the Frontera (Arch. Cal., P. S. P., 13: 333–334), though it was present in San Diego (*ibid.*: 323–326). The ravages of all sorts of sickness were doubtless increased by the weakened resistance of the confined Indians to the white man's diseases.

Serious events followed the Mexican Revolution. The whole patriarchal system of the padres was incompatible with the newly established Republic, and this fact accelerated the decline of the missions. It is said that Governor Echeandía, passing through the Frontera in 1825 (*sic*), gave the Indians their first lesson in the principles of independence and republican equality (Rojo: 74; as though they had not known and fought for such principles long before the Revolution!). In consequence, work at the missions almost stopped, and the Indians, no longer under compulsion, gave themselves over to drink, gambling, and laziness

---

[5] There were enough Santa Catalina Indians remaining in 1852 to be called a "tribe."—Doc. Orig., 2:535.

[6] According to an abstract of title examined by the writer.

(Lassepas: 12). The careful instruction at the missions had taught the Indians something of the white man's civilization, to be sure, but it had not taught them how to maintain it without supervision.

In 1830, when the missions of the old Jesuit area were extinguished by decree, San Fernando, Rosario, Santo Domingo, San Vicente, Santo Tomás, San Miguel, and Santa Catalina were ordered to remain as missions "because of having in their charge a considerable number of catechumens" (*ibid.:* 203–204), though Rosario had only forty-one and Santo Domingo seventy-eight in that year (*ibid.:* 104–105). The secularization of all mission property by the congressional decree of 1833 seems to have had little if any effect upon the Dominican missions. The missionaries were not recalled nor replaced by secular clergy, and urgent petitions resulted in a restoration of the old status by a new law in 1835 (*ibid.:* 18–19).

After the Revolution, only two padres served in the Frontera, and after 1839 only one remained in the field. The final blow to Santo Tomás, the last religious center of the Dominicans in the Frontera, came through the discovery of gold in Alta California, a disaster which the padres had always feared. On June 10, 1849, Agustín Mansilla y Gamboa, at Santo Tomás, wrote to his brother, Fray Tomás, then at San Diego, a letter which stated that robberies by people passing through (on the way to the newly opened gold mines) were on the increase; that the lawlessness was communicating itself to the Indians; and, finally, that an Indian had just stolen the altar valuables of the church and sold them to a passer-by who was headed north (Arch. San Diego, 1826–1850). This event determined the abandonment of the Frontera by its last missionary.

XVIII. POST-MISSION LANDSCAPES

VALLEY SETTLEMENTS

MANY of the mission valleys, formerly the nerve centers of the Frontera, have continued to support small pueblos of irrigators, though all these pueblos together now have no more inhabitants than formerly a single large mission had. Rosario and Santo Tomás are the only two with more than one hundred. At Rosario most of the inhabitants live in the area between the two old missions. At Santo Tomás the population is grouped into two parts: La Misión, occupying the final site of the mission and using the water from the yet flowing springs of the mission; and El Pueblito, at the lower end of the valley, using the flowing arroyo water by the first mission site. The San Vicente locality is occupied by about two dozen families, half of them living at the big bend of the arroyo near the mission, and the rest scattered along the lower cañon at occasional small patches of irrigable land (fig. 12). The sites of Santo Domingo and Descanso missions and San Telmo Chapel are each occupied by a small community of fewer than a dozen families, grouped compactly near the old religious buildings at Santo Domingo and at San Telmo, and scattered along the valley for three miles in the vicinity of Descanso. San Pedro Mártir Mission Valley is now unoccupied.

Whatever else the missions may have handed down, they left an area which was nearly cleared of Indians and made ready for unopposed occupation by settlers. Many of the present cultivators of the mission valleys are Mexicans whose ancestors drifted in from the south after the collapse of the missions. Only at Rosario and Santo Domingo among the coastal valleys are there two or three families descended in part from the mission Indians. A few of the descendants of the mission troops live in the mission valleys, though most of these people scorn cultivation of the soil as "Indian work." The products of the valleys, little changed from mission days, include corn, wheat, barley, and beans, and figs, grapes, apricots, olives, pomegranates, and pears. Descanso still practices dry farming and has no irrigated orchards. The greater part of the valley production is used for local consumption, as in mission days, but an outside market (Ensenada) is now absorbing Santo Tomás wine and San Telmo pears. In Santo Domingo, part of the old mission's irrigating ditch is still in use. In all the other mission valleys the present canal is lower than the original one, so that not so large an area can be irrigated as formerly. The modern canals lack the careful construction of the padres; they are simply diversions from the main source of water, without any dams to raise the water to higher levels as in mission days. The entire irrigation system is inferior to that of the missions, partly, perhaps, because of loss of land by arroyo cutting.

The ruined walls of the mission buildings still overlook the present pueblos. No attempt has been made to preserve them. Rain and treasure seekers are fast obliterating the adobe ruins, and at Santo Tomás and Guadalupe the sites of the principal mission buildings have been completely plowed up. At Santa Catalina only a low outlined mound remains. The best preserved of the mission ruins are at Santo Domingo, some of the rooms there having been kept roofed until a few years ago.

GATHERING OF WILD PRODUCTS

Systematic exploitation of the wild food products of the land is practiced now only in the area still predominantly occupied by Indians. At the time of the writer's investigations in 1929, there were 45 native Indian families within the old Dominican area, all of them in the interior, besides half a dozen scattered individuals at and near Santo Domingo and Rosario—a rough total of 225 Indians. Most of them live in the areas where the missions were destroyed before the population had entirely succumbed to disease, that is, in the Santa Catalina (36 families) and Guadalupe (8 families) areas.

These Indians still eat acorn mush, roasted mescal hearts, yucca fruit, and biznaga cactus buds, besides more modern foods such as corn, wheat, and coffee. Rabbits, taken with gun or throwing-stick, and deer, shot with rifles, are also eaten when obtainable. Pine nuts, gathered in the Sierras Juarez and San Pedro Mártir, are not generally eaten by the Indians now, but are sold to outside traders for cash or goods. Wild honey and beeswax bring in a little cash.

Systematic gathering of shellfish for the settlements of the coastal terrace lands seems to have died out with the coastal Indians, though clams, mussels, and abalones are as available as ever. Small commercial abalone camps are in operation on the rough outer parts of Punta Banda, and canneries have been operated now and then at various places along the coast, the latest one near El Sausal. Much commercial fishing is carried on in the waters off the coast by fleets with headquarters in San Diego and San Pedro, but shore fishing, which had been so important for the large coastal villages of the Indians, is almost non-existent.

GRAZING

Many of the soldiers, upon retirement from active duty, bought ranches in the Frontera or gained them by grant. A few of these private ranches began to appear even before the end of the mission period. Thus, in 1804, Ensign José Manuel Ruiz received a large ranch for cattle raising at Ensenada, a place midway between Santo Tomás and San Miguel and therefore not needed by either of these missions (above, p. 94). Later, as the mission ranches and rancherías declined, and as the missions themselves were secularized, one piece of land after another fell into private hands. The first sale of developed mission territory seems to have been the sale of San Telmo to Jesús Arce, in 1834 (Lassepas: 122) ; the first mission site reported sold was that of Guadalupe, in 1845, to Juan Bandini (*ibid.*: 143), though others may have been sold before. San

Rafael Valley was occupied at least as early as 1844 by Agustín Mancilla (*ibid.*: 124), the brother of the missionary who had charge of it; Valle Trinidad, by 1846, by Tomás Warner (*ibid.*: 143); and various other tracts about the same period. (Bandini and Warner were Alta Californians.) The period of private ranches was well under way before the last mission had been abandoned in 1849.

Some of the ranches were kept by the original grantees or purchasers, while others were resold immediately, generally to men of San Diego or Los Angeles, as statements by Lassepas and Castro show. The final use to which most of the ranch lands were put was cattle raising, as in mission days. Even now the greater part of the Frontera is given over to grazing, most of the ranchers limiting themselves to raising cattle, the industry with which they are most familiar. Cattle, furthermore, can range over a longer radius from water holes than sheep, they need less constant attention than sheep, and are less susceptible to the depredations of coyotes. Sheep herding prevails now only in the north and interior of the Frontera where a foreign element, the ubiquitous Basque, runs flocks of thousands of sheep from winter quarters in Tijuana Valley to grassy summer pasture in the San Pedro Mártir Sierra by way of the Álamo Plain.

During the early pastoral period just after the mission period, the chief centers of population remained the little agricultural pueblos in the former mission valleys. The capital of the Frontera shifted from one to another of these pueblos. After the abandonment of the old mission capital, San Vicente, Rosario appears to have been chosen as the administrative center.[7] A decree of June 20, 1848, created a military colony at Rosario (Castro: 368). The colony actually remained here only a few months, from March to July, 1849, and moved then to Santo Tomás (Negrete: 349), which remained the capital for about twenty-five years. The reasons given for the shift to Santo Tomás were extent and fertility of land, abundance of water, favorableness of climate, and nearness to the port of Ensenada, through which supplies could be received by ship (Castro: 369–370). From the time of this military colony at Santo Tomás down to the present, the settlement, with 119 gente de razón in 1851, besides Indians (Doc. Orig., 2:157–163), has remained of substantially the same size and kind: a community of modest numbers, occupied in farming and stock raising.

NEW CULTURE ELEMENTS: GOLD AND PORTS

Grazing and small-scale irrigation, forms of land use introduced in mission days, continued to dominate the Frontera with little change until 1872. The elements of the physical landscape that had been critical for the missions remained critical, and permanent water remained the most important. In 1872, with discovery of rich placer deposits in the northern margins of the San Rafael Valley (Zárate and Nuñez, 1925), gold

[7] Though it is asserted by David Zárate that for a short period, about this time, El Sausal de Camacho was the capital, too.

became a new attraction of the Frontera. Whereas foreign influence had previously been slight, in 1872, foreigners, mostly from California, began to flock to the gold fields by thousands, and the isolation of Lower California was temporarily broken. Almost overnight the center of the Frontera shifted from the coastal district to the interior. Santo Tomás, the little agricultural capital of northern Lower California, found itself marginal to the main center of interest, and the government about this time transferred its seat to Real del Castillo, a new town on the gold fields, where the officials and troops were most needed.[8]

In 1888 another gold rush developed with a strike at Álamo (Zárate y Nuñez), in the Álamo Plain west of Santa Catalina. Smaller placer deposits were found and worked from time to time at Socorro (near the western foot of San Pedro Mártir Mountain), Valladares, and other localities. The known deposits have been in large part worked out by now, and have long since ceased to be important.

An indirect but lasting effect of the gold discoveries was the development of a town at Ensenada (pl. 9b). From a ranch headquarters, Ensenada became an important port through which supplies could be sent to Real del Castillo. Its official opening as a port of entry took place in 1877, and in 1882, because of the continuing growth and importance of its port, Ensenada replaced Real del Castillo as the capital of the Northern District of Lower California and occupied that position for thirty-three years. Ensenada has remained the leading town of the old Dominican area down to the present time. By 1910 its population had passed the two thousand mark. The site of Ensenada had been avoided by the mission founders chiefly because it lacked a supply of water suitable for irrigation. The town now gets its supply of water from deep wells, which were not a part of the mission pattern.

San Quintín Bay, the second best port of the Frontera, had also failed of permanent settlement in mission days because of the absence of fresh water. For a while, starting just before 1890, a newly established town of San Quintín, on the east side of the bay, was a busy center of an ambitious attempt at land colonization. Earlier efforts, starting with large grants of land from the government, had been made by American companies to colonize and develop the Frontera, but without success. An English company made the principal effort to develop the San Quintín district, based upon the raising of wheat in San Quintín Plain by dry farming. Large sums of money were spent in building a flour mill at the edge of the bay to grind the wheat, a railroad to ship the grain to the mill,[9] and a hotel and large, wooden dwellings in and near the town. A customhouse was created at San Quintín by the Government to handle the immigration of the colonists and the importations of their supplies and equipment. Unfortunately, the wheat which was to support the

[8] That the transfer of the capital to Real del Castillo was accomplished at least by 1875 is proved by the inscriptions on official documents now on file at Ensenada.

[9] The railroad was torn up years ago, though it still appears on many maps.

colony was not forthcoming. After the extravagant investments had
been made, it was found that the rainfall was insufficient for the growth
of grain crops except after unusually wet winters, and the colony failed.

Only two of the colony ranches now remain occupied: one a cattle
ranch, and the other (the Hamilton Ranch, in San Ramón Valley) a
garden, fruit patch, and traveler's haven, using water from deep wells.
The town of San Quintín has been abandoned by all except a few families
of Government officials connected with a virtually inoperative customhouse. Aside from occasional importations of supplies for the widely
spaced ranches or the little settlements by the Santo Domingo River, the
business of the customhouse is chiefly connected with the exploitation by
a California company of the salt deposits just north of the bay. The salt
is trucked to the old flour mill for storage and shipped out through
the port. The trucking is hampered by poor roads.

LARGE-SCALE AGRICULTURE

In the low coastal plains of Maneadero and San Antonio del Mar, ranchers from the United States are raising field crops, especially beans, depending upon the modest winter rains and heavy summer fogs for most
of the water. More important, ever since 1905 a colony of Russians has
been established in Guadalupe Valley, raising wheat in large quantities
(Schmieder, 1928). The northern part of the Frontera is capable of
raising wheat crops by dry farming, though the crop is greatly reduced
in dry seasons. The wheat is grown not only in Guadalupe Valley, but
also upon the fertile "trays" south of San Miguel, on the coastal terraces
just to the south, and even on the Ensenada Plain. At Ensenada, satisfactory crops can be obtained approximately every other year. With a
seasonal rainfall of more than 10 inches, an average crop is generally obtained; one seasonal rainfall of 8.8 inches produced half a crop; seasons
with 5 to 5.5 inches produce no crops. The intensity and distribution
of the storms also affect the yields.[10] Total annual production by the
forty Russian families (originally one hundred) varies from 40,000 to
125,000 bushels of wheat—an amount many times as great as the total
annual grain production of all the Dominican missions combined. The
missions, however, attempting to be self-supporting in all directions,
were concerned merely with producing enough food for their own needs,
whereas the Russians are producing for export.

The latest great agricultural development in the Northern District
of Lower California has been the raising of cotton. This has been done,
not in the area developed by the Dominicans, but in the lowlands of the
Colorado River, a district which once was the goal of Dominican advance, but from which settlement was excluded by the hostility of the
Colorado Indians. Arrillaga (1796, October 20), in his hurried exploration to the Colorado River in 1796, remarked that "cotton could yield
very well if it were planted." He was right. Cotton, irrigated by the

---

[10] Carefully kept observations of David Goldbaum.

waters of the Colorado River, has become the most important crop of the Northern District. The cultural center of gravity of the district shifted away at last from the old Frontera, and in 1915 Mexicali, a town in the Colorado lowlands at the United States border, replaced Ensenada as the seat of government of the Territory.

INFLUENCES FROM THE NORTH

Lower California is an island, and always has been, so far as contact with the rest of Mexico is concerned. Physically, the Northern District of Lower California is much more closely bound to the United States than to Mexico. The only barrier to easy communication with the former is the international boundary line. Most of the economic contacts of the old Frontera area are with California, a condition which holds true at present more than it did when Alta and Baja California were both a part of the same nation and managed by friendly religious orders. Nearly all the exports and imports of the Northern District are to or from California.

For years, even for decades, the Frontera has been a recreation ground for small numbers of visitors from California. Sportsmen have found it an unspoiled field for hunting deer, mountain sheep, quail, duck, and other game. Besides transient parties of hunters, gun clubs, the members of which hail from San Diego and Los Angeles, have been organized in the Frontera. Such a club, the Old Mission Gun Club, now leases the valley of the former mission San Miguel (Misión Vieja). Other clubs have their headquarters at the southern end of Todos Santos Bay, at Laguna Hanson in the Sierra Juarez, and at other places. Some travelers come to enjoy the freedom of this thinly settled frontier land, others for a healthful camping trip or vacation at some ranch, others to take advantage of the delightful bathing along the beautiful ten-mile sweep of beach at Ensenada, and yet others simply to get a taste of the "atmosphere" of a foreign land.

The Eighteenth Amendment to the Constitution did more than anything else to direct a flow of California visitors to Lower California. Every week-end, thousands of thirsty citizens crossed the border for liquid refreshment, and on special holidays, such as Memorial Day and Independence Day, they came in tens of thousands. Cash from the pockets of these Americans has supported saloon and hotel keepers, brewers, distillers, wine makers, and other businessmen south of the line, and the taxes upon business gave the government of the Territory a dependable revenue. From 1910 to 1930 the population of the Northern District of Lower California increased 485 per cent (Wittich: 249), a much larger percentage than in any other state or territory of the Republic, and most of the increase was subsequent to 1920, the date when prohibition became effective. Prohibition and cotton were the leading factors in the greater part of this phenomenal growth.

The most marked cultural developments resulting from prohibition have taken place outside the limits of the old Frontera. Following the establishment of the United States-Mexico boundary north of the former Franciscan-Dominican boundary, a strip of land, formerly of negligible significance, has been settled. Here is Tijuana, with its saloon-dancehall-lined streets, its race track, and its recently acquired fashionable neighbor, Agua Caliente. Ensenada is far enough from the United States to have retained some of its dignified character as a normal Mexican town; the travelers who visit it in increasing numbers, by the seventy-mile automobile road from Tijuana or by steamer excursions from Los Angeles, are not always concerned with dissipation.

The road connecting Tijuana and Ensenada, following in the main the coastal route of the padres, is dotted with bars and auto camps, often using old names of mission days, resulting in such incongruities as "Descanso Bar," "Mégano Bar," and "Rosarito Beach Resort." The tourists of week-end hordes rarely wander away from the single highway, and few ever go south or east of Ensenada. In spite of the increasing American influence, such towns as Santo Domingo and Rosario still contain no one who can speak English; and on the borders of Valle Trinidad are Indian children in their teens who cannot even speak Spanish. The culture landscape of most of the Frontera, with the exceptions already noted, has changed but little since 1849, and the population density of the Northern District is still less than two to the square mile. Mining activity has died down, and the developments associated with the two powerful factors of prohibition and cotton raising have taken place, as noted above, beyond the borders of the Frontera. The old occupations of stock raising and small-scale valley irrigation continue to dominate the culture landscape, as they have dominated it ever since their introduction by the Dominican missionaries.

THE FUTURE

Lower California is dry, and this fact is bound to continue to affect the utilization of the Frontera. A large part of the surface is fit only for scant pasturage and wild game. Stock raising seems likely to remain the sole method of utilizing great stretches of the area.

The humid Sierras Juarez and San Pedro Mártir, however, have permanent streams of water, and irrigation is sure to be kept up and likely to be greatly extended. Some of the primitive diversion systems now in use in the small valleys of the Frontera can be replaced by large-scale modern dams and canals, which will make possible the irrigation of extensive tracts of land now out of reach of water. The most extensive stretches of arable land that would be available for such irrigation projects are the coastal terraces and plains. Already, a large dam, the García Dam, is under construction across the Tijuana River. This dam is intended to be used for irrigating about five thousand acres in the broad Tijuana Valley near the town of Tijuana. Other dams farther up the same river are contemplated. A site has also been surveyed for a dam on the Santo Domingo River, the water to be used for irrigating the San Quintín Plain and San Ramón Valley. By coincidence, the principal stream of the Frontera adjoins the principal coastal plain of the Frontera. If needed, the extensive valleys of Guadalupe, San Rafael, San Telmo, and Santo Tomás might also be irrigated by water from dammed streams which head in the sierras. The broad coastal plains of Ensenada and Rosarito and the floor of Médano Valley might be partly irrigated from reservoirs, but the streams available there are short and have only small drainage basins. The development of such large irrigation projects has been slow in the past because of limited funds available for dam building, but eventually such projects will probably be important elements of the culture landscape.

The most accessible gold deposits have been exploited, but possibly large-scale methods could, with proper management, still be profitably employed at some of the mines. Small copper mines have been worked in times of high prices, but no important deposits are known. The San Quintín salt fields may become well established as a partial source of supply for California if the tariff question can be satisfactorily arranged. The great deposits of salt on Carmen Island, in the Gulf of California, eliminate mainland Mexico as a buyer of San Quintín salt. The excellent timber of San Pedro Mártir Mountain is too inaccessible to be considered as a future source of lumber, but the Sierra Juarez forests, which could be easily reached by a railroad to the west, might be exploited. All the limited forest lands of the Frontera should be carefully preserved, for they will some day have great value as vacation areas for the sun-scorched people of the surrounding arid regions, and in the meantime they will continue to protect the watershed which is vital to the existence of the west-coast communities.

All indications point to an increasing value of the Frontera as a resort area for people of the United States. Even with the modification of our liquor laws tourists of many types will continue to visit the west coast.[11] Ensenada, in particular, has the potentialities of a great summer or winter resort, with equable oceanic climate, a sheltered yacht harbor, a beautiful bathing beach, and the possibility of near-by hunting and fishing. A modern concrete highway from the Border to Ensenada is under construction. Investment of United States capital is discouraged by the laws against ownership of land by foreigners and by the fear of extortionate taxes upon any successful enterprise; but the government of the District realizes the cash value of the tourist business and welcomes American visitors. Probably in the long run the Territory will be better off, from the Mexican viewpoint, if American capital is not permitted to become unduly influential.

---

[11] Fred H. Stanley, Ensenada businessman, estimates that by 1934 40 per cent of the Tijuana saloons had closed because of the depression and the repeal of prohibition in the United States. The Mexican anti-gambling law of 1935, too, has reduced the influx of a certain type of tourist.

APPENDIX

WEIGHTS AND MEASURES

THE GREAT LACK OF UNIFORMITY among writers in reducing the old Mexican measures to modern equivalents makes it desirable to append the following tables. They are derived, except where otherwise noted, from the lengthy tables in volume 10, pages 195–252, of the *Boletín de Geografía y Estadística* (1863), which gives the old Mexican measures and their metric equivalents. This is the most complete, detailed, and authoritative source which the writer has seen.

	OLD MEXICAN	METRIC	ENGLISH
Linear	1 legua*..	4190 meters	2.6 miles
	1 vara=4 palmos=3 pies=36 pulgadas=48 dedos....................................	.838 meters	33 inches
Square (*agrarian measures*)			
	1 sitio de ganado mayor..........................	1755 hectares	4336.6 acres
	1 sitio de ganado menor..........................	780 hectares	1927.4 acres
	1 criadero de ganado mayor..................	438 hectares	1082.3 acres
	1 criadero de ganado menor...................	195 hectares	481.8 acres
	1 fanega de sembradura de maiz..........	3 hectares	7.413 acres
Dry	1 carga=2 fanegas		
	1 fanega†=2 medios=12 almudes= 48 cuartillos...	90.815 liters	2.6 bushels
Liquid (*wine, etc., but not oil*)			
	1 cuartillo=2 medios=4 cuartos..........	.456 liters	.48 quarts
	1 tinaja‡..	....	12.75 gallons
Weight	1 quintal=4 arrobas=100 libras= 1600 onzas=921,600 granos..................	46.0246 kilograms	101.44 pounds
	1 arroba..	11.506 kilograms	25.36 pounds

Running water—

    The amount of water running in a spring or stream, a very important factor in the settlement of an arid region, was commonly described in terms of a natural object with cross-section approximately equal to that of the current of water. The rate of flow of the water was disregarded. The following terms were thus used:

    buey de agua   a large flow of water, the volume of which is similar to the corpulence of an ox§

    naranja de agua an orange-sized flow

    lima de agua   a lime-sized flow

    limón de agua a small, lemon-sized flow

    braza de agua probably a stream of water one *braza* (1 fathom or 6 feet) wide

---

   * The legua seems ordinarily to have been considered to be about the distance covered in an hour's travel, but two travelers seldom made exactly the same estimates of distance even on the same route.

   † The ratio 1 fanega=12 almudes is the same as that given by Sales himself (part 3, p. 103). Some modern writers use 1=8.

   Rodriguez (1922) agrees to the ratio of 1 fanega to 2.6 bushels, saying that in Mexico 1 fanega=91 liters, though many modern writers use the Spanish fanega of 1.6 bushels. Certainly 2.6 bushels of corn would more nearly suffice to sow a "*fanega de sembradura*" than 1.6 bushels.

   ‡ Ulloa (1878).   § *Ibid.*

TABLE 1

CROPS AND HERDS

| Year | Cattle | Sheep | Goats | Pigs | Horses | Mules and Burros | Bu., @ 2.6 bu. per fanega | | | | Other data | Source |
							Wheat	Barley	Corn	Beans		
							ROSARIO					
1775	1	172	149	....	35	10	312	52	169	......	59 A. cult.	a
1776	18	340	268	....	38	9	546	26	1820	......	3BG, 250PW, 104 A. cult.	b
1780	48	377	226	15	......	24	....	....	....	......	2yokesoxen	c
1782	140	358	70	....	74	19	23	520	1043	......		d
1784	167	883	155	55	61	14	All grains		3658	......		e
1785	121	728	113	59	56	15	390	520	650	179		f
1786	266	989	144	....	54	14	62	676	5590	312		g
1787	287	1008	117	....	35	35	....	156	3640	52		h
1793	134	800	134	80	38	32	780	780	3900	312	47BG	i
1794	172	560	146	94	45	28	130	486	3500	159	13 BG	j
1800	300	650	140	30	76	36	52	78	260	10		k
1801	270	400	200	20	115	26	31	....	156	5		l
1830	....	....	......	....	......	....	....	....	302	8	29B lentils	m
							SANTO DOMINGO					
1780	176	139	116	7	16	61	....	....	....	......	1 yoke oxen	c
1782	167	8	45	....	52	38	....	....	....	......		d
1784	130	8	55	20	42	41	650	....	416	......		e
1785	39	11	28	12	38	35	988	....	182	21		f
1786	172	10	28	5	51	35	1482	....	442	......	140gal.wine	g
1787	194	—49—		15	39	28	1482	....	260	......	57BG&peas	h
1788	146	86	30	7	28	27	650	....	130	......		n
1793	300	150	50	12	46	30	1820	....	520	130		i
1794	300	100	100	20	30	25	2080	....	1300	73	75BG	j
1800	500	1000	100	30	141	25	2600	....	1300	260	52BG	k
1801	660	600	100	40	119	41	1560	....	1040	52	10BG	l
1805	....	....	......	....	......	....	(3900)	....	....	......		o
1830	....	....	......	....	......	....	364	130	....	31		m
							SAN VICENTE					
1792	56	114	27	....	6	40	520	65	5	5		d
1784	178	517	141	....	63	34	650	....	676	......		e
1785	153	457	27	....	59	33	354	....	614	......		f
1786	170	603	31	....	76	40	783	....	1568	......		g
1787	150	—633—		....	65	25	468	....	598	......		h
1788	152	—644—		....	75	25	....	....	....	......		n
1793	178	748	69	....	155	50	780	....	1040	52		i
1794	242	548	69	....	157	61	192	....	1560	......		j
1800	750	1150	150	....	113	48	910	....	1040	26		k
1801	364	800	347	....	161	54	780	83	1040	......		l
1835	....	....	......	....	......	....	....	....	208	26		m

TABLE 1—(*Concluded*)

Year	Cattle	Sheep	Goats	Pigs	Horses	Mules and Burros	Bu., @ 2.6 bu. per fanega				Other data	Source
							Wheat	Barley	Corn	Beans		
						SAN MIGUEL						
1788	59	120	371	....	20	27	....	....	....	......		n
1793	250	250	197	36	96	22	582	....	1300	47		i
1794	445	848	204	44	83	22	634	1056	832	44	8BG	j
1800	1350	1644	7	26	300	28	1170	541	520	26	21BG	k
1801	1600	2104	12	30	253	63	281	572	780	31		l
1834	3500	1500	......	....	50	10	624	819	18	......		m
						SANTO TOMÁS						
1793	350	500	150	60	124	48	520	650	468	31	26BG	i
1794	507	430	120	70	157	23	182	....	1820	31		j
1800	1070	2000	400	....	115	72	1560	1040	1300	130		k
1801	1200	2646	40	....	168	41	1560	1040	1040	104		l
1825	13	....	......	....	15	18	156	26	104	5		m
						SAN PEDRO MÁRTIR						
1800	600	400	300	50	113	27	130	....	780	208	13BG	k
1801	700	500	150	50	144	25	52	26	780	109	5BG	l
						SANTA CATALINA						
1800	315	210	102	....	120	25	16	....	65	......		k
1801	364	205	91	....	149	26	52	....	16	......		l
1834	1000	600	......	......	......		....	....	78	......		m

Abbreviations: A, acres; B, bushels; G, garbanzos; P, pounds; W, wool.

Key to sources used:

a. Peramas, June 30, 1775, MS
b. Peramas, 1776, MS
c. Croix, May, 1780, MS
d. Arch. Cal., S.P., 1:22
e. —— 31-32
f. —— 37
g. —— 43-44
h. —— 51

i. Arch. Cal., S.P., 1: 126-131
j. —— 2: 9-10
k. Bandini, May 21, 1801, MS
l. ——, June 29, 1802, MS
m. Lassepas (1859)
n. Arch. Cal., S.P., 1: 55-57, MS
o. Cleland: 477

TABLE 2
POPULATION

Year	Rosario	Santo Domingo	San Vicente	Santo Tomás	San Miguel	San Pedro Mártir	Santa Catalina	Source of data
1775	207 (June)							a
1776	564 (June)							b
1782	251	79						c
1785			83					c
1787	(328)	(271)	257		137			d
1790	(348)	205	(317)	96				c
1791		194						c
1793	390	296	179		171			c
1794				151	206	60	133	c
1800	257	315	246	262	224	92	223	e
1801	252	278	259	256	206	94		f
1805	(200–300)	(200–300)	(200–300)	(200–300)	(200–300)	(200–300)	(200–300)	g
1824	(130–150)	(300+)	(300)	(400+)	(350–400)		(600+)	h
1829	38		142					i
1830	41	78						j
1834			176	(254)	(254)			j
1835		25	7	60			250	j
1849	25				40 plus 25 at Descanso			k
1852	12			192				l
1853	24	39			1	1		m
1855		19	40	24	5	2		j
1857	18						0	j
1860		8	12	16	10 plus 10 (Descanso) plus 8 (Guadalupe)		0	n

Sources of the foregoing census figures:

a. Peramas, June 30, 1775, MS
b. Peramas, 1776, MS
c. Bancroft (1884b)
d. Sales (1794)
e. Bandini, May 21, 1801, MS
f. Bandini, June 29, 1802, MS
g. Cleland (1922); Shaler account
h. Troncoso, *in* Escudero (1849)
i. Arch. Cal., S. P., Miss., 6: 9
j. Lassepas (1859)
k. Castro (1849), MS
l. Doc. Orig. para la Hist. de la B. Cfa., vol. 2, no. 157, MS
m. Negrete (1859)
n. Alric (1866)

NOTE.—Figures of doubtful accuracy are enclosed in parentheses in the table. Figures of obvious exaggeration, such as those of Pattie and Mofras, are not included.

BIBLIOGRAPHY

PUBLISHED WORKS

ALRIC, H. J.
1866. Dix ans de residence d'un missionaire dans les deux Californies (Mexico City).
Mostly Upper California. Mission statistics unreliable.

BAEGERT, JAKOB
1773. Nachrichten von der amerikanischen Halbinsel Californien: mit einem zweyfachen Anhang falscher Nachrichten (Mannheim).
Fundamental work on the Jesuit area of Lower California.

BANCROFT, H. H.
1883– History of Mexico (San Francisco). 6 vols.
1884a. History of California (San Francisco), vol. 1.
1884b. History of the North Mexican States and Texas (San Francisco). 2 vols.
Volume 1 is a fundamental historical source for Lower California. It contains numerous inaccuracies of details.
1886. History of the Northwest Coast (San Francisco), vol. 1.
1888. California Pastoral (San Francisco).

BLACKMAR, F. W.
1891. Spanish Institutions of the Southwest (Baltimore).
Valuable analysis of the mission system in general.
Boletín de la Sociedad Mexicana de Geografía y Estadística (Mexico).
Contains Negrete's journey (see below); table of old Mexican weights and measures and their metric equivalents in vol. 10, pp. 195–252; also see index, vol. 8, for scattered data.

BOLTON, H. E.
1913. Guide to Materials for the History of the United States in the Principal Archives of Mexico. Carnegie Institute, Publ. no. 163 (Washington).
1926. Historical Memoirs of New California, by Fray Francisco Palóu (Berkeley).
1927. Fray Juan Crespi: Missionary Explorer on the Pacific Coast, 1769–1774 (Berkeley).
1930. Anza's California Expedition (Berkeley).

BÖSE, E., and WITTICH, E.
1913. Memoria de la Comisión del Instituto Geológico de México que Exploró la Región Norte de la Baja California. Parergones del Inst. Geol. de Mex. (Mexico), vol. 4, nos. 2–10.
Contains useful geological and climatological data.

BROWNE, J. ROSS
1868. Explorations in Lower California. Harper's New Monthly Magazine, vol. 37, pp. 577–591, 740–752; vol. 38, pp. 9–23.
Mostly on the Southern District of Lower California.
1869a. Resources of the Pacific Slope (New York).
A valuable early summary of Lower California geography.
1869b. A Sketch of the Settlement and Exploration of Lower California (New York).
A mine of valuable information on the Peninsula. Its most useful parts include:
TAYLOR, A. S. Historical Summary of Lower California, from its Discovery in 1532 to 1867, pp. 3–77.
An interesting pioneer work. Lacks adequate documentation.

BROWNE, J. ROSS *(Continued)*
　1869*b*. *(Continued)*
　　　GABB, W. M. Exploration of Lower California, pp. 82–122.
　　　　Good descriptions of the country and notes on trails and missions in
　　　　1867.
　　　SCAMMON, CAPT. C. M. Report on the West Coast of Lower California,
　　　　pp. 123–131.
　　　HAWKS, J. D. Journal of an Expedition through Lower California in the
　　　　Late Summer of 1849, pp. 132–142.
　　　　Some good notes on conditions at the very end of the Dominican
　　　　mission period.
　　　CLAVIJERO, J. History of Lower California, pp. 155–172.
　　　　Extracts dealing with natural history.

BRYAN, KIRK
　1925. Date of Channel Trenching (Arroyo Cutting) in the Arid Southwest.
　　　Science, n.s., 62:338–344.

BURNEY, JAMES
　1806. A Chronological History of the Voyages and Discoveries in the South
　　　Sea or Pacific Ocean (London).
　　　Contains a condensed copy of Viscaino's charts.

CARPENTER, F. A.
　1913. The Climate and Weather of San Diego, California (San Diego).

CARRASCO Y GUISASOLA, D. F.
　1882. Documentos Referentes al Reconocimiento de las Costas de las Californias
　　　... (Madrid).
　　　Document 28 is an account of Viscaino's voyage.

CHAPMAN, C. E.
　1916. The Founding of Spanish California: The Northwestward Expansion of
　　　New Spain, 1687–1783 (New York).
　1919. Catalogue of Materials in the Archivo General de Indias for the History
　　　of the Pacific Coast and the American Southwest (Berkeley).
　　　Many items on the Dominicans before their arrival in California. Careful
　　　annotations give a good idea of the content of the items mentioned.
　1923. A History of California: The Spanish Period (New York).

CHAPPE D'AUTEROCHE, JEAN
　1778. A Voyage to California to Observe the Transit of Venus (London edition).
　　　Contains a few notes on sea travel and epidemics at the southern end of
　　　Lower California in 1769.

CLAVIGERO, F. J.
　1852. Historia de la Antigua ó Baja California (Mexico. First edition, Venice,
　　　1789).
　　　A fundamental source for the Jesuit area. Contains accounts of the ex-
　　　plorations of Consag and Link.

CLELAND, R. G.
　1922. A History of California: The American Period (New York).
　　　Of special value for Lower California are:
　　　Appendix B: Shaler's Description of California. On the basis of a voy-
　　　　age in 1805.
　　　Appendix C: SMITH, W. C. S. A Forty-Niner in Lower California.
　　　Especially good for the area south of the Dominican foundations, but
　　　touches upon the Frontera too.

COOPER, W. S.
    1922. The Broad-Sclerophyll Vegetation of California. Carnegie Institute, Publ.
        no. 319 (Washington).
        Important for its discussion of vegetation formations which extend into
        Lower California.

COSBY, S. W.
    1929. Notes on a Map of the Laguna Salada Basin, Baja California, Mexico.
        Geog. Rev., 19:613–620.
        A good description, based upon intensive soil field work, of the area
        along the northeastern border of the Dominican area.

COSTANSÓ, MIGUEL
    1910. The Narrative of the Portolá Expedition of 1769–1770. Edited by A. van
        Hemert-Engert and F. J. Teggart. Publ. Acad. Pac. Coast Hist., 1:91–
        159 (Berkeley).
        Costansó was cosmographer of the party which reached San Diego by
        sea. Vicente Vila (captain of the ship) and Lieutenant Pedro Fages
        were also members of the sea party.
    1911. The Portolá Expedition of 1769–1770. Diary of Miguel Costansó. Edited
        by F. J. Teggart. *Ibid.*, 2:161–327 (Berkeley).
        Useful for its frontispiece map of 1770 by Costansó.

CRESPI. *See* Bolton, 1927. Crespi's diary is also contained in Palóu's "Noticias."

D. P. E. P.
    1801. El Viagero Universal ó Noticia del Mundo Antiguo y Nuevo (Madrid),
        vol. 26.
        Long quotations from Sales, and some notes on the founding of San
        Miguel not contained in Sales.

DAVIDSON, GEORGE
    1887. Examination of Some of the Early Voyages of Discovery and Explora-
        tion on the Northwest Coast of America (1539–1603). U. S. Coast Geod.
        Surv. Ann. Rep., 1886, App. 7 (Washington).
        Particularly valuable for its identifications of the places mentioned by
        Cabrillo and Viscaino.

DIXON, GEORGE
    1789. A Voyage Round the World (especially to Northwest America), 1785–
        1788 (ed. 2; London).
        Contains useful notes on sea otters.

DUFLOT DE MOFRAS
    1844. Exploration du territoire de l'Orégon, des Californies, et de la Mer Ver-
        meille en 1840, '41 et '42 (Paris). 2 vols.
        Mission statistics not reliable.

ENGELHARDT, ZEPHYRIN
    1908. The Missions and Missionaries of California, vol. 1: Lower California
        (San Francisco).
        The principal compendium of historical facts on the missions. Some of
        the data included here are not to be found elsewhere, the originals
        having been destroyed in the 1906 fire at San Francisco.
    1920. San Diego Mission (San Francisco).
        Contains a few notes on the northern part of the Frontera.
    1929. The Missions and Missionaries of California, vol. 1: Lower California
        (Santa Barbara).
        Contains a little additional material, but also lacks some of the geo-
        graphically useful items of the edition of 1908.

Escudero, J. A.
  1849. Noticias Estadísticas de Sonora y Cinaloa (Mexico).
         In the back part of this volume are the independently numbered pages
         by Troncoso (see below).

Forbes, Alexander
  1839. California: A History of Upper and Lower California (London).
         For Lower California based in large measure upon Venegas.

Gabb. *See* Browne, 1869*b*.

Goldman, E. A.
  1916. Plant Records of an Expedition to Lower California. Smithsonian Inst.,
         U. S. Nat. Mus., Contrib. U. S. Nat. Herb., vol. 16, pt. 14 (Washington).
         A useful, illustrated series of descriptions of some of the distinctive
         plants of Lower California.

Gonzales Cabrera Bueno, José
  1734. Navegación Especulativa y Práctica (Manila).
         Contains important early accounts of Lower California.

Greenhow, R.
  1844. History of Oregon and California (Boston).
         Has a few notes on sea otters.

Hart, G. H., and Guilbert, H. R.
  1928. Factors Influencing Percentage Calf Crop in Range Herds. Univ. Calif.
         Coll. Agr., Agr. Exp. Sta. Bull. 458 (Berkeley).

Hawks. *See* Browne 1869*b*.

Hendry, G. W.
  1926. Francisco Palóu's Boundary Marker: A Record of the Discovery of the
         First Boundary between Upper and Lower California. Calif. Hist. Soc.
         Quar., December, 1926 (San Francisco).
  1931. The Adobe Brick as a Historical Source. Agr. Hist., vol. 5, no. 3.

Hittell, T. H.
  1885. History of California (San Francisco). 4 vols.
         An important early history. Some of the facts given are not to be found
         elsewhere, the original sources, in the Archives of California, having
         disappeared.

Humboldt, Alexander de
  1811. Essai politique sur le Royaume de la Nouvelle Espagne (Paris. Also
         published in London the same year). 2 vols. and atlas.

Hunt, J. A.
  1911. Early Dominican Missions in California. *In* Dominican Year-Book, 1911.
         An account of the journey into Lower California in 1889 by Father
         Newell.
         See also Engelhardt, 1929:600–601.

Husmann, G. C.
  1905. Some Uses of the Grapevine and Its Fruit. *In* U. S. Dept. Agr. Yearbook,
         1904:366, pl. 44 (Washington).
         Age and size of mission grapevine near Santa Barbara.

James, G. W.
  1906. In and Out of the Old Missions of California (Boston).
         A popular description of the Upper California missions.

KNIFFEN, F. B.

1931. Lower Californian Studies. III. The Primitive Cultural Landscape of the Colorado Delta. Univ. Calif. Publ. Geog., 5:43–66 (Berkeley).

1932. Lower Californian Studies. IV. The Natural Landscape of the Colorado Delta. *Ibid.*, 5:149–244 (Berkeley).

KÖPPEN, WLADIMIR

1931. Grundriss der Klimakunde. (Second edition of Die Klimate der Erde, 1923).

KROEBER, A. L.

1925. Handbook of the Indians of California. Smithsonian Inst., Bur. of Am. Ethn., Bull. 78 (Washington).
Of value to the present volume for its description of neighboring tribes and discussion of methods of estimating aboriginal populations.

LASSEPAS, U. U.

1859. Historia de la Colonización de la Baja California (Mexico).
Of great value, especially for the last years of the mission period and the early years of private ranches. Some inaccuracies of details, particularly of dates.

Literary Digest, 108:13–14 (Feb. 21, 1931).
Proposed purchase of Lower California by the United States.

MEARES, JOHN

1790. Voyages Made in the Years 1788 and 1789 (London).
Contains interesting notes on sea-otter catching, though not in Lower California waters.

MERRIAM, C. H.

1905. The Indian Population of California. Am. Anthr., n.s., 7:594–606.
An estimate of aboriginal population; dissected by Kroeber (1925).

MORRELL, BENJAMIN

1832. A Narrative of Four Voyages, ... from the Year 1822 to 1831 (New York).
Contains some notes on what appears to be Rosario Bay.

MURR, C. G.

1809–1811. Nachrichten von verschiedenen Ländern Spanischen Amerikas (Halle).
Contains a condensed description of California, mostly on the Jesuit area. Good notes on sea otters.

NEGRETE, F. C.

1859. Geografía y Estadística de la Baja California, 1853. *In* Bol. Soc. Mex. Geog. y. Estad., 7:338–359 (Mexico).
An important and useful work.

NELSON, E. W.

1922. Lower California and Its Natural Resources. Mem. Nat. Acad. Sci., vol. 16, mem. 1 (Washington).
The chief source book on the physical geography of the Peninsula. Contains a bibliography, particularly of scientific writings, to 1919.

NEWCOMB, REXFORD

1915. European Precedents in Mission Architecture. Construction Details, 7: 37–62, 69–93.

NORDHOFF, CHARLES

1888. Peninsular California (New York).
Written to attract settlers, but has some useful notes on the natural landscape.

NORTH, A. W.
    1906–1907a. The Mother of California. Sunset Mag., 18 (1906–07) : 33–41, 145–
        155, 177–188.
        Sketchy and inaccurate.
    1907b. The Uncharted Sierra of San Pedro Mártir. Bull. Am. Geog. Soc., 39:
        544–554; map, p. 769.
        Contains some useful notes, including an interesting reference to Link.
    1908. The Mother of California (San Francisco).
        A popular history of Lower California. Inaccurate and undocumented.
        Has a bibliography.
    1910. Camp and Camino in Lower California (New York).
        A popular account of a trip in 1905–1906.

ORTEGA, JOSÉ
    1887. Historia del Nayarít, Sonora, Sinaloa, y Ambas Californias (Mexico;
        first published in Barcelona, 1754, as "Apostólicos Afanes de la Com-
        pañia de Jesus").
        Contains a valuable account of the explorations of Consag.

PALÓU, FRANCISCO
    1787. Relación Histórica de la Vida y Apostólicas Tareas del Venerable Padre
        Fray Junípero Serra (Mexico).
        Concerns chiefly the brief Franciscan régime in Lower California. A
        good note on Link.
    1874. Noticias de la Nueva California. (San Francisco. Also published in Mexico,
        in 1857; and in Berkeley, 1926, edited by Bolton; *see under* BOLTON).
        4 vols.

PATTIE, J. O.
    1905. Pattie's Personal Narrative of a Voyage to the Pacific and in Mexico,
        June 20, 1824–August 30, 1830. *In* Thwaites, R. G., Early Western
        Travels, 1748–1846, vol. 18 (Cleveland).
        First-hand but exaggerated accounts of Santa Catalina, San Vicente,
        Santo Tomás, and San Miguel.

PEROUSE, J. F. G. DE LA
    1799. A Voyage Round the World (London).

PORTOLÁ, GASPAR DE
    1909. Diary of Gaspar de Portolá during the California Expedition of 1769–
        1770. Edited by Smith, D. E., and Teggart, F. J. Publ. Acad. Pac. Coast
        Hist., 1:31–89 (Berkeley).

PRIESTLEY, H. I.
    1916. José de Gálvez: Visitor General of New Spain (1765–1771). Univ. Calif.
        Publ. Hist., 5:xiv + 449 (Berkeley).
        Presents the circumstances surrounding the decision of the Franciscans
        to admit the Dominicans to Lower California.

RALSTON, J. H.
    1902. United States vs. Mexico. 57 Cong., 2 Sess., Sen. Doc. no. 28 (Washington).
        Discussion of the Pious Fund. Uses population figures from Lassepas.

REEVE, J. K.
    1894. The Peninsula of Lower California. Lippincott's Mag., 53:71–78.
        A summary of current conditions, based on a rapid trip.

RICHMAN, I. B.
    1911. California under Spain and Mexico, 1535–1847 (Boston and New York).
        A critical, useful history, with some new material.

RIVEROLL, TEODORO. *See* Viosca.

RODRIGUEZ, GUSTAVO
1922. Las Pesas y Medidas del Mundo (Habana).

ROMERO, MATÍAS. *See* Viosca.

RUSSELL, R. J.
1926. Climates of California. Univ. Calif. Publ. Geog., 2:73–84 (Berkeley).
       A scientific classification of climates.
1931. Dry Climates of the United States. I. Climatic Map. *Ibid.*, 5:1–41
       (Berkeley).
       Extensions and refinements of the earlier paper (1926).

SALES, LUIS
1794. Noticias de la Provincia de Californias. En tres Cartas de un Sacerdote
       Religioso a un Amigo Suyo (Valencia).
       The only book on the Dominican area in Lower California by one of the
       Dominican padres. Of considerable geographic and anthropologic value.

SAUER, C. O.
1929. Land Forms in the Peninsular Range of California as Developed about
       Warner's Hot Springs and Mesa Grande. Univ. Calif. Publ. Geog., 3:199–
       290 (Berkeley).
       Analysis of an area similar in some respects to parts of near-by Lower
       California.

SAUER, C. O., and MEIGS, P.
1927. Lower California Studies. I. Site and Culture at San Fernando de Velicatá.
       Ibid., 2:271–302 (Berkeley).
       Historical geography of the area just southeast of the Dominican area.

SCAMMON, C. M.
1874. The Marine Mammals of the North-western Coast of North America
       (San Francisco).
       Interesting and authoritative. Contains a detailed discussion of the
       sea otter.

SCHMIEDER, OSCAR
1928. Lower Californian Studies. II. The Russian Colony of Guadalupe Valley.
       Univ. Calif. Publ. Geog., 2:409–434 (Berkeley).
       Mostly on modern culture landscape.

SEEMAN, BERTHOLD
1853. Narrative of H. M. S. Herald, 1845–51 (London).
       Contains some observations on the coasts of Lower California.

SERRA, JUNÍPERO
1902. Diary: Loreto to San Diego, March 28–June 30, 1769. Out West, 16
       (1902): 293–296, 399–406, 513–518; 17(1902):69–76.

SUDWORTH, G. B.
1908. Forest Trees of the Pacific Slope (Washington).

"Sutil y Mexicana"
1802. Atlas para el Viage de las Goletas . . . en 1792 (Madrid).

TAYLOR, A. S.
1860. Indianology of California. California Farmer, May 18, 1860.
       Some valuable notes on Indians and rancherías of San Miguel Mission,
       Lower California.
1864. Précis India Californicus. *In* KNIGHT, W. H., Handbook Almanac for the
       Pacific States, pp. 27–41 (San Francisco).
       Includes scattered notes on Lower California Indians.
       Historical Summary of Lower California (*see* BROWNE, 1869*b*).

TORQUEMADA, JUAN DE
   1723. Los Veinte I Un Libros Rituales I Monarchia Indiana . . . , vol. 1 (Madrid).
      A detailed account of Viscaino's expedition.

TRONCOSO, FRANCISCO
   1849. (Information on Lower California in 1824.) *In* ESCUDERO (which see), back
      section, pp. 13–24.
      Authoritative, valuable notes on the condition of the Dominican mis-
      sions in a period for which there are few other sources of information
      available.

ULLOA, AUGUSTO, AND OTHERS
   1878. Diccionario Encyclopédico de la Lengua Española (Madrid).

United States Hydrographic Office
   1880. The West Coast of Mexico. Bur. of Navigation, publ. 56 (Washington).
      This edition is more useful than those of later coast pilots because of its
      pictures of the Lower Californian coast.

URIBE, J. B.
   1925. Tijuana. El Hispano Americano (San Diego), September 16, 1925.
      Some interesting historico-legendary notes.

VANCOUVER, GEORGE
   1798. A Voyage of Discovery to the North Pacific Ocean . . . in the Years
      1790–95. Atlas (London).

VENEGAS, MIGUEL
   1759. A Natural and Civil History of California (London; first edition, Madrid,
      1757).
      A fundamental source for the Jesuit area. Baegert points out numerous
      inaccuracies. For the Frontera, the most useful parts are the accounts
      of the voyages of Consag in the Gulf of California (1746) and of
      Viscaino (from Torquemada's version), apps. 3 and 2, respectively.

Viagero Universal, El, *See* D. P. E. P.

VILA, VICENTE
   1911. The Portolá Expedition of 1769–1770. Diary of Vicente Vila. Edited by
      Rose, R. S. Publ. Acad. Pac. Coast Hist., 2:1–119 (Berkeley).
      Gives a detailed account of the difficulties of navigation from La Paz to
      San Diego.

VIOSCA, S.
   Ca. 1863. Historical Outline of Lower California (and other articles) (San Fran-
      cisco).
      The most valuable part is the detailed account of an expedition of ex-
      ploration in the Jesuit area in 1862, sent by Governor Riveroll. Gabb
      quotes Viosca as the writer (e.g., Browne, 1869*b*, p. 95).

VISCAINO, SEBASTIÁN. *See* Carrasco y Guisasola, Davidson, Torquemada, and Vene-
      gas.

WICKSON, E. J.
   1926. The California Fruits (San Francisco).
      Includes some notes on mission fruits.

WITTICH, ERNST
   1931. Die Volkzählung in der Republik Mexiko im Mai 1930. Pet. Mitt., 77, nos.
      9–10: 249–254.
      Census figures and discussion of population changes.

ZÁRATE, DAVID, and NUÑEZ, JULIO
   1925. Ensenada y Su Origen. El Hispano Americano (San Diego), September 16,
      1925.

MANUSCRIPTS

Unless otherwise noted, the following manuscripts are to be found in the Bancroft Library of the University of California. Listings are therefore made so as to afford ease of locating in that library. Though the older materials of the Bancroft Library have been worked and reworked by historians, some items of much geographical but little historical interest have not as yet been published. The usefulness of a detailed check list such as is here supplied is believed to justify the space given to it. The California Transcripts, many of which are listed below, include much material recently acquired by the Bancroft Library from Mexican and Spanish archives and not hitherto used. This collection is still growing.

ARCHIVO DEL ARZOBISPADO DE SAN FRANCISCO—

CARTAS DE LOS MISIONEROS DE CALIFORNIA

Vol.   pp.

I   82 Pallas and Grijalva. Apr. 28, 1794. *S. P. Mártir: founding*

     112 Pallas. Jan. 22, 1795. *S. Catalina: site recommended*

     183 Valdellon. Jan. 23, 1798. *S. Catalina: slow progress*

     187 Loriente and Lopez. June 23, 1798. *S. Tomás: S. Rafael ranch*

     225 Belda. Jan. 8, 1799. *Retirement of padres*

     238 Belda. May 30, 1799. *Retirement of padres*

II   23–6 Arviña. Nov. 15, 1802. *Cruelty to Indians*

     49 Ruiz. May 6, 1803. *Dry winter. Indians murder sergeant*

   52–3 Ruiz. May 19, 1803. *S. Tomás: murder*

     54 Ruiz. May 13, 1803. *S. Tomás: murder*

     55 Ruiz. May, 1803. *S. Quintín: foreign vessels in port*

     61 Ruiz. June 1, 1803. *S. Tomás: murder*

     70 Ruiz. June 11, 1803. *S. Tomás: Indian uprising*

   146 Gallego. July 15, 1806. *S. Vicente: mission headquarters*

V part 2, pp. 30–31. Señan. Dec., 1822. *S. Diego: estado*

ARCHIVO DE CALIFORNIA—

PROVINCIAL RECORDS

Vol.   pp.

I   13 Neve. Mar. 23, 1775. *Rosario: statistics: pop. and corn*

   33–4 Neve. Sept. 19, 1777. *Number of troops. Frontera and Loreto*

   62–3 Neve. 1776. *S. Domingo, Rosario, S. Fernando: statistics*

   359 Neve. Aug. 10, 1775. *S. Domingo: attractiveness of site*

   377 Neve. Nov. 29, 1775. *S. Domingo: founding*

  516–7 Fages. May 4, 1785. *New road north of San Vicente*

 517–20 Fages. May 4, 1785. *S. Miguel: exploration*

  632–3 Arrillaga. Aug. 24, 1793. *S. Tomás, S. Miguel: site change*

  633 Arrillaga. Aug. 24, 1793. *S. P. Mártir: preliminaries*

II 77–81 Neve. Oct. 24, 1780. *S. Vicente: founding*

  417–9 Fages. May 2, 1785. *New road. Colorado region*

  468–9 Fages. Aug. 28, 1786. *S. Miguel, S. Tomás: sites*

III 27 Fages. June 22, 1786. *Nutria-catching by soldiers*

  28 Fages. June 20, 1787. *S. Miguel-S. Diego relationship*

  642–6 Fages. Apr. 4, 1787. *S. Miguel: instructions for founding*

Vol.   pp.

    547–52, 576–7 Arrillaga. Dec. 10, 1795. *Summarizes Bernal diary*

    553–5 Ruiz. Dec. 1, 1795. *Report of Bernal trip by another member of the expedition*

    556–7 Borica. July 27, 1795. *Instructions to Bernal for Santa Catalina exploration*

    585–90 Grajera. Oct. 10, 1795. *S. Miguel: Rosario Plain. Trade with English ship*

XXI   193–5 Arrillaga. Nov. 3, 1792. *S. Tomás: sites described*

    202–10 Arrillaga. Nov. 7, 1792. *Sierra sites discussed*

    283 Arrillaga. Aug. 17, 1793. *S. Tomás: change of site*

    321 Arrillaga. Jan. 15, 1794. *Sierra sites*

    434 Arrilaga. May 31, 1794. *S. P. Mártir: founding*

PROVINCIAL STATE PAPERS. BENICIA. MILITARY

Vol.   pp.

XX   304 Revillagigedo. Mar. 27, 1793. *S. Tomás: site change*

PROVINCIAL STATE PAPERS. BENICIA. MISCELLANEOUS. 1770–1821

Vol.   pp.

I   21 Link. Mar. 27, 1766. *Diary of Voyage Feb. 20– Mar. 27. Title only*

STATE PAPERS. MISSIONS

Vol.   pp.

I   9–17 Fages. Aug., 1796. *Report on southern missions. Good*

    22 Unsigned. 1782. *Estado*

    31 Unsigned. 1784. *Estado*

    44 Unsigned. 1786. *Estado*

    51 Unsigned. 1787. *Estado*

    57 Unsigned. 1788. *Estado*

    126 Unsigned. 1793. *Estado*

    131 Arrillaga. Sept. 9, 1794. *Estado*

II   9 Garcia. Dec. 31, 1794

    33–6 Arrillaga. Apr. 8, 1795. *Report on Frontera missions*

    37 Unsigned. 1794. *S. Tomás: change of site*

    115 Loriente. Nov. 12, 1797. *S. Catalina: founding*

    115–7 Ruiz. Nov. 12, 1797. *S. Catalina: a child baptized*

VI   9 Arce. Dec. 31, 1829. *Rosario: census*

    9 Mancilla. Dec. 31, 1829. *S. Vicente: census*

STATE PAPERS. MISSIONS AND COLONIZATION

Vol.   pp.

I   8–14 Revillagigedo. Dec. 27, 1793. *Decadence in south*

    92–4 Arrillaga. June 8, 1786. *Good report. Plenty of rain in N, three dry years in S*

    281–323 Revillagigedo. Dec. 27, 1793. *General information. Dates inaccurate*

STATE PAPERS. SACRAMENTO

Vol.   pp.

I   103–4 Revillagigedo. Oct. 4, 1791. *S. Tomás: founding. Future plans*

IV   652–9 Borica. Sept. 11, 1796. *Proposed division of Californias*

V   846–7 Gomez. Apr. 29, 1791. *S. Tomás: early days*

IX   306–8 Pallas. July 19, 1794. *S. P. Mártir: change of site*

    312–7 Pallas. July 18, 1794. *S. P. Mártir: change of site*

    322–5 Pallas. July 29, 1794. *S. P. Mártir: change of site*

ARCHIVO DE LAS MISIONES. PAPELES ORIGINALES. 1826–1856–

Vol. pp.
II 903 Caballero. June 25, 1839. *Proof that Guadalupe was a mission*

ARCHIVOS DEL CONDADO DE SAN DIEGO. 1826–1850 (copied by Benjamin Hayes)—

pp.
 3 (Commerce and Revenues, 1820–43) Aug. 12, 1836. *Hides from Lower California to S. Diego*
 10 (Miscellaneous Papers, 1830–43) *Early land grants*
 110 (Documents of 1836) May 31, 1836. *Owners of Rosario (N.) Tecate, Ti-Juan mentioned*
 260 Osio. Aug. 20, 1840. *Santa Catalina: burned*
 353 (Documents of 1849) Mancilla, A. June 10, 1849. *S. Tomás: robbery*
 356 Arcuello. Aug. 4, 1849. *Ti-Juan ranch mentioned*

ARCHIVO DEL OBISPADO DE MONTEREY Y LOS ANGELES—

Vol. pp.
 99–119 Unsigned. Dec. 13, 1816. *Estado of San Buenaventura*

ARCHIVO DE SANTA BARBARA—

Vol. pp.
I 18 Galvez. Nov. 23, 1768. *Indians: change in mode of life*
 83–118 Serra. May 21, 1773. *San Fernando as the frontier*
 154 Serra. 1774. *Yields of crops, Alta California*

ARMONA, MATÍAS DE. June 30, 1770. Letter to Croix. (Calif. Transcripts.)
Comments upon gap in the mission chain.

ARRILLAGA, J. J. DE. Dec. 31, 1786. An estado. (Calif. Transcripts.)
Dec. 9, 1796. Diario de los Reconocimientos verificados por el Capitán de Loreto de Orden Superior en la Frontera. (Calif. Transcripts.)
Interesting and important explorations.

BANDINI, JUAN. 1776–1864. Documentos para la Historia de California.
Contains two estados by Arrillaga: May 21, 1801, and June 29, 1802.

BUCARELY Y URZUA, ANTONIO. Dec. 27, 1772. Letter commenting on the state of the Californias. (Calif. Transcripts.)

CAÑIZARES, JOSEPH DE. July 3, 1769. Diario, Villacata to San Diego. (Calif. Transcripts.)
Contains details of journey not given in the published diaries of the other members of the party.

CASTRO, MANUEL. 1849. Derrotero formado por el Capitán Don Manuel Castro desde San José del Cabo hasta la nueva linea de occidente, en la Baja California. *In* Doc. Orig. para la Hist. de la B. Cfa., vol. 2, pp. 360–372.
Includes important description of the Frontera in the last year of mission existence there.

COLEGIO DE SAN FERNANDO, MEXICO. Feb. 26, 1776. Da cuenta de los descubrimientos y las misiones de Californias, 1769–1776. (Calif. Transcripts.)
Mentions danger from Indians on Frontera route.

CROIX [MARQUIS DE]. May, 1780. Estado. (Calif. Transcripts.)
Includes interesting comments: amount of cultivated lands.

DIEGO, OBISPO. May 14, 1769. Letter to Pedro de Rada. (Gálvez Transcripts.)
Emphasizes the poverty of Lower California.

Documentos Originales para la Historia de la Baja California, 1849–52. Vol. 2.
> Mostly on the Military Colony at Santo Tomás. Items of use to the present work include:
> pp.
>> 38 Vidal. Feb. 7, 1851. *S. Tomás: passing of men to California mines*
>> 157–63 A sergeant. July 28, 1851. *S. Tomás: census*
>> 199 Espinosa. July 8, 1851. *Steamer wrecked near Rosario*
>> 258–61 Castro. Mar., 1852. *"Ex-misión de Guadalupe" mentioned*
>> 360–72 Castro. Diary. (*See* above under heading "Castro.")
>> 409 Arce. Dec. 23, 1835. *S. Tomás, S. Vicente, S. José mentioned*
>> 411 Bona. Aug. 10, 1850. *S. Vicente: still the capital*
>> 412 Pico. July 26, 1846. *S. Tomás*
>> 416–9 Bona. June 7, 1850. *S. Tomás: limits*
>> 458 Unsigned. Apr. 29, 1851. *Guadalupe, 1845*
>> 535 Castro. Feb. 13, 1852. *S. Catalina: appointment of Indian capitán*

ECHEANDÍA, J. M. May 14, 1829. Letter. (Calif. Transcripts.) *S. Quintín: salt*

Gálvez Transcripts.
> Important for antecedents of Dominican area, but thoroughly used by Priestley (1916).

[GÁLVEZ, JOSÉ DE.] Aug., 1773. Breve noticias de las principales expediciones y providencias de visita que promovió Don . . . (Gálvez Transcripts).
> Poverty of Lower California emphasized.

GENTIL, IGNACIO. Sept. 8, 1800. Documents relative to the missions of California. (Calif. Transcripts.)
> Important summary of progress and plans of the missions.

Hayes Papers. *See* Archivos del Condado de San Diego.

Libros de bautizmos, casamientos, y entierros.
> Includes baptismal, marriage, and burial books, for San Fernando, Rosario, and Santo Domingo, and baptismal and burial books for San Vicente, and a detailed census of Santa Catalina.
> These, the original mission books, are at present in the library of St. Dominic's Monastery, Benicia, California.

MORA, VICENTE DE. June 26, 1774. Diary . . . formed on the visits which he has made of the Missions of the North since November 4, 1773. (Calif. Transcripts.)
> Valuable account of the detailed explorations for the site of Rosario Mission.

PALACIOS. *See* RINN

PERAMÁS, MELCHOR DE. Feb. 24, 1775. An estado. (Calif. Transcripts.)
> June 30, 1775. An estado. (Calif. Transcripts.)
> 1776. An estado. (Calif. Transcripts.)
> May 27, 1777. An estado. (Calif. Transcripts.)

REVILLAGIGEDO. Nov. 26, 1789. Provisions for establishing new missions . . . (Calif. Transcripts).

RINN, I. L. The Voyages of Vizcaino. Master's thesis in history, Univ. of Calif. Library.
> Contains the excellent account by Palacios, chief cosmographer of the expedition.

ROJO, M. C. 1879. Apuntes Históricos de la Baja California, Suministrados en 1879.
> Valuable notes on the later missions, particularly Guadalupe, and on the troops of the Frontera.

RUBÍ, EL MARQUÉS DE. April 3, 1768. State of the Provinces. (Calif. Transcripts.)

SERRA, JUNÍPERO. Nov. 3, 1768. Estado. (Calif. Transcripts.)

U. S. CONSULATE, Ensenada. Records of exports (in the Ensenada office).

VASADRE, A. V. DE. Apr. 11, 1791. Documents relative to project of . . . (Calif. Transcripts).
The project was an unsuccessful nutria monopoly.

VERGER, RAFAEL. Aug. 3, 1771. Letter. (Calif. Transcripts.)
Concerns the proposed five missions north of Velicatá.

VELAZQUEZ, JOSEPH. 1770. Diario que hizo el Correo que vino de Monterrey y llamado Jph. Velazquez. (Gálvez Transcripts.)
Valuable account of route and Indians in Frontera.
Nov. 17–26, 1775. Diary of an expedition of Joseph Velazquez sent out by order of Neve to explore the coast of the North . . . (Calif. Transcripts).
Illiterate but meaty account of the first explorations in the San Pedro Mártir Sierra.

VISCAINO, SEBASTIÁN. 1603. Map and description of coast, copied from the original by Enrico Martínez, 1603. (Photostat in Bancroft Library.)
See RINN.

INDEX

INDEX

Abalones. *See* Shellfish

Acorns. *See* Foods

Acre, Jesús, sale of San Telmo to, 158

Adobe bricks, 43, 51

Agriculture, 43, 161; dry farming at Rosario, 52, at San Telmo Abajo, 76, at San Vicente, 85, at Santo Tomás, 92, at San Miguel, 100, at Descanso Mission, 106, 107, at Santa Catalina, 121, in northern part of the Frontera, 161

Aguagito, caves of, Indian shell mounds at, 59

Ahumada, Fray Tomás de, statements by, concerning San Miguel Mission, 37

Álamo Plain, location of, 119

Álamo region: excellent sites for settlement in, 16–17; gallery forests of, 16–17

Animal life: deer, 41, 58, 162; ducks, 162; mountain sheep, 41, 162; quail, 162; rabbits, 41, 58; sea lions, 86; sea otters, 64, 65, 118. *See also* Livestock

Arrillaga, José Joaquín de: expeditions of, 34 ff.; original survey of, 120; exploration of Colorado River region by, 161. *See also* Explorations

Arroyo: Grande, 123; León, 123

Balsas, crude tule, 41, 64, 101

Banda, Cerro, shell mounds found on or near, 94

Bandini, Juan, sale of Guadalupe Mission site to, 158

Barley. *See* Crops

Barri, Governor Felipe, interference of, with management of mission Indians, 4

Beans. *See* Crops

Bernal, Ensign Ildefonso. *See* Explorations

Burros. *See* Livestock

Caballero, Fray Felix, 37; results of energy of, 115; a most active missionary, 117

Cactus growth at San Vicente, 84, 86. *See also* Foods; Vegetation

Cañizares, José de, 10, n. 13

Casas, Bartolomé de las, 2

Catalina Mesas, 119

Cattle. *See* Livestock

Cemeteries, location of, 51

Clams. *See* Shellfish

Clavigero, Francisco Javier, account of Link's work by, 9

Climate: gulf storms, 2, 5, n. 2; thunderstorms, 17, 44, 119; rainfall, 18, 33 *passim*, 65, 76, 94, 100, 119, 143, 161; frosts, 30; cold with north winds, 33; snow, 33, 119; fogs, 52, 76, 77, 86, 89, 161; effect of, on vegetation, 54–55, 113; temperature differences at San Telmo, 77, and at Santo Tomás, 89; dew at Santo Tomás, 89; winds, 95, 108; at Descanso Mission, 107; temperature, 108, humidity, 108, sea breeze, 108, and dew, 108; maximum precipitation, 119; Sierran, 126; at San Isidoro Ranch, 129; drought, 134, 144

Coast. *See* Terrace region

Cocopa Indians, hostile, 121 *passim*

Colorado Desert: early explorations in, 7; region least suited for missions, 16; population of, area, 142

Colorado River: good land near, 36; cotton grown in lowlands of, 161

Colorado settlement, projected, 29, 36, 37, 93

Communications: at Rosario, 61; of the Santo Domingo area, 77; main lines of, from San Vicente, 87; at San Miguel, 103; summary of routes of, and distances, 148–149; nature of traffic, 149

Consag, Fernando: expeditions of, 7–8, 11; place-names given by, 7–8; value of work of, to explorers, 7; exploration of Dominican frontier by, 8 *passim*

Córdova, Vicar Pedro de, 2

Corn. *See* Crops

Cotton raising, 161

Crespi, Fray Juan, 7, 9; diary of, cited, 10; mission sites recommended by, and Serra, 11; observations of, on journey to San Diego, 18; description of San Vicente Mission site by, 24; good judgment of, in selection of sites, 26; final site of Santo Tomás discovered and described by, 28; recommended site in Descanso Valley, 38; description of El Salado by, 79

Crops: at *Mission Rosario*, wheat and beans, 52, 53; irrigation used to raise, 52; maize the principal crop, 52; corn, barley, 53; average yields, 53; figs, grapes, 53; tomatoes, 54; at *Mission Santo Domingo*, fruit trees, 69; wheat, 69, 77; corn, beans, 69; yield for most successful year, 69; garbanzos, peas, 69; at *San Telmo Mission*, wheat, barley, corn, beans, 76; at *San Vicente*, wheat, 84, 85; corn, beans, barley, 85; largest yield, 85; at *Santo Tomás*, corn, 91, 92; fruit, 91–92; wheat, barley, beans, 92; onions, calabazas, 97; at *San Miguel*, wheat, 100, 105; barley, 100; corn, beans, garbanzos, 105;

PLATES

PLATE 1

a. A stand of mescal (*agave*) at the edge of a cliff overlooking the sea just south of the Rosario Plain, near the northern range of this species. The plant most important to the Indians. The heart of the plant, roasted, was a major food, and the fiber of the thick leaves, or pencas, was used for making nets and sandals. This species thrives in the foggy coastal lands.

b. Ruins of the first Rosario Mission on a vidrío-covered fragment of the Upper Terrace, facing south-southeast. The opening to the right of the center in the background is the Cañada de San Fernando, through which led the main trail to San Fernando de Velicatá and the south. The huts on the far side of the valley belong to Yaqui immigrants.

a

b

PLATE 2

a. Looking north up a side cañon east of the first mission, Rosario Valley. The Lower and Upper valley-floor terraces, the 100-foot and 300-foot older valley terraces, and at least one other terrace are here represented, out of reach of the erosive attacks of the Rosario River. At the head of the cañon can be seen the southern edge of the main 800-foot north mesa. Note the striking sparseness of vegetation on these steep, south-facing, desert slopes.

b. Typical shell heap at the outer edge of the Upper Terrace of Rosario Valley, east of the first mission. Such a distribution of Indian middens occurs in the valley for a distance of at least eight miles from the sea.

a

b

PLATE 3

a. Ruins of the second Rosario Mission, from the north, in 1926. Note the massiveness of the walls, the pointed Gothic arch of the doorway and niche, the patches of plaster on the walls, and the mission bells partly visible beside the girl. The floor of the mission and the tops of the walls to the right are covered with vidrío.

b. Large Indian shell heap on the terrace at the south edge of Socorro Valley. The site of one of the Rosario rancherías. Looking northeast. In the background, forming the north wall of Socorro Valley, is the sand-dune barrier that has always been a great obstacle to north-south travel.

a

b

PLATE 4

a. San Quintín Plain. Looking west from the high terrace at the eastern edge of the plain. San Quintín Bay in the distance, protected from the ocean by a chain of recent volcanoes.

b. The salt lagoons north of San Quintín Bay. Looking southwest from a small cinder cone. These deposits have been of continuous importance as a source of salt for the aborigines, mission population, navigators, and others. The fields were being worked on a commercial scale at the time this picture was taken (1926). In the distance is the volcanic island, San Martín.

c. Red Rock, at the southern portal of Santo Domingo Cañon. Viewed from the floor of San Ramón Valley to the west. The mouth of the cañon is just to the left of the rock. Hamilton Ranch houses are to the right. The cave in which the mission services were said to have been first held is not visible in the picture, being in the left (northern) face of the rock.

Monte de Ceniza   M. de Kenton
M. de Riveroll

a

b

c

PLATE 5

Santo Domingo Mission ruins. Looking southeast. Main quadrangle is in right foreground. Cemetery is to left, farther up the
alluvial fan. Just across the road were the irrigated lands of
the mission, including the tuna-surrounded huerta still visible
to the right. The buildings across the road were all erected by
villagers of post-mission date. The banana groves east of the
huerta are recent importations, but seem to succeed in this
environment.

PLATE 6

a. San Telmo Basin (Arriba). Looking west. San Telmo Chapel, a subsidiary of Santo Domingo Mission, was in this basin. About sixty acres of land were irrigated here. Both inlet and outlet of the basin are at the extreme right of the picture.

b. The tule-rimmed Poza de San Telmo, in the narrows between San Telmo Valley and the San Telmo Basin. Looking north. Crespi's route and the mission trail ascended the cañon in the center background.

c. El Salado, alkaline flat at the south edge of San Vicente Basin. Looking southwest toward the head of El Salado Cañon, which is one of the drainage outlets of the basin through the mountains to the sea. The marsh- and salt-grass flat merges without break into the head of the cañon. Note the sharpness of intersection of plain and mountains.

a

b

c

PLATE 7

a. San Isidro Mesa, the coastal terrace west of San Vicente. North of the arroyo. The height of the sea cliff, entirely of unconsolidated material, may be realized by a comparison with the one-story house at the top of the cliff toward the left.

b. San Isidro Mesa, along the coast south of the arroyo. At this point the unconsolidated material of the marine terrace is underlain by a basalt floor. Storm waves have driven back the front of the unconsolidated material, exposing a hard basalt platform along the water's edge.

a

b

PLATE 8

a. Live-oak and sycamore grove in the cañon near the lower end of Santo Tomás Valley. Oaks are not found at the coastal missions farther south.

b. Ruins of the first mission, Santo Tomás, on a small fan terrace on the northern side of the lower end of Santo Tomás Valley. Looking southeast. The cultivated valley floor with its groves of willows and cottonwoods along the arroyo, occupies the middle of the picture. Across the valley, along the base of the north-facing valley wall on the right, may be seen a sprinkling of dark live oaks, thinning out and disappearing toward the drier east.

a

b

PLATE 9

a. The mission huerta, Santo Tomás. Some of the tuna and olive trees are said to date from the mission period. At the edge of the road can be seen the stones of part of the irrigation ditch that led from the springs. The mission buildings (second mission) were near the large eucalyptus trees a little left of the center of the picture.

b. Ensenada Plain and the Bay (Ensenada) of Todos Santos. Always an important port of the Frontera. Note the sweeping curve of the broad beach, and the long protecting arm of Punta Banda in the distance. Looking southwest. The town of Ensenada may be seen nestling at the foot of the ridge that terminates the plain on the north (right). The greater part of the plain visible here was granted very early (1804) as a private ranch.

a

b

C. Banda

PLATE 10

a. Level floor, basalt rim, and sharp rim notch at northern edge of a tray. The notch here leads by a steep cañon down into San Miguel Valley.

b. San Miguel Valley. Looking seaward. Note the rolling sag-pond zone transitional between the valley floor and the summit of the 700-foot south wall of the valley, to the left. The mission ruins are barely discernible as a light, worn spot a little above the valley floor.

c. Hut in use at present by old Indian women at San José, a former ranchería of Guadalupe Mission. Small brush huts even lower than this are still in use among the Keliwas in the interior.

a

Mission

b

c

PLATE 11

a. View across Descanso Valley from the north. The cultivable, mustard-covered (dark) valley floor is being progressively destroyed by winter attacks of the arroyo from the east (left). The light area in the middle of the valley is a reëntrant which was cut in the previous winter (1927). Shallow channels, cut by floods which jumped their arroyo banks, can be detected in the valley floor below the reëntrant. The trail to the south across the high mesas can be seen ascending the farther slope, from right to left.

b. Ruins of the Descanso Mission. Looking southward across the valley. The fort of the mission, and other buildings, lie at the top of the slope on the southern side of the valley. The old trail can be seen climbing the slope diagonally, starting below the fort and rising to the left. Modern coastal highway and Descanso Bar at the right.

a

Fort

b

a. Sandstone cliffs, etched by differential erosion of waves and wind-driven sand, on the coast north of Médano Valley. Similar sandstone is the basal material of the landscape between Descanso and Mount Médano.

b. Badland in coastal terrace north of Descanso.

a

b

PLATE 13

a. Mount Médano and El Coronel (left) from the north. Part of the range originally designated as the boundary between Dominican and Franciscan territory.

b. Rincón de los Encinos, live-oak grove in eastern part of Guadalupe Valley, site of important ranchería of Guadalupe Mission. Looking southeast. Cerro San Antonio (4432 feet) in right background, with knobcone pines on the skyline of its eastern ridge.

a

b

PLATE 14

a. Ojá Cuñúrr, the rock which gave the Guadalupe Mission site its name. The overhang of the rock bears colored pictographs.

b. The Álamo Plain. Looking northeast across the town of Álamo from Cerro Tomasa. Sierra Juarez and Catalina mesas in distant right background.

a

b

PLATE 15

a. View, southeastward, into the desertic Valle Trinidad, the chief break in the mountain backbone of the Frontera. Sierra San Pedro Mártir in the center distance.

b. View of the Mission Plain, looking northeast from Santa Catalina Mission. The sage-covered flat in the foreground, with young junipers just getting established, is believed to have been a wheat field in mission days. The trees in the middle of the flat mark the important, permanent little stream which was the principal basis for the selection of the site for a mission. The Catalina mesas in the background form the abrupt eastern termination of the Álamo Plain. Cerro de la Ciénega at left.

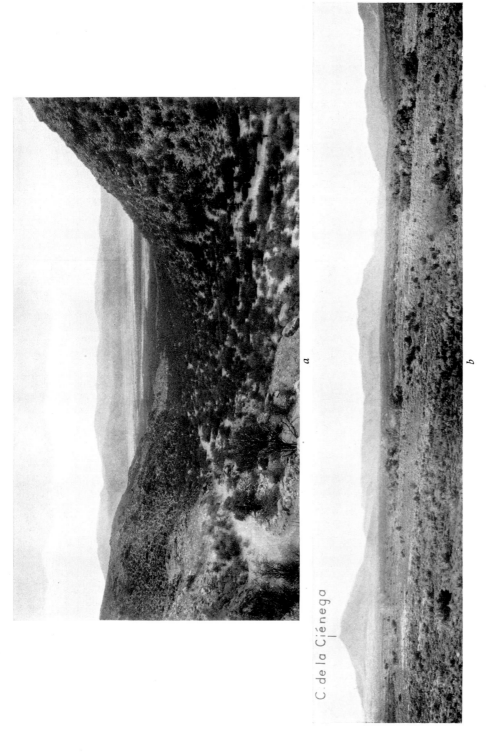

a

C. de la Ciénega

b

PLATE 16

a. San Matías Pass, an eastward continuation of Valle Trinidad. Looking southeast from near Niay Wey. Piñon trees in foreground. San Felipe Desert, at foot of San Pedro Mártir Sierra, in left distance.

b. Santa Catalina Mission ruins. Looking east. The outline of the quadrangle is marked by mere mounds, all that remain of the mission walls. The men are standing upon the ruins. In the distant right background is the Portezuelo, an important pass to the Colorado lowlands. Characteristic cactus and mescal on the rocky mission platform in the foreground.

a

b

PLATE 17

a. Grassy opening in yellow-pine forest, Sierra Juarez. Elevation about 4900 feet.

b. Granite-surrounded Santa Catalina Valley, from the south. Upon the lower slopes of the dark, rounded, low lava hill just north of and overlooking the valley are the ruins of the mission, barely distinguishable in this view. Cerro de la Ciénega and the Catalina mesas in the background.

c. Summer *ramada* of an Indian family, Santa Catalina Valley, 1929. Several Indian families are still living here and at San Miguel.

a

b

c

PLATE 18

a. The broad, even surface of the plateau of the Sierra San Pedro Mártir. Looking south 20° west from the highest, eastern edge of the mountain. The forest here is in large part lodgepole pine, and the opening in the forest in the middle of the picture is the grassy Vallecito (elevation more than 8000 feet).

b. The granite- and pine-surrounded mountain meadow of La Encantada (elevation more than 7000 feet), Sierra San Pedro Mártir. Looking south 20° east.

a

b

PLATE 19

a. Picacho de la Providencia (also known as Picacho del Diablo, Las Tres Palomas, Calamahue Mountain), highest point of Lower California (10,126 feet). Looking south 55° east from a point near the high eastern rim of the San Pedro Mártir Plateau. The sharp, steep drop to the east at the edge of the plateau is apparent in the middle of the picture.

b. Santo Tomás Valley (elevation 6250 feet). Looking west (downstream) from a point six miles east of the San Pedro Mártir Mission. Situated near the lower, southern edge of the plateau, where a scattered growth of yellow pine and piñon is the sole representative of the dense forest of higher altitudes. The steep slopes support a thick growth of high monte, and the moister valley floor, covered with grass and willow thickets, provided pasturage for the mission herds. The landscape here is similar to that of the mission valley.

a

b